On Rereading

 *On Rereading*

PATRICIA MEYER SPACKS

THE BELKNAP PRESS *of* HARVARD UNIVERSITY PRESS

Cambridge, Massachusetts, and London, England · 2011

Library of Congress Cataloging-in-Publication Data
Spacks, Patricia Ann Meyer.

  On rereading / Patricia Meyer Spacks.

     p.   cm.

  Includes bibliographical references and index.

  ISBN 978-0-674-06222-1 (alk. paper)

  1. Spacks, Patricia Ann Meyer—Books and reading.   2. Books and
reading—United States.   3. Books and reading—Psychological aspects.
4. Fiction—Psychological aspects.   I. Title.

  z1003.2.s63   2011

  028'.9—dc23   2011023305

In memory of Liliane Greene

Contents

On Rereading

Always a Stranger?

IF YOU'RE A PARENT, grandparent, aunt, uncle, cousin, or friend of the family, you've perhaps endured the fury of a toddler compelled to listen to her favorite book with a word missed or a picture skipped. The point of the favorite book, for the listener, is that it remains the same. The more often the three-year-old hears the familiar sentences, the more content she appears. When a word changes, pleasure recedes: a beloved book has lost its identity.

Trying to account for this passion for sameness, we may say that it reveals the toddler's need for security. In a world crammed with new experiences, exciting yet unpredictable, the child treasures what she can hold on to. If even the book turns unpredictable, she loses what she has depended on. A friend's personality has changed.

We smile grown-up smiles at the child's demand for perfect re-iteration even if we retain that childish need in more acceptable form, addicted to our own rereadings. Diverse impulses motivate us rereaders, desire for security among them. Consider Larry Mc-Murtry, writing in his early seventies: "If I once read for adventure, I now read for security. How nice to be able to return to what won't change." McMurtry reports that publishers keep sending him new books to comment on. He sends them back, preferring the books he already knows. "When I sit down at dinner with a given book," McMurtry writes, "I want to know what I'm going to find."

2 ·

We always find frustration: early in life, the adults we depend on won't read the book to us exactly as it should be each time; later, we realize the impossibility of rereading, re-encountering, regrasping, everything we have already perused. But we may discover, also, the special, increasingly complicated pleasure of literary re-encounters. Rereading: a treat, a form of escape, a device for getting to sleep or for distracting oneself, a way to evoke memories (not only of the text but of one's life and of past selves), a reminder of half-forgotten truths, an inlet to new insight. It rouses or soothes, provokes or reassures. And, as McMurtry reminds us, it can provide security.

What kind of security, exactly? McMurtry suggests that a book reread offers what will not change—but for most readers, rereading provides, in contrast, an experience of repeated unexpected change. We remember Hansel and Gretel making their trail of bread crumbs, but it may come as a surprise to reread the Grimm brothers' version of the story and find the witch licking her lips over the prospect of eating the children on toast. Only a tiny detail, that, but one that complicates the story's flavor and makes it memorable in a new way. That allusion to toast makes the reader suddenly aware that the witch really *is* planning to eat those children. She's thinking about the meal to come. I read the tale anew in the battered copy of *Grimm's Fairy Tales* that survives from my childhood and come upon this unexpected moment. Did I fail to remember it because once it scared me by its specificity? Who knows?

Change occurs not only as a result of noticing new details but also because interpretations alter. In a youthful reading of *Crime and Punishment*, Raskolnikov seems a daring young man, exciting in his willingness to defy convention. As a grown-up rereader, I think him a fool, or a monster. I read the novel again: he has become an object of sympathetic pity tinged with horror. I find myself enthralled for new reasons.

Sometimes a book changes for the worse. Vivian Gornick: "When I read Colette in my twenties, I said to myself, That is exactly the way it is. Now I read her and I find myself thinking, How much smaller this all seems than it once did—cold, brilliant, limited—and silently I am saying to her, Why aren't you making more sense of things?" We read to recapture the thrill of a book first encountered twenty years earlier, and the thrill has mysteriously vanished. We remember a wonderful story, and the story has turned into a cliché. The change may attest to our maturity, but it feels like loss.

Or, perhaps, provocation. As Verlyn Klinkenborg puts it, writing in the *New York Times*, "The real secret of rereading is simply this: it is impossible. The characters remain the same, and the words never change, but the reader always does. Pip is always there to be revisited, but you, the reader, are a little like the convict who surprises him in the graveyard—always a stranger" ("Some Thoughts on the Pleasures of Being a Re-Reader," May 30, 2009). Klinkenborg claims that the books he repeatedly rereads provide not a canon but a refuge. In other words, this special group matters to him not because he judges its members to be of particular merit but because its books supply a certain kind of emotional satisfaction. His manifest excitement at the role of the reader—always a stranger—suggests, however, that his satisfaction involves more than refuge.

The question of what kind of security rereading offers gives way to another: How can rereading provide security at all? How can a rereader who remains "always a stranger" expect reassurance? If books keep changing along with their readers, they possess no stability and would seem to offer no security. Seeing former classmates at a twenty-fifth high school reunion can come as a shock; so can reseeing a once beloved book. Yet the claim of security carries conviction. It reminds us that in every book, though much may change, much stays the same. The plot no longer thrills, but it remains the plot that thrilled us once. The characters appear more or less reprehensible than they did before, but like those high school classmates, they continue to possess traits we recognize.

Reread books offer another kind of reassurance as well: that of remembering our past selves. "In reading a book which is an old favourite with me," the nineteenth-century essayist William Hazlitt writes,

> (say the first novel I ever read) I not only have the pleasure of imagination and of a critical relish of the work, but the pleasures of memory added to it. It recalls the same feelings and associations which I had in first reading it, and which I can never have again in any other way. Standard productions of this kind are links in the chain of our conscious being. They bind together the different scattered divisions of our personal identity.

In other words, the stability of reread books helps to create a solid sense of self. That important claim suggests another profound aspect of rereading as experience: the degree to which it records both the development and the continuity of the self. If the activity helps to consolidate identity, as Hazlitt suggests, it also helps to measure personal change.

The dynamic tension between stability and change lies at the heart of rereading. Every renewed exchange between book and reader contains elements of both, and both provide pleasure. Our psychic needs vary, and reread books answer different needs at different times. Seeking solace, we return to a treasured children's book. A beloved piece of light fiction answers our yearning for pure recreation. We find excitement in a rousing plot even though we already know how it will turn out; we contemplate our past as we reread something first encountered in adolescence.

The results of a British survey of readers encourage fantasy about sources of rereading pleasure. Conducted by Costa, an English coffee company, but also the funder of an important national book award, the survey asked some 2,000 readers about whether and what they reread. Tabulated into a list of the twenty works most often reread, the answers prove arresting. The Bible ranks sixteenth on the list of twenty. Shakespeare does not appear at all. The top three, in order, are the Harry Potter series, *The Lord of the Rings,* and *Pride and Prejudice.*

I have no idea how scientifically this survey was designed. I received it in an e-mail message from a friend; some items on the list make me suspect that respondents simply listed any title they could think of. How the answerers were chosen, who they were: I don't know. So I don't offer this list as real evidence of anything—only as a stimulus to the imagination.

For the collection of titles fairly demands that you make up stories about it. Four of the twenty books listed are conventionally children's reading: Harry Potter, of course; and *The Hobbit; The Lion, the Witch and the Wardrobe;* and *Black Beauty.* Twenty percent seems a rather high proportion, and *Black Beauty* something of a surprise, but there it is. Then there are four nineteenth-century classics, *Jane Eyre, Wuthering Heights,* and *Great Expectations* joining *Pride and Prejudice;* and a twentieth-century classic, *1984.* Several books seem peculiarly American, surprising choices for British respondents: *Catch-22, To Kill a Mockingbird,* and *Gone with the Wind.* Two, I must confess, I had never heard of: *Flowers in the Attic,* by V. C. Andrews, and *Good Omens,* by Neil Gaiman and Terry Pratchett.

The mind rushes to produce plausible explanations. Surely the relatively large number of children's books speaks of nostalgia. Harry Potter would be at the top because he is much in the news—maybe adults reread the books in reading them aloud to children. *The Lion, the Witch and the Wardrobe,* at the time of the 2007 poll, was a recent movie, a fact that might have sent people back to the original. Possibly the American books seem glamorous and sophisticated, conversation pieces. Those classics? Well, perhaps the English know better than Americans do what a really good read they are. I can't, however, come up with any theory at all for the inclusion of *The Da Vinci Code,* a work so badly written that I couldn't get beyond the second paragraph in my attempt at a first reading.

Each individual among the 2,000 may have a different reason from any other individual for rereading a given work. You read a C. S. Lewis children's book because of the movie, or because you suddenly noticed it in the bookcase, or because your niece mentioned that she was enjoying the book. You return to *Gone with the Wind* because some green curtains reminded you of Scarlett O'Hara. The immediate causes, or pretexts, for rereading are infinite—like the possible rewards. Yet those rewards generally cluster around the promise of change or of stability. The green curtains will be there every time you return to the novel; the dress Scarlett makes out of them will never change; what your imagination makes of them may shift repeatedly. Those curtains thus illustrate the double promise that rereading holds, of sameness and of difference.

Vagaries of memory play a large part in the dramas of rereading. I register the detail about the witch wanting to eat Hansel and

Gretel on toast and think, I never noticed that before. All I can accurately say, though, is that I don't remember having noticed it before. Perhaps I wasn't scared at all; maybe I delighted in it many years ago as I delight in it today, but faulty memory, which has erased that pleasure, allows it now to be experienced as altogether new. I might read the story again, say five years hence, and this time recall both my current enjoyment of the unexpected detail and the satisfaction it gave me a long time ago—that satisfaction that I, hypothetically, have at the moment forgotten. There are presumably reasons for remembering at one time and not another, but those reasons are rarely accessible. The unpredictability of re-reading derives largely from memory's mysterious operations.

An idea like stability thus becomes complicated. The small child who hears the same story every night—hears it, indeed, sometimes several times in a single evening—won't forget any of its details, but the adult who has read many books over a long period may have memories sufficiently blurred that a book reread after a gap of years offers nothing recognizable. Its words, we know, remain the same, yet *they* seem strangers: strangers though, miraculously, friends as well. Repeated rereadings of the same text, the adult equivalent of the toddler's treasured experience, provide more dependable recall. I know several people who read Jane Austen's novels every year or so. They thus create their own security.

The security that McMurtry seeks, then, is always available, but for at least some readers, it may depend on several iterations of a single work. "When I take up a work that I have read before (the oftener the better) I know what I have to expect," Hazlitt writes. The parentheses contain the salient point: the more often one reads something, the more one knows what to expect—although surprise can always erupt, and usually does. That lasting possibility of surprise in rereading is one reason the subject seems worth investigating. Another is that to study rereading may shed light on why and how we read in the first place.

For one thing, the dynamic of stasis and change that I've been talking about calls attention to the intricate processes of exchange between reader and text that mark every act of reading. When I speak, or Vivian Gornick speaks, of apparent change in a reread work, of changing relationships between reader and text, of alterations in what we see, we necessarily allude to changes in the reader. The book's words remain those that we read before. We may, however, notice language that we have not previously attended to as we read again, or the words may carry new meaning. Such possibilities probably register, at least in part, how our minds, hearts, experience, personal and cultural situation, or all of the above—or maybe just our mood—have changed since the last time we read those words. Reading a book, or rereading it, we enter into relation not only with the text but with an imagined author. Rereading, we relate also to one or more version of our past selves. Examining the textures of these relationships, we learn both about ourselves and about complicated connections informing the mysterious process of reading.

We may learn, too, about the varying kinds as well as degrees of attention we pay to a text. As we discover new things in new readings of familiar words, we must realize the difference that *how* we read makes. A single individual, reading in various ways, thus understands various aspects of a work. Meaning varies as we interpret according to the state of our emotions, intellect, and situation at a given moment. Hence the experience of rereading implies questions about the limits of interpretation. To what extent, and how, does the nature of the text, as opposed to the nature and situation of the reader, control the possibilities of interpretation? To what extent do we create the books we read? Such questions may loom large for any reader; they become virtually inescapable for the rereader.

I've already mentioned memory more than once as a component of rereading, and I will frequently mention it again. To reflect on the large place of memory in rereading may entice us to consider its importance in all acts of reading. Fiction, my preoccupation in this book, especially challenges memory, as the reader consciously or unconsciously assesses every detail on the page against her own experience in life. Understanding, as we grow, more and more about the nature of human beings, we both apply what we have learned to our encounters with people on the page and draw on what we have read in evaluating those we meet in the world.

Experience in life, that standard against which we judge whatever we find in a book, includes experience of other books, which, like direct knowledge of social actualities, contributes to the assessment of each new text. In rereading, demands on memory multiply. Not only do we engage the wisdom acquired by diverse experience of books and of life; we also, by the power of memory, feel the influence of our previous reading of the book now before us. Even if our recollection of particulars has become vague over the years, retained knowledge informs our response to a new exchange with the text. Memory of our past selves in this response originates in but goes beyond memory of our selves as earlier readers of the particular web of language again before us. Reading something for the first time may also evoke past selves, inasmuch as we recall bygone experience, of books and of life outside books, when vicariously experiencing the lives of imaginary others. Rereading brings us more sharply in contact with how we—like the books we reread—have both changed and remained the same. Books help to constitute our identity. They also, as we reread them, measure identity's changes with the passage of time.

To think about rereading encourages particular focus on the relation between outsides and insides that shapes all literary experience. Reading stimulates the inner life. It encourages fantasy: eighteenth-century moralists, for exactly this reason, thought the reading of novels dangerous for young women. (Their fantasies might—horrors!—be sexual, given novelists' propensity for writing about love. And they might lead to action.) The line between reading and daydreaming often blurs. The act of silent reading feels private, an intimate encounter between a narrator's mind and heart and a reader's, its process altogether interior. True, the interior process stems from absorbing words that exist in more or less permanent form, but the reader tends to lose consciousness of those words as objective facts in the rush of thoughts and feelings they induce. A powerful novel makes its reader feel as though she literally inhabits its world and participates in its action.

Yet the words on paper exist, an author exists or has existed, other readers have read the same words before and will read them after any individual enjoyer of the text. Consciously or unconsciously, readers evaluate the happenings in a fiction against their knowledge of real events, assess the characters by their own experience of how people operate. Actualities are actual, and the realm of reading cannot long remain independent of them. We seek in fiction illumination of life experience, insight into the workings of minds and hearts, representations of the learning that life provides; but we also test what we read against what we already know from the world beyond the text.

I seem to have moved from the "how" of reading—the exchange between reader and text, the functions of memory, the position of the outside world—to the "why," which will figure importantly in this book. Indeed, "why" questions keep multiplying. If I say that we seek illumination and insight in fiction, a corollary question comes promptly to mind: "Why not seek such values, rather, in writing that purports to deal with facts?" Suspicion of the misleading possibilities of imaginative literature goes back a long way—at least to Plato, who notoriously banished poets from his ideal republic. Defenses of the imagination are almost equally ancient. They typically claim—as I would claim—that imagina-tive writing can tell a deeper truth than that promulgated by the kind of prose that sticks rigorously to demonstrable fact.

• 11

Theoretical defenses of the imagination, however, tend to sound, to twenty-first-century readers, only rhetorical: fine lan-guage, dubious substance. Particularities, I surmise, would have more persuasive force. Rereading, looking again at what one has previously seen, reveals what carries meaning for the individual doing the seeing. It heightens the experienced value of particulars. If it tells the reader something new, it also reminds her of truth it has told in the past. It may not provoke a formulated apologia for fiction, but it enforces realization of fiction's power. In investi-gating my own responses to rereading, I hope to demonstrate that power.

The "why" of reading fiction, however, involves more than the power of truth. It includes also the power of pleasure, an aspect of reading generally neglected in academic discourse and one that nonacademic readers often deprecate. "I'm just reading for plea-sure": that sounds frivolous, suggesting that one is reading "junk." From classic times through at least the eighteenth century, though, major critics agreed that pleasure and instruction define the dual purpose of reading, and both matter. It is noteworthy that Dr. Johnson, moral arbiter as well as literary critic, assesses each of his subjects in his mammoth work *Lives of the Poets* partly on the ba-sis of the degree of pleasure the poet's work evokes. Pleasure, in the many varieties that reading can produce, is worth being taken seriously by serious readers. I shall delight in talking about it in this book.

In rereading, the interchange of external and internal that I have sketched becomes complicated by the past, and by memory. Feelings from the past lie in wait for the reader in the present, so that feeling becomes insistently the purpose of reading. New feelings may intensify or conflict with the old ones; new judgments may attempt to deny old feelings. The subjective reality of the book being read for the second or fifth or tenth time assumes more than ordinary power. The accumulation of personal experience over time complicates individual responses to words in print; layers of past encounters with the same book infuse new readings of it.

Alternatively, the second or fifth reading allows the reader fuller awareness of the book as something outside herself. Less overwhelmed than she was the first time by the energy of plot and characters, she may have psychic space now to evaluate, to analyze, to understand rather than only to feel. She may become more conscious of possible divergences between the author's intent and her responses; she may think more widely about the book's bearing on past and present social and political circumstance and about its relation to what she knows of human psychology. Successive rereadings enlarge the space of freedom around a book, and thus the possibilities for a reader's reactions.

Rereading can intensify and focus questions of value. Professional literary critics have in recent times often shied away from the intricate and uncertain effort of evaluating what they discuss. The Norton anthology of "world masterpieces" changed its title (now it's the multivolume *Norton Anthology of World Literature*): presumably its editors found the "masterpiece" label too controversial. Amateur critics reflect comparable uneasiness when they declare a book "interesting" rather than "good."

Of course rereaders, too, can and do resort to such evasions. But the act of purposefully returning to something read already, read perhaps more than once before, in the face of guilt-inducing awareness of all the other books that you should have read at least once but haven't—that act in itself urges thought about *why*. What kind of value does a work have to make you come back to it? Is the value only personal, the result of some individual idiosyncrasy, or does it inhere in the text? What are the appropriate standards of literary judgment? My own reflections about matters of value have become increasingly perplexed as a result of the experiments recorded in this book, but I have also become convinced that efforts to discriminate the worth of a literary production not only constitute a useful critical discipline but also contribute to the endless search for self-knowledge.

Despite the rhapsodies that the very thought of rereading can induce in aficionados like me, some people remain impervious to the charms of such activity. Some even express moral disapproval. One needs to read so many more books than one can possibly manage, they say—accurately—that it's wrong to squander valuable time on reading a book more than once. A graduate student who told me that she had "strong opinions" (pro) on the subject of rereading explained that when she developed as a passionate reader in her childhood and early adolescence, her mother would rebuke her if she found the girl rereading something. According to the mother, her daughter's mind would stagnate or weaken if she didn't keep seeking out new and increasingly difficult reading matter. The student kept a journal in which she wrote, among other things, about her reading, and she noticed how her interpretations changed with successive encounters. Different interpretations, she believed, had to mean growth. Hence her continued defiance of her mother; hence her strong opinions as an adult. Her mother, however, likewise had strong opinions, about the meretriciousness of what the daughter considered valuable.

Roger Angell, in a *New Yorker* essay, economically expresses the rereader's response to such criticism: "There's a sweet dab of guilt attached to rereading. Yes, we really should be into something new, for we need to know all about credit-default swaps and Darwin and steroids and the rest, but not just now, please." No reader can fail to agree that the number of books she needs to read far exceeds her capacities, but when the passion for rereading kicks in, the faint guilt that therefore attends the indulgence only intensifies its sweetness.

Yet in some moods that sense of guilt can become painful. I think my impulse to write about rereading originated in a need to justify my own self-indulgence—sinful self-indulgence, I feel at times. Is rereading, I wonder in bad moments, only a form of laziness, unwillingness to confront the hard work of coming to terms with a new and difficult book? If not, precisely what value can one claim for it as a process, apart from the nature of the particular book read? I want to use rereading as a way to think about reading, as I have already said, but questions about the worth of rereading as an act in itself lie at the heart of my present investigation, which aspires to discover the significance and consequence of this activity. Rereading can appear like avoidance, yet I believe that it constitutes a form of engagement. But engagement with what, exactly? The questions multiply. Any engagement involved in acts of rereading must in the nature of things be *re*-engagement, and why should re-engagement be necessary, given attentive reading in the first place? I hope through acts of conscious rereading to clarify, for myself and for others, just what rereading provides that first readings cannot supply. I don't expect to persuade people like my student's mother, people who don't enjoy rereading or who think it a useless or misguided activity, although I'd like at least to insert a bit of doubt into their cavalier rejections of this mode of experience. Mainly, though, I aspire to gratify those who reread already—with or without guilt about all those books they should be reading instead—and who might enjoy reflecting about what they're doing.

My readers' reflections, however, probably will—and probably should—differ from mine. I want them to think about their own experience as readers and rereaders and to realize how exceedingly personal that experience is. From my point of view, outrage at what I have to say—"That's not what it's like at all!"—is as desirable a response as agreement, since it reveals the responder's cogitation about an activity rarely examined. Ideally, conversation about rereading might be both lengthy and complicated.

The subsequent chapters deal with particular varieties of pleasure and enlightenment that rereading entails, attempting to define their nature by investigating experimental instances. These chapters also illustrate ways that the process of rereading intensifies gratifications always inherent in reading. In reading we seek emotional and intellectual stimulation. We hope to find wisdom. We enter into a relation of trust with authors, carrying on with them a constant, more or less conscious, dialogue. We look for enjoyment. Presumably we reread fiction, for the most part, because we have found stimulation, wisdom, or enjoyment in our previous encounter or encounters with a text. All, I will maintain on the basis largely of personal experience, can recur more intensely in new exchanges with familiar texts.

I am my own guinea pig in these endeavors. For this reason, my efforts to creep up, as it were, on the rereading process cannot constitute a natural experiment. When I reread self-consciously, in order to ascertain what's going on as I read, I obviously interfere with the process: it's not the same as random recreational rereading, however hard I try to make it so. Moreover, I am a professional critic. I have spent many years teaching and writing about books. In order to do so, I have reread many books many times, and reread them as one seeking a thesis, an argument through which I might persuade my own readers, or my students, to read the book in question as I do. This personal history necessarily inflects my ways of reading.

Yet I have also been a recreational rereader, and I've had many of the experiences that other rereaders record: finding a childhood favorite no longer compelling or, alternately, discovering new riches in it; understanding a beloved work differently every time I read it; unearthing correspondences between my experience and that delineated on the page. Moreover, I have frequently reread, just for pleasure, books that I've taught or written about: I can't get along without *Pride and Prejudice* for more than a year or so, although I've probably read it forty times.

When I write about my own experience of books, though, I write necessarily as a reader of a certain kind. I am one who "takes a book apart"—a phrase often used by those who think of this activity as the antithesis of "just enjoying." I think—I feel—I *know* that taking a book apart, making myself conscious of how the elements of its construction work with one another to generate emotional, moral, and intellectual effects, is itself a powerful mode of pleasure. The more I understand, the more I enjoy. The more questions I ask of myself and of the book, the more I can see; the more I see, the more I feel.

Rereading, for me, is a process of heightened attention, even when it feels most relaxed; and paying attention is the fundamental action of literary criticism. I don't mean that I deliberately focus my attention on particular moments or sequences when I reread. The passive voice seems appropriate: attention is paid. I do not feel as though I choose what I freshly notice; rather, the text demands my attention in new places, thus revealing itself anew. Rereading, therefore, arouses my critical faculties.

For this reason, my enterprise is both extended and analytical. I hope to articulate a series of discoveries and to develop an extensive argument for rereading as a way of learning and of knowing and as an inlet to particular forms of pleasure. Emerging by a process of accretion, that argument depends on feeling as well as on reason—just as rereading itself does. In part an argument for the centrality of reading in the examined life, it makes a case also for the importance and the special power of a particular way of pondering what one has read.

I am not writing, however, in my voice as professional critic. I have made no systematic effort to produce coherent interpretations of the books I've reread. Rather, I've tried as much as possible to read in a state of relaxation, welcoming whatever comes into my mind as a result. I typically set down a series of reflections that may illuminate facets of what I've read but that rarely add up to a systematic "reading."

These reflections, however, often carry me well beyond the text, recalling me to perplexing questions about the justifications for rereading—and, indeed, adding to them. For instance, I have found repeated gaps between my judgment of literary worth and my personal taste. I reread something I once enjoyed, enjoy it no longer, yet admire it for its craft, its perceptions, its energy. The converse also holds: I enjoy a book but think it virtually devoid of literary value. Such discrepancy is by no means inevitable: often my judgment and my taste coincide. The intermittent presence of a chasm dividing them, however, can puzzle and alarm me.

Partly because I here cultivate my consciousness of such feelings and their import, this is, as I said before, not pure recreational rereading, reading just for fun or for comfort or for memory's sake. Although in some respects very like what I have always done for a living, recreational reading has a different inflection. I think I have approached the recreational position, but I haven't quite achieved it. My choice of reading, like my way of reading, is highly personal. In the succeeding chapters, as I discuss various kinds of rereading and my own experience of them, I will necessarily be writing autobiography, but not an autobiography primarily about happenings and not really an intellectual autobiography either. This will be an autobiography of thoughts and feelings elicited by novels. Rereading of course can involve other genres besides novels: the rereading of poetry offers special satisfactions, and many (including me) reread memoirs, plays, essays—just about anything they have enjoyed once and might enjoy again, or anything that has puzzled them once and that they might be able to figure out now, or anything they remember having read but don't remember the contents of. I focus now on novels alone for the sake of coherence, because I reread them more often than any other form, and because I think they provide a significant source of pleasure for a great many people.

My claim to be writing autobiography requires immediate qualification. I have been surprised, as I have pursued the reading for this book, to discover that I rarely remember the circumstances of my first readings. I remember the general impression a book made on me but not, usually, specific reasons for that impression. What remains most vividly in my mind after many years (and I return to most of the books I reread here after first reading them long ago) is awareness of the other books, or the other kinds of books, I was reading at the time. It's as though my life in books has superseded every other aspect of life, so that what autobiography I offer is largely mediated by literary works.

I propose to discuss various kinds of rereading and questions particularly associated with them. Rereading of children's books makes a good starting point, partly because a special sense of guilt gets associated with it: you're not only reading for the tenth time something you've read before; you're reading something intended for ten-year-olds. What laziness! To think about why such indulgence can feel so pleasurable may begin to unlock the mysteries of rereading.

But children's books are only the beginning. Then there is rereading of Jane Austen, a special case, as I realized sharply in conversation with a friend who claimed that she hated to reread. When I pointed out that I have known her to reread Jane Austen, she looked surprised. "*Everyone* rereads Jane Austen," she said. I think that's approximately true: but why? To think about Austen in this connection raises fundamental questions of value. Many people read and reread her novels, with various alleged reasons for doing so. Such great popularity, across time and space, reveals a remarkable range of appeal. To locate its basis—to uncover, perhaps, the sources of pleasure in this reading, reading that often turns into rereading—might suggest one ground for according high value to a book or an author.

I pursue two exercises that call attention to divergence of taste and judgment: the rereading of books that I didn't like the first time I read them, although I thought I *should* like them, and the rereading of books that I have felt embarrassed about liking. I investigate some specific sources of pleasure in rereading. I explore a couple of special cases. One is the experience of rereading alone books that I read the first time in the company of others engaged with the same book. This relatively unusual situation brings up the possibility that relationships outside those between narrator and reader can influence reactions to books read. To reread, all by myself, books originally read in a context of shared responses dramatizes the difference that diverse life situations can make to the apparent import of a printed text. Finally, I consider "professional" rereading as a topic in itself, attempting to suggest by example how different its results are from those of even approximate recreational rereading.

A few of the rereadings I record were genuinely spontaneous and recreational. I happened to have reread *Emma* and *Pride and Prejudice* recently, so I set down reflections that occurred to me as a result. Most of my comments on individual works, though, share an artificial context: they result from specific assignments. In this case, I have made assignments to myself, thinking of problems I wanted to ponder (would I still like the books I was vaguely ashamed of having liked? If I really thought about the children's books I reread, how would they hold up?) and then seeking books through which to explore them. Although they provided abundant recreation, these assignments could not result in purely recreational rereading. They produced a lot of self-questioning, some tentative answers, and a few firm conclusions. Among other things, they repeatedly substantiated the perception that the pleasures of rereading derive fundamentally from the paradoxical combination of stability and change.

The rest of this book will explore more fully the claims made in the present chapter about the sources of pleasure and profit in the activity of rereading. I will examine my repeated encounters with various books, ranging from the widely familiar to the obscure, from accessible to demanding, in order to show something of what I have learned and felt and how I have developed during a lifetime of rereading for pleasure as well as for professional reasons.

The choice of specific texts is almost entirely arbitrary—purposely arbitrary. I wanted to avoid concentration on books of a single kind, to range as widely as possible among the many novels that I have read for pleasure over the years. I started with books that lived on my shelves, having survived several changes of residence, each of which required condensation of my library. After that, what happened to come into my head pretty much dictated my choices. By no means do I wish to urge that these particular novels should be universally read. Rather, I want to suggest the heterogeneity of my own taste and the general usefulness of rereading all sorts of things. If a reader of this book should feel drawn to read, say, *Middlemarch* for the first time—well, that would be great. But if my account of *Middlemarch* instead encourages her to take another try at *The Mill on the Floss,* or maybe a Trollope novel, or, for that matter, something by Philip Roth, or something by Sara Paretsky: equally great.

I try to discuss mainly works that will be widely familiar, but on occasion I stray into more esoteric realms. My academic specialty—and my hobby horse—is eighteenth-century English literature, and I cannot entirely forgo writing about my passion. Most of the books I read, though, are nineteenth- and twentieth-century products. Considering them, *re*considering them, I offer a sampling of the fresh insights that come with repeated literary encounters.

My interest focuses both on those insights themselves and on reflections about rereading as an activity—a way of knowledge and of pleasure. To write about the activity and its consequences recapitulates both kinds of reward. Indeed, writing about rereading does more than recapitulate. Rather, it multiplies: the process of articulating enlarges insight and recalls delight. Perhaps reading about rereading may have comparable effects.

I must confess that a certain polemic purpose guides me in this enterprise. As a book about rereading, this is, as I have suggested, most essentially a treatment of reading: indeed, a defense of reading. It attempts to demonstrate how reading gets inside your head and what it does when it gets there. My experiment ponders questions of value. Its fundamental assumptions do not diverge from those of classical times: reading, which should instruct and delight, is to be valued inasmuch as it accomplishes those aims. Such terms—"instruct," "delight," even "reading"—have little meaning in the abstract. Reading exists primarily in countless individual, particular exchanges. Instruction and delight have innumerable shapes. By writing of some of them, I hope to stimulate readers' reflection about their own experience and to encourage the pleasure of reading in all its particularity.

2

Once Upon a Time

LOTS OF PEOPLE ENJOY rereading children's books—and why not? The books of our childhood often have glowing memories attached to them. Rereading them helps us recall a time almost certainly less stressful and more protected than the present and may enable us at least partially to recall selves from that distant past. Moreover, the works themselves offer special satisfactions. They evoke a realm where clear lines divide good from evil and the good guys always win. Although scary threats abound and frightening things may happen, everything will turn out all right. To read or reread these works provides relative simplicity and clarity—as well as, often, comedy, adventure, and excitement. For those of us who reread for pleasure and relaxation, children's books supply dependable fare.

It would seem, then, that for grown-ups engaged in rereading, children's books occupy the stability end of the continuum between stability and change. Relatively uncomplicated as they are, we can hardly expect them to reveal striking new aspects. Moreover, the strong expectation of stability does much to create the anticipated condition: we find, often, what we seek. Wanting to recapture a bygone experience, we feel predisposed to do so. And we yearn for this kind of rereading to provide escape from adult complexities.

In practice, though, rereading children's books, like other kinds of rereading, may offer unexpected rewards rather than the predictable or hoped-for ones, as well as, on occasion, unexpected disappointments. Possibly the book that we imagined as soothing in its simplicity turns out to be entirely too simple to provide grown-up satisfactions: we must cross it off our list. At the opposite extreme, we may discover that a work remembered as straightforward in the pleasures it supplies offers surprising complexities. Almost always in rereading children's books, we risk discovering new things about ourselves. In other words, the stability-change continuum is no more predictable in children's literature than in any other variety.

Children read their books for the first time in a space outside history, culture, and community. I first read *Alice in Wonderland* for myself around the age of six. It was not a happy period in my life: after moving from Chicago to Florida in the middle of the school year, I had been placed in the "dumb second grade," as everyone called it—the class for slow learners and for children repeating the grade—because the local authorities didn't approve of my having been allowed to skip the first grade in Illinois. The dumb second grade bored and embarrassed me. I had been reading since before I was three, and reading now became my rescue operation. We lived only two blocks from the public library, to which I walked every day after school. I read and read, going more or less systematically through the shelves of the children's section. Nancy Drew, the Bobbsey Twins, the Little Colonel, Elsie Dinsmore, the Oz books—with varying degrees of enthusiasm, I read them all.

And I found *Alice in Wonderland*, which enchanted me. Lewis

Carroll was, as far as I was concerned, only a name on a title page. I had no idea who he was, nor did I care. If I'd known about Charles Dodgson, I might have felt interested in the idea of someone's using a false name as an author, but the actuality of an Oxford mathematician would have meant little to me. I didn't imagine that anyone else had read the wonderful words that presented themselves. It didn't occur to me that Alice came from an earlier era; I probably didn't yet know distinctly that earlier eras—times before I was alive—had existed. Alice was my contemporary, my friend, almost my double—or, at any rate, the double of the little girl I wanted to be.

Alice in Wonderland, I felt, belonged to me alone. Not the physical book: eventually given a copy by a benevolent courtesy uncle, I felt my possession of it almost irrelevant in comparison with my ownership of its contents. I owned those words because I felt them so profoundly; I knew exactly what they meant. Even though I missed all the literary allusions and didn't comprehend some of the vocabulary, I understood the experience the language recorded: that of being left alone to make your own discoveries. This was not an experience I had myself undergone, or so I felt, but one for which I longed. To be sure, Alice repeatedly finds herself the victim of bossy or complaining others—caterpillars and duchesses and gryphons—beings that seemed like grumpy grown-ups. But she never allows herself to remain a victim for long. Although she cries rather a lot, her intrepidity and resourcefulness awed me. They also roused in me a determination to perform likewise. That determination would not pay off for many years: life appeared to provide few opportunities for intrepidity. Still, Alice solidified what had previously been only a vague dream of possibility. It's not that I wanted to grow up to be Alice. I wanted to be Alice *right now.*

I don't think I talked about all this with my parents. My mother was already worrying that I liked reading too much. (I mean both that I liked it too much and that I read too much.) This fact was convenient for her: well before the era of television, she always had a ready way to entertain me and to keep me from being a nuisance. She, however, had little interest in books and considerable anxiety about the dangers of bookishness (not, in the small-town South of those days, a desirable characteristic, especially for girls). My father told me stories, so he might have been a more likely recipient of confidences about my wonderful discovery, but as I recall it felt private to me, not something to be shared.

It's OK to be curious, *Alice in Wonderland* informed me. Alice's adventures begin because, "burning with curiosity," she follows a White Rabbit who has both a waistcoat pocket and a watch to take out of it: two phenomena she has never seen before. It's OK to cry but not necessary to cry all the time. Much depends on size: when I grew taller, I'd have more power. You should take advantage of whatever opportunity offers—magic mushrooms, golden keys, Cheshire cats. If you insult someone by accident (as Alice repeatedly insults small animals by speaking affectionately of her mouse-eating cat or her dog), their feelings may be hurt, but the hurt feelings won't last forever. If a baby turns into a pig in your arms, don't worry about it; just let the pig trot away. The book was rich in instruction but devoid of irritating morals.

Rich also in pure pleasure. I already understood that talking animals did not actually exist. I knew the unlikelihood of meeting a rabbit wearing a waistcoat or a mouse that tells a tale about his distaste for cats. *Alice* was "just a story," but a story so full of delight that I could hardly get enough of it. I felt disappointed that it turned out all to be a dream, but that was my only complaint. I think I reread the book almost immediately after I finished my first reading, and I reread it repeatedly during my childhood, finding it always delicious and discovering new sources of pleasure as I came to know more about the world and about other books. *Alice in Wonderland* became my talisman.

The year I turned eleven, I was in seventh grade. The school system of my small Florida town dealt with bright kids by having them skip grades (despite its disapproval of skipping first grade), so I was ahead of myself. I began studying Spanish and was enthralled by the notion that you could say things differently in different languages and be understood by different people. I entertained myself by trying to translate bits of poetry and prose—an enterprise made difficult by the fact that I knew little of my new language at this point. *Alice in Wonderland* remained one of my favorite books, although by this time I had read many more grown-up works.

I must have been pestering my mother about Christmas, trying to figure out what was in store for me. At any rate, she said she'd tell me about one present. She was going to give me, she said, a copy of *Alice in Wonderland* in Spanish.

The idea that two passions might be simultaneously satisfied thrilled me. My mother had never given me a book. If she was going to do so, perhaps her disapproval of my reading didn't run as deep as I had thought. On Christmas morning I waited expectantly through lesser gifts, believing that the best was being saved for last. The presents came to an end, though, and no Spanish *Alice in Wonderland* had appeared. I inquired, and my mother said that had been a joke, designed to make me stop nagging her; she didn't even know if any such work existed.

It seems an odd idea now, the notion of *Alice in Wonderland* in Spanish, but at the time I could imagine nothing more satisfying. My disappointment remains vivid to me after more than six decades. The idea of such a book would not have occurred to me without my mother's suggestion, but once that idea existed, its lack of realization felt like deprivation. I continued to read *Alice* in

English from time to time, but with a vague sense of disappointment.

I graduated from high school; I went to college, then graduate school; for several years I abandoned Lewis Carroll. The next time I read *Alice,* I think, was when, during the 1960s, I taught at Wellesley College a seminar called The Independent Woman. As I pondered the construction of a syllabus, my youthful role model returned to my mind. *Alice in Wonderland* joined works by such writers as Doris Lessing to become a central text in the course.

I don't remember details about what I found in Carroll's book during that particular rereading, although I remember well the students' enthusiasm over it, but I have recently read *Alice* yet again. Doing so reminded me of past pleasures I had almost forgotten: for instance, the sheer comedy of such scenes as the Mock Turtle's tearful attempts to tell his story or the game of croquet with flamingos as mallets and hedgehogs as balls. And the delicious word play: the classical master, an old crab (literally), teaches Laughing and Grief; students also, according to the Mock Turtle, have to learn Mystery, ancient and modern, as well as Drawling from the Drawling-master. I must have loved this as a child: the discovery that words can become jokes just because, sounding alike, they may mean such different things.

As an adult, I can't recapture the excitement of first discovering the games that can be played with words, but I have the advantage of knowledge that children lack: of history, culture, and community. Memories of what I have read about Victorian girls' schools enrich the idea of a Drawling-master. I imagine what it might have been like for a late-nineteenth-century child to read Carroll's words; I hope that children in the present are sharing my delight in reading them yet again. Musings about past and present culture mingle with my direct response to the comedy of the Mock Turtle and the Gryphon, whose interplay suggests that everything is up for grabs—language, action, sanity itself—in the wonderful world Carroll has evoked.

Alice in Wonderland provides another new source of pleasure this time through. For the first time, I notice how much of the heroine's experience takes place in her mind. She talks a lot, but often she talks to herself, making her interior life audible. If many of her reflections are trivial (Do cats eat bats? Do bats eat cats?), almost all convey her lively awareness and curiosity about the world and her eagerness to make use of whatever she knows. She wonders what latitude or longitude she's reached as she falls slowly down the rabbit hole, although she doesn't know what either term designates. She knows, though, that they are "nice grand words to say." She imagines the possibility of shutting up like a telescope; she looks for poison labels on bottles because she knows that poison would probably disagree with her. More important, she wonders who she is. She feels different; she keeps changing sizes; she finds her experience now unlike any she has had before. Perhaps she has become someone else she knows: not Ada, who has ringlets, as she herself doesn't, but maybe Mabel, who is terribly ignorant. If she has turned into Mabel, she decides, she will just stay at the bottom of the rabbit hole: life there seems more gratifying than the prospect of existence in Mabel's "poky little house."

Questions about her identity occur rather often to Alice, partly in response to inquiries by the strange folk she meets in Wonderland. She thinks like a child, not like a metaphysician, so she considers the problem not in the abstract but as an immediate difficulty in her encounters and in her reflections. Inasmuch as such recourse is possible, given the peculiarities of her environment, she remains consistently pragmatic, confronting her difficulties on the basis of her previous experience. Not only is she admirable as a child heroine: she models an approach to life that adults, too, might find useful.

Her problems of identity derive entirely from her immediate

situation. A striking aspect of Alice's course through the underground world is how firmly she in fact remains herself, despite the insubordination of her language when she tries to recite a poem and despite the pressure that the beings she meets exert upon her in various ways and various directions. When, during the ridiculous trial of the Knave of Hearts, she cries, "Stuff and nonsense!" and then responds, "I won't!" to the Queen's command that she hold her tongue, she asserts her own superiority—in size, but also in acumen—to the creatures whom she subsequently dismisses with the statement, "You're nothing but a pack of cards!" Insisting that she knows better, *thinks* better, than they, she thus claims her own power. Doing so precipitates her out of Wonderland, into a world where she gets sent off to tea, leaving her sister in sentimental musings over her.

Alice's reflectiveness, her constant, often vocal, meditation about what's happening to her, thus ends in judgment: assertion of the trial's injustice and of the insubstantiality of its cast of characters. Such assertion necessarily involves self-assertion: a firm claim of identity as the dream comes to its end.

In other words, the two aspects of the story that struck me in this most recent reading relate closely to each other in a Cartesian equation: Alice thinks, therefore she is. Her doubts about her identity dissipate in the course of her responsive reflections about what is happening to her. For a long time, she does not judge: she accepts the Mock Turtle and the Gryphon on their own terms, although she has qualms about the wisdom of the March Hare's proceedings. When she finally issues her judgment, the result of her watching and pondering of the court's activities, that judgment is solid—and so is she.

I had altogether forgotten the musings by Alice's sister that conclude the narrative, no doubt because they strike me as an unsatisfactory ending to Carroll's story, which could easily have concluded, a couple of pages earlier, with Alice thinking about what a wonderful dream she had had. What's at issue here, though, involves more than narrative technique. The unnamed older sister's thoughts and feelings about Alice seem an authorial effort to repudiate the implications of the child's experience as the story has evoked it. Her sister pictures Alice as a grown woman,

> and how she would keep, through all her riper years, the simple and loving heart of her childhood; and how she would gather about her other little children, and make *their* eyes bright and eager with many a strange tale, perhaps even with the dream of Wonderland long ago; and how she would feel with all their simple sorrows, and find a pleasure in all their simple joys, remembering her own child-life, and the happy summer days.

These are the final words of *Alice in Wonderland*.

The emphasis on Alice's "simple and loving heart," with the double reiteration of "simple" as an adjective for the sorrows and joys of Alice's hypothetical children, may suggest a view of the little girl at odds with my emphasis on her reflectiveness and her problems about identity. A simple and loving heart is not incompatible with a lively intelligence, but to characterize the story's heroine thus stresses her participation in a generic myth of childhood innocence and purity rather than her individualized intelligence, practicality, and eagerness. My version of Alice interests me a lot more than her sister's vision does. But my Alice—the Alice, I would argue, that Carroll depicted—has rebellious potential. If the creatures of Wonderland are parodic versions of Victorian elders, Alice's willingness to ask herself mental questions about them hints at the possibility of a child's challenging established hierarchies. The sister's meditations at the end promulgate a less threatening little girl (emphasis on *little:* what harm, after all, can an innocent child do?) than readers perhaps have glimpsed. If we think more about that simple and loving heart, we will think less about the mind that works its way to overturning a courtroom.

To talk about pragmatism, identity, and Cartesian equations may seem inappropriate in dealing with a children's book. Certainly such matters have little bearing on the ways that actual children would respond to *Alice in Wonderland*—little bearing, indeed, on the ways I remember responding myself.

Or am I wrong here? I think maybe I am. My early response to Alice as a confronter and solver of problems in fact had a good deal to do with pragmatism, and probably with identity. I have wondered why, unlike others with whom I have discussed childhood reading, I never felt scared by the bizarre transformations that Alice endured—expanding, for instance, to the extent of filling up a whole house. I was certainly not immune to terror when I read what I thought "scary" books, but *Alice* wasn't one of them. My imperviousness, I now suspect, may have come from the fact that I was more interested in Alice's responses than in what actually happened to her. The equation between thinking and being almost certainly had its subterranean effect on me as a juvenile ponderer. Children would not put their reactions in such highfalutin terms, but it may be that I actually knew from the beginning what I have only consciously realized now.

It doesn't matter, though, whether I did or not. To find serious import in books that ostensibly claim only to entertain children may suggest why they endure so powerfully—for children and for adults. Four out of twenty of the most frequently reread books in Great Britain, remember, are conventionally considered works for children. We rereaders of juvenile literature may say that we read for comfort, ease, relaxation, and so we do: *Alice in Wonderland*, like *Black Beauty* or even Harry Potter, makes few obvious demands and seems peculiarly satisfying for just that reason, a book to be read when one doesn't want to have to think too hard. But I don't think I would have read *Alice* so often had it not offered deeper satisfactions. One need not articulate such pleasures in order to experience them, but putting words to the meanings that lie beneath the surface of apparently simple texts allows a reader to experience more sharply what may have been previously blurred.

Such articulation also allows the making of connections that would otherwise remain hidden. To see Alice as a Cartesian heroine may encourage us to discover her unexpected resemblance to some other figure from the works accumulated in that miscellaneous collection in our heads. To think of her as having identity problems makes her suddenly, comically, congruent with a host of modern and postmodern characters. In other words, talking about such matters as pragmatism and identity in connection with a children's book can heighten the reader's consciousness, and to heighten consciousness enlarges the inlets of pleasure. The more I think about Alice, the more interesting she becomes to me. A book's propensity to provoke thought, for me, stands high among its virtues.

But other virtues stand high as well, the capacity to generate immediate pleasure among them. Readers and rereaders who find in *Alice in Wonderland* only such pleasure find a great deal. Although people reread on occasion in order to understand better some text that seemed obscure the first time around, or to understand in a new way something first read long ago, habitual rereaders most often, I'd guess (and I include myself among them), pursue the activity as a form of self-indulgence or pure relaxation. Sometimes we yearn for diminished rather than heightened consciousness. The knowledge that books—the same books—can provide either satisfaction, depending on the state of mind we bring to them, is a delight of rereading. I would contend, though, that those meanings lying beneath the surface operate even when we seek and find pure relaxation in the activity of rereading. They contribute to our pleasure; they enrich the text we encounter even if we don't allow them to provoke thought.

Reading a book for the first time can rarely if ever offer the kind of relaxed pleasure that comes with previous knowledge of how everything is going to turn out. It is equally true that reading a book for the first time rarely stimulates the kind of subtle discriminations that become possible when much in the text feels familiar. Children's books as well as grown-up ones provoke such discrimination.

Sometimes, though, a work that has delighted one's childhood does not reward adult attempts at analysis. My main source of books as a little girl, apart from the public library, was that rich courtesy uncle I have mentioned, whose tastes were firmly rooted in the Victorian Age. (I remember his reading Kipling's "If" to me, with great expression, as a guide to conduct.) He gave me several sumptuous volumes, most of which I still own, tattered though they are. One of these belonged to the large category of *Alice*-imitations. *Davy and the Goblin*, indeed, declared its allegiance in its subtitle: *Or What Followed Reading "Alice's Adventures in Wonderland."* Googling its author, Charles Edward Carryl, I discover that he was an American millionaire who held a seat on the New York Stock Exchange for thirty-four years. The information, of course unknown to me as a child, has no apparent relevance to *Davy and the Goblin*, but *Alice* has a great deal. Like its predecessor, *Davy* abounds in peculiar creatures, unaccountable transformations, and nonsense verse. Its male protagonist feels as bewildered as Carroll's female one. The wondrous experiences the book offers him turn out, like Alice's, all to be a dream.

Although I loved the book as a child and read at least parts of it over and over, I found rereading it as an adult tedious. The tedium resulted, I think, from the respects in which Carryl's tribute differed from its model. As a writer of nonsense verse, this millionaire excels. I used to recite with great pleasure verses from "A Capital Ship for an Ocean Trip," which offered a rollicking meter that made it easy to remember, as well as a satisfyingly comic series of events. And then there was the poem by the irritated giant, annoyed at feeling disrespected by the smaller beings who have awakened him from his nap. He admonishes them, in words that I have found useful myself from time to time:

> Don't reply that I was drowsy,
> For my nap was but a kind
> Of dramatic illustration
> Of a peaceful state of mind.

Such textual moments owe nothing to *Alice* beyond the idea of versifying characters' responses to immediate situations, and they remain gratifying in themselves.

In its larger scheme, however, *Davy and the Goblin* now seems inadequate. Unlike Alice, Davy does not ponder the implications of his adventures and his encounters. One episode gives way to another, invariably, by arbitrary transformation. Although characters may reappear, they challenge the protagonist briefly, if at all, and no situation gets resolved. Davy does not develop in any way, except that presumably by the end he believes in the possibility of goblins. (He begins, the narrator tells us, as a thorough skeptic, although we see no evidence of his skepticism.) He faces no problems that require of him independent action or thought. The book offers no stimulus for thinking about such matters as Cartesian equations and identity problems.

For a child, rollicking verse and unconnected comic adventures may suffice to provide abundant entertainment. They do not necessarily supply adequate satisfaction for the adult, who does not demand identity problems but who perhaps prefers at least minimal characterization for a story's protagonist and finds interest lagging if ludicrous episodes succeed one another indefinitely without logic or apparent meaning. *Davy and the Goblin* has changed for the worse since the last time I read it, and I'm sorry to lose some of the delight I earlier experienced with it.

It occurs to me, though, that perhaps my self-conscious rereading, rereading in deliberate pursuit of critical judgment, is to blame for my loss of pleasure. I claimed earlier that an analytic frame of mind, far from spoiling my enjoyment of reading, only adds to it; and I absolutely believe that to be true as a general proposition. Children's books, however, may constitute a special case, inasmuch as rereading them typically involves a state of conscious or unconscious regression. Powerful nostalgia for childhood necessarily informs much adult rereading of books from the distant past and provides a rich source of delight as one captures a bit of a long-gone state of mind and feeling. To reread *Davy and the Goblin* purposefully, in the immediate context of *Alice in Wonderland*, overrides nostalgia and regression and thus weakens pleasure. It seems likely, then, that I can hope again to recapture the sheer fun of it in some future, more random rereading.

In at least one instance, I recaptured the fun of a childhood book of surpassing simplicity—recaptured the fun and experienced the nostalgia, despite my purposeful reading. I'm thinking of *The Story of Ferdinand*, another early favorite of mine, not a novel in length but arguably one in miniature, and, I now believe, a masterpiece. The author of this tale, Munro Leaf, was a friend of my father, so we probably received the book as soon as it was published, in 1936. I was old enough for *Alice in Wonderland*, and *Ferdinand* seemed intended for much younger children. It had only a few hundred words of text, with many large and charming pictures, line drawings by Robert Lawson. Its plot can be readily summarized: a Spanish bull named Ferdinand has no interest in other bulls or their activities; he prefers to sit under a cork tree and smell the flowers. When scouts come in search of the strongest, fiercest bull for the Madrid bullfights, however, Ferdinand chances to sit on a bee, whose sting causes him to go into a fury of bucking and leaping. The scouts therefore think him an ideal candidate. At the actual fight, the audience includes many ladies wearing flowers in their hair. Ferdinand enters the ring and sits down to smell the flowers. Since he can't be provoked into fighting, he is sent back to his field, where he presumably lives happily ever after.

My mother and my father seemed to enjoy this story as much as I did. In 1936, they presumably saw deeper meanings in the fable; I did not. (As it turns out, Leaf's book was attacked as "communist" and as a satire of pacifism. The author said he had nothing in mind but a good story.) When I read *Ferdinand* now (it takes about five minutes), I still find it delightful. I take it on its own terms: although I realize that it could be read as political allegory, what interests me is the flawless clarity and logic of the simple tale.

Like Alice, even more than Alice, Ferdinand stays always and distinctly himself. He doesn't question established ways of doing things; he simply remains unaffected by conventional expectations, with his mother's full support. He seems effortlessly happy. The drawings are wonderful. The book demands almost nothing of its adult reader, and it delivers great satisfaction. A fundamental source of that satisfaction is the extreme ease with which everything works out. A bullfight hardly seems more sinister than a bee sting, and someone who doesn't want to fight doesn't have to. Surely the wish that life might be less difficult crosses every mind: *Ferdinand* fulfills that wish. It also reminds us of a time when we didn't even know that life was hard.

Rereading the little book now, I think of it in ways that would not have been available to me as a child; I articulate sources of appeal that I must have responded to earlier without needing to wonder why. It has been enriched, while remaining the story that I loved long ago.

All of which is to say that children's books, like grown-up books, offer a variety of delights, some of which depend on a reader's state of mind, some of which may vividly alter states of mind and feeling. It would be impossible to exhaust the different kinds of juvenile literature that reward renewed attention in adulthood, but I will linger on two more varieties: the tale of pure adventure and the series composed of several related works. The series, with its reiterated promise of further developments, holds a special kind of fascination. But so does the adventure story, which offers the temptation of pure excitement.

On my ninth birthday I received as a gift (an inscription in the book tells me so) Robert Louis Stevenson's *Kidnapped*, less well known than *Treasure Island*, but from a child's point of view (and, it turns out, an adult's as well) at least equally exciting. Of the books that survive from my childhood, this is the most tattered: I read it repeatedly, though I don't believe that I have read it again since I went to college. It was, I now realize, a "boy's book," but that fact made little difference to me at the age of nine. Although I got particular pleasure from the fact that Alice was a girl like me (or like the girl I wanted to be), I did not find it at all difficult to identify with male protagonists.

David Balfour was particularly easy to identify with because his qualities were ones I admired and aspired to. Seventeen years old, he sets off into an unknown world, an orphan with uncertain prospects and no knowledge of his own family: like Alice, seeking himself by means of random encounters. By the novel's end, he has discovered his membership in a distinguished family, has come into an inheritance, and has in conspicuous ways grown up. Between the beginning and the end, David exists in almost constant danger of death, engaged in a series of unexpected and perilous adventures.

The book's title suggests victimization. In fact, though, kidnapping only inaugurates a sequence of happenings by which David, gaining confidence through adversity, achieves his maturity. His miserly uncle, wrongful possessor of the family fortune, arranges for his kidnapping: lured aboard a ship, then promptly knocked unconscious, he is to be sold as a slave in North Carolina. It is 1751: Great Britain is still unsettled by the threat of a royal claimant in France. In 1745, the son of the deposed King James, Bonnie Prince Charlie, had landed an invading force in Scotland. Many Scots joined him in marching south toward London, to be disastrously defeated at the Battle of Culloden. Scots lairds who had participated in the rebellion paid with their lives. The wearing of tartan and of kilts was banned, as was possession of weapons. Numerous Scots, nonetheless, remained loyal to "the king over the water."

I knew nothing of all this at the age of nine, and the history is important to Stevenson's book. I hated dialect stories—we had been made to read Uncle Remus in school, and I found the tales intensely irritating because of their language. Many of Stevenson's characters speak in Scots dialect. For all my historical ignorance and my linguistic prejudice, however, I loved the novel.

I call it a novel because Stevenson wrote it as one. He did not seek a juvenile audience. The book I was given, however, with a copyright date of 1913, was obviously intended for young readers, with large type and abundant full-page illustrations by the popular children's illustrator N. C. Wyeth, so children had discovered *Kidnapped* within fifty years of its first publication in 1886. Amazon currently advertises the work as appropriate for readers from the sixth grade up. There is, of course, a special charm for children in reading books that appear planned for grown-ups, and I probably enjoyed the fact that I didn't really understand the historical context in which events took place: since I could grasp, at least in a general sense, what was going on, I had the illusion that I was figuring it all out.

In his kidnapped condition, David finds himself serving as cabin boy after his predecessor is murdered. When the captain and crew plot to murder a man they think wealthy, the only survivor from a small boat that the ship has plowed into, David allies himself with the survivor and with him defeats fifteen opponents, killing one of them. Most of the rest of the novel consists of a series of prolonged, unpredictable, arduous, dangerous journeys. First, after the ship is wrecked off the coast of the Highlands, David travels alone toward Alan Breck, the man at whose side he has fought. The two together flee pursuit for a murder that neither has committed, then make their way toward the Lowlands, where David finds safety and wealth that enable him to send Alan back to France, his intended destination in the original boat.

The novel is preoccupied with male bonding. At one point a wife sits by the fireside and weeps while her husband makes plans; at another, a serving girl in a tavern provides a boat, which she rows herself, for the final stage of the comrades' escape to the Lowlands. These are the only females in speaking roles, and the roles are tiny. The relation between David and Alan, which springs from their first fight together, gradually becomes more complex and more compelling. David has in a sense rescued Alan at the start—the older man (his age is never specified) could not have held off the ship's crew alone. Afterwards, though, Alan becomes increasingly the guide and caretaker. He gives David a silver button as a sign of his commitment. When the boy finally makes his way to human habitation after being shipwrecked alone, he discovers that Alan has left instructions along the way to guide the "lad with the silver button" to him. Apparently indefatigable, the native Highlander runs, creeps, and climbs to make his way through dangerous territory, and he draws David as well to unanticipated feats of physical endurance. When David sickens, Alan cares for him. When David shows his ignorance, Alan instructs him.

David has previously been instructed mainly by the local minister, a warm and devout man. With this moral guidance in his background, he finds himself frequently puzzled by Alan's morality, which operates by intricate arguments leading to perverse conclusions. For instance, when the two of them witness a murder, Alan knows the murderer's identity. He will not, however, divulge it, although his silence places both him and the boy he has befriended in mortal danger. Moreover, he deliberately attracts soldiers' attention, so that they pursue him and David rather than the true culprit. The guilty, he points out, are at higher risk than the innocent, if they are captured. "Alan's morals were all tail-first," David observes; "but he was ready to give his life for them, such as they were." In general, the boy admires more than he disapproves the principles by which the older man operates.

When, however, his own moral principles clash sharply with Alan's—and when, to boot, Alan inadvertently harms him—trouble ensues. David lies sick in a Highland hut, while Alan plays cards with their host. David has previously declined to play, announcing that gambling is against his principles. Alan first wins, then loses, then asks half-conscious David for a loan, and takes the small remaining amount of money that the boy has, only to lose it as well. The two cannot travel without money. Their host returns the money he has won, thus humiliating David. Although he contains his anger at Alan for a time, it bursts forth on the subsequent journey, causing a rupture that is healed only when David, at the point of collapse, asks for physical help. At that moment Alan announces that he has previously liked his companion because the youth never gets angry, but now he likes him even better because he has done exactly what he "never" does.

David feels vindicated in his principles and strengthened in his friendship. For the rest of their time together, the couple (and they seem like a couple in the deepest sense) continue to struggle against outside forces but feel no disharmony between themselves.

The aspects of the book that attracted me most as a girl continue to appeal to me now. There was a time in my childhood when I would answer people who asked me what I wanted to be when I grew up by saying that I really wanted to be a soldier, but since girls couldn't be soldiers, I'd be a nurse. I had little notion what soldiers did; what I really wanted to be was a knight. Uncle Joe had given me a volume of Howard Pyle's stories based on Arthurian legends. Enthralled, I sought out from the library other tales of knights and their ladies. What got me was not the fighting or the dragons. It was the embodied ideals of honor, integrity, loyalty, and courage. I wanted to be a knight because knights—at least in the children's versions of the stories—were *good*, in ways to which I aspired. A soldier, I thought, would be the modern equivalent of a knight.

This may sound like a digression from *Kidnapped*, but in fact it isn't. I found in Stevenson's story what I loved in the Arthurian tales: relationships predicated on idealistic commitments. In the final third of the narrative, David realizes for the first time that his personal danger would greatly diminish if he parted company with Alan. He feels tempted to separate himself, but his sense of loyalty intervenes. Although the continued companionship of the two men is foolhardy from the point of view of expediency, honor makes it necessary—and affection makes it attractive. Like the Arthurian knights, these men speak rarely of affection. When they part at last, they hardly speak at all. They make practical arrangements; then "the words seemed to leave us; and though I would seek to jest with Alan . . ., and he with me . . ., you could feel very well that we were nearer tears than laughter." Then: "'Well, goodbye,' said Alan, and held out his left hand. 'Good-bye,' said I, and gave the hand a little grasp, and went off down hill." Such is their parting. David feels like crying, but he doesn't do so; he feels "a cold gnawing in my inside like a remorse for something wrong," but he doesn't analyze it. He goes about his business, doing what he is supposed to do.

Men with strong feelings, who control those feelings in order to fulfill their responsibilities; men who put loyalty before self-interest; men capable, like Alan, of passionate commitment to a cause: such figures captured my imagination as a child. (Of course girls of the same sort were even better—but my reading provided few examples of female nobility.) When I reread *Kidnapped* now, I realize how central to Stevenson's enterprise the ideals of honor, loyalty, and commitment are. The adventures provided by a fast-moving plot are means to the end of demonstrating these ideals in action.

Though I still find the novel's version of heroism compelling, I now also see aspects of *Kidnapped* that give me pause. By now I have had some real-life experience of men who claim to have strong feelings but never express them, and I find such men rather less attractive in fiction than I once did. The figure of the woman who weeps over her husband's predicament but can offer no suggestions for alleviating it now troubles me, as does that of the girl who appears for long enough to be beguiled into helping the travelers and then vanishes forever. Stock characters abound, and many of them have names that seem a little too good to be true: "Alan" and "David" for the straightforward, manly protagonists; "Ebenezer"—surely with overtones of Ebenezer Scrooge—for the crabbed uncle.

Uncle Ebenezer, an unredeemable villain, strikes me as cartoonish. A few minutes after first meeting his nephew, he sends him off on an expedition that will lead him to certain death. Only a well-timed flash of lightning saves the youth from a fatal fall: the stairs he has been ordered to ascend in the dark end in mid-air. Since Ebenezer's subsequent machinations show him invariably concerned not to have blood on his hands, this maneuver seems implausible in relation to the character, if useful for the author. In fact, conveniences of plot rather than deep imaginings of plot's significance often appear to dictate the book's happenings.

None of this bothered me as a child, and, surprisingly, it bothers me little now. I've suggested some serious narrative flaws, as well as a moral weakness revealed in the treatment of women; but the narrative, flaws regardless, remains compelling in its onward rush, and the moral scheme implicit in the protagonists' manly virtues retains its appeal because of its very simplicity and clarity—simplicity and clarity that come at the expense of shutting out the inconvenient complexities of another gender. It occurs to me that the attractions of *Kidnapped* bear some relation to those of the Harry Potter books. I was immediately struck, reading the early books in the Potter series, by their fundamental similarity to Victorian boys' books like *Tom Brown's Schooldays*. Harry Potter's school offers a lot more excitement than its Victorian counterpart, with magic rather than math as an object of study, but loyalty, honesty, integrity, and courage are the virtues celebrated. No longer are they figured as only "manly": girls participate too, manifesting the same qualities of character, although the hero is male. The appeal of clear, straightforward virtue, however, remains powerful.

And so it is with *Kidnapped*. I rather doubt if kids read it now. Its vocabulary would be daunting, and it seems unlikely that young readers would think the historical facts worth figuring out or even surmising. If they struggled through it, though, I suspect it would still exercise its power over the imagination. At any rate, rereading it proved entertaining for me.

Still, that rereading raised questions about my younger self. How did I really process that female absence at the center of the narrative? Obviously, I knew that some activities were, in the real world, forbidden to girls: I couldn't be a soldier, much less a knight, but only a nurse. What kind of identification could I have felt with David Balfour? I might thrill to his exploits, and to his loyalty and courage, but the fantasy of identifying with such a man, like the more familiar girlish fantasy of being a princess, must have seemed something that belonged only to the world of books. For the time of reading, one could imagine oneself exhibiting courage and honor, but possibly in actuality—this must have been, at some level, the fear—loyalty and courage, like clambering through the Highlands, were impossible for girls.

I can only speculate; I can't really remember exactly how I dealt with narratives of male experience. Even the possibility of such speculation, though, reveals that childhood reading is not always the simple pleasure that we may nostalgically recall. Nostalgia filters out discordant elements in order to allow the gratification of happy, hazy memory. Memories of childhood reading may depend heavily on haziness. Serious rereading of childhood books should perhaps endeavor to clear away, if possible, some of the haze. Or maybe "should" is beside the point: preservation of the haze may be rereading's real purpose.

Nostalgia almost inevitably composes part of the experience of rereading childhood books. Thinking of that fact, I suggested earlier that books from childhood were likely to remain largely the same in rereadings, if only because, given nostalgia's power, one so much wants them to do just that. Having contemplated closely a sample of my own rereadings, however, I could equally well argue the opposite. Given the difference in development, in life experience, and in book experience, the responses of a six-year-old and of the same person decades later will surely differ.

The wonder of rereading beloved books from childhood is that both situations, superficially contradictory though they are, can exist simultaneously. I reread *Alice in Wonderland*, having read it often before (although not for a long time), and recapture the delight of my original readings, with the kind of freshness I associate primarily with reading something for the first time. But that delight has an overlay—an enrichment, in fact—of new insight. Thinking now of Alice's inwardness and its effects on the narrative, I understand part of the reason the book gives me such pleasure.

As a child, I greedily absorbed the many books I read as visions of alternate lives. Now, still capable on occasion of the same sort of greedy absorption, I am also aware of books as structures of language and of specific problems that they set out to address. I feel *Alice* as pure delight at the same time that I think about how her questions about identity are addressed in the text. I read *Kidnapped* with the excitement that attends good adventure stories, but also with a good deal of knowledge about eighteenth-century history—knowledge that deepens but does not threaten my immediate emotional response. The sense of having it both ways, of preserving the joy that is the object of nostalgia while possessing new powers of understanding, makes the rereading of treasures from long ago especially satisfying.

I have little nostalgia about The Chronicles of Narnia, since I didn't first read the seven books as a child. They didn't exist when I was the right age for reading them. I discovered them during my first grown-up teaching job, at Indiana University, when the powers that be decided that I should teach a course in children's literature. All I knew about children's literature came from having been a child. Although I was only in my early twenties, much had happened in the literary world since I had first read *Alice in Wonderland*. Relying heavily on syllabi from previous teachers of the class who, unlike me, knew what they were doing, I gave myself a crash course in recent works intended for children, the Narnia books among them.

I devoured those books. Despite the fact that I was reading specifically to prepare for a class, I took in the story with the uncritical ravenousness of a bookish child. I learned that when you read a compelling children's book for the first time as an adult, you can have the astonishing experience of reading like a child once more, even though you're simultaneously reading as a grown-up. Once more I felt the direct appeal of encountering an imaginary world in which the powers of good unquestionably dominated. Appearances might be ambiguous—a wicked witch might briefly seem a kind, beautiful woman—but they didn't remain so for long. The imaginary world, Narnia, belonged to children: the various human children granted access to it learned that they could not return after they got too old. And it was a world full of adventures that demanded of children—boys and girls alike—courage, honesty, loyalty, and honor: those virtues that had thrilled me as a child. Individual adventures didn't last too long; they succeeded one another in great variety. The stories abounded in delightful, often unexpected, detail. As an adult, I could understand the Christian allegory that informed the series, but the child's consciousness that I still possessed allowed me to consume the adventures for their own sake. The figure of Aslan, the huge, benevolent lion-deity who consistently saves the human children and their Narnian allies at points of extremity, carries imaginative power even without reference to his Christian meaning, as does the fable itself.

I taught the books enthusiastically. In due time, my husband

and I read them to our five-year-old daughter, in whom they stimulated a good deal of theological speculation. I have reread some or all of them occasionally, in times of stress, always achieving through them a state of comfortable regression.

48 ·

Now, though, I've reread them again with a more critical eye, and I realize for the first time that they exemplify the difficulties as well as the possibilities of an extended series. *The Lion, the Witch and the Wardrobe*, the first of the seven, is unquestionably the strongest. It introduces four schoolchildren, siblings, two boys and two girls, who make their way into the magic land of Narnia by means of an old wardrobe. (Several books later, in *The Magician's Nephew*, we learn that the wood of the wardrobe belonged to a tree that grew from a Narnian apple core: hence, presumably, its liminal power.) There one of them, Edmund, encounters temptation and falls to it; the others ally themselves with benign talking animals, learn to love Aslan, and witness his self-sacrifice as he gives his life for that of the betrayer, Edmund. They also see his resurrection, which coincides with that of icebound Narnia. Edmund repents and reforms, and all four are crowned kings and queens of Narnia, with Peter, the eldest, as High King.

No subtle or detailed characterization differentiates the children. Edmund shows signs from the beginning of being sulky, envious, and weak, but his easy betrayal of the others provides him with no gratification, and his suffering at the hands of the witch who has entrapped him, combined with a single chastening conversation with Aslan, suffices to make him seem just like his siblings. Girls, in Lewis's universe, have more domestic interests than boys do, and not until the final volume is one of them allowed to participate fully in battle. (In that final volume, too, it turns out that Susan, one of the original two girls, is no longer a friend of Narnia: she has turned, rather, to "nylons and lipstick and invitations.") Although individual books have individual casts of characters, all the boys seem much alike, as do all the girls. The talking animals, in contrast, are strongly individuated.

The Lion, the Witch and the Wardrobe, however, leaves its reader little psychic room to respond to inadequacies of characterization or dubious gender politics. The speed and unexpectedness of its individual episodes compel attention and create delight. From the moment Lucy first emerges from the wardrobe into a snowy alternative universe until the final sequence, in which the four kings and queens—talking now like kings and queens, or Arthurian knights, not at all like children—pursue an adventure that leads them back to the wardrobe, new characters, new dilemmas, and new spectacles succeed one another in sequences that make moral and psychological sense but that nonetheless offer constant surprise. I found the story absorbing the first time I read it; I find it absorbing now. The ingenuity with which Lewis has imagined the lion as a Christ figure—a force of wisdom and of salvation, but also a furry beast with sweet breath and a playful tail; the attention he has devoted to beavers and fauns who play their parts in the children's adventures; the dramatized malevolence of his chief figure of evil, the Ice Witch; the brilliant sense of detail that makes scenes come to life: such elements of the narrative can hardly fail to keep the reader's interest. Aslan's supernatural role is clear from the first time he is mentioned. Mr. and Mrs. Beaver tell the children about the great Lion, causing Lucy to worry about whether he's "safe." "'Course he isn't safe," responds Mr. Beaver. "But he's good. He's the King, I tell you." Aslan's metaphorical crucifixion and resurrection therefore come as no real surprise, yet it would be difficult to predict in advance how these great events can be brought about.

The book's achievement, on first reading and on rereading, involves more than entertainment. It is not necessary to understand or to approve of the Christian allegory to feel that something mo-

· 49

mentous is at stake in the conflict between Aslan and the Witch, played out through the children, but also in vivid battle involving all the creatures of Narnia. Despite the coyness of some of his first-person interventions, the narrator preserves a moral seriousness that controls the story. When the four children find themselves back again in the professor's house, where their adventure began, the reader is likely to feel that something significant has happened to them, although the text makes no attempt to specify what that "something" might be.

The same tone and the same kinds of narrative device work less well, however, as the series continues. In *The Lion, the Witch and the Wardrobe*, the great lion figure comes as a surprise, and we cannot know in advance the nature of his interventions. As the tales succeed one another, though, Aslan's role becomes predictable. We know that he will rescue the virtuous in the nick of time; we know that he will appear in the hour of need; we know how the children will respond to his presence. They are not always the same children. Although the four siblings reappear in *Prince Caspian*, second in the series, only two of them return to Narnia in *The Voyage of the Dawn Treader*. Joining them is an unpleasant cousin named Eustace Scrubbs, who, after being turned into a dragon for a time, reforms and becomes just like everyone else among the protagonists. In *The Silver Chair*, Eustace fills the protagonist role along with a new girl, Jill Pole. The two of them are indistinguishable in character and in speech patterns from the original children. Even Shasta, the Narnian hero of *The Horse and His Boy*, strongly resembles the others.

Unexpected details continue to enliven the narrative sequence: I particularly like the bit during the creation sequence of *The Magician's Nephew* where an iron crowbar that has played a part in the action, tossed on the ground, grows into a lamppost with a lamp on top—the lamppost that serves as a marker for the children in the first two volumes of the series. Lewis goes back and fills in the blanks of his story: he gives us the creation of Narnia as a world and the world's final destruction, when stars and sun go out; he explains where the first king and queen came from; he accounts for Narnian events a long time (that is, a long Narnian time: in England, few years have passed) after the original adventures. He also invents a series of happenings that fill in Narnian history and geography: *The Voyage of the Dawn Treader*, for instance, takes the voyagers to the ends of Narnian earth. But the stories seem increasingly thin, and willed rather than inspired. Despite their inventiveness, the later books in the series strike me now as predictable.

The child reader, I strongly suspect—drawing on my own experience as a child/adult reader—responds positively to predictability of the sort that Lewis's series offers. Remembering older, duller series from my own childhood—the endless Nancy Drew books, the even more innocuous careers of the Bobbsey Twins—I realize that predictability, which marks all these works, constitutes part of their appeal. Books in series offer some of rereading's pleasures, combined with greater novelty. Reading them even for the first time, like rereading unconnected works, provides the sense of security that Larry McMurtry reports finding. You want them to go on forever, precisely because you know ahead of time just what pleasures they will give.

Still, the fact is that the Narnia series appears to have worn out for me. The emptiness of the characterizations, which I noted long ago, has finally started to bother me enough that I can no longer be carried along by imaginative detail. What I would have thrilled to as a child in the Narnia books is what I thrilled to in *Kidnapped* and in the Arthurian tales, a different version of what I loved in *Alice:* a vision of a realm that offered constant challenges to those within it and that rewarded such virtues as courage, loyalty, and honesty, as well as curiosity and enterprise. Stories of such realms suggested a context in which I myself might conceivably thrive, in which I would be encouraged to be my best self and allowed to test that self. I still find that vision in the Narnia books, but it no longer engages me deeply—as it still does in *Kidnapped*, for example. I'm a little sorry to have read Lewis's fictions once again. I probably won't give them another try.

Having read them now, though, I realize sharply that for me "security" is not a sufficient reward for rereading. The Narnia books have stayed too completely the same: that's why I won't read them again. The first time I read them I was able to formulate the nature of their appeal to me, to appreciate the details, and to take note of the flabby characterization and sexism that marred the stories but didn't spoil them; I have seen nothing new in my recent reading. To read the books now, it seems, provides only a stodgy sort of comfort—no fresh interest.

It has become clear to me, as a result of this new encounter with several examples of juvenile fiction, what I was looking for when I read as a child. Rereading children's books, for me, has meant above all rereading my younger self. The sameness, the stability that we seek in rereading involves more than the solidity of a text: it entails also the solidity of personality. I see with some surprise, rereading *Kidnapped* and *Alice* and the rest, how much still remains of my child-self. I see also to what a great extent I read, from my early youth on, in order to affirm that self. I have demonstrated to myself anew the power of rereading as discovery.

I've formulated these observations in the first person because I have no idea how generalizable they are. Do all children, or most children, who read avidly read to discover and affirm their selves? I don't know. What I *do* know, or think I know, is that children, like adults, read to fill psychic needs. Perhaps they get comfort and reassurance from reading about happy families; perhaps they want to read what's scary in order to realize the safety of their own situation; perhaps they yearn for vicarious adventure. Long after the time when they insist that caregivers reread their favorite books and then reread them some more, many children reread for themselves the works that offer them security.

To reread as an adult those treasured books provides an undemanding and soothing experience partly because of what I earlier called the haze of nostalgia. It also can supply the joy of unexpected insight: of discovering that much more goes on in familiar books than we could glimpse at the time of first reading. The most profound pleasure of such rereading, though, perhaps derives from the thrill of rediscovering a past self, a self that we may have thought lost.

3

A Civilized World

WHAT IS IT ABOUT Jane Austen? "Everyone" reads and rereads her, although not everyone rereads George Eliot or Charles Dickens or other great nineteenth-century novelists. They, to be sure, write longer books, but comparative brevity hardly suffices to explain Austen's popularity. Teenage girls delight in *Pride and Prejudice*, despite the fact that Austen writes distinctly for grown-ups. When I recently taught a freshman seminar on Austen, fully half the class of seventeen- and eighteen-year-olds had already read *Pride and Prejudice* more than once—and had seen more than one of the movie versions. By now the films have helped to make the books accessible, but the novels' large audience predates (and indeed helps to account for) the movies. The movies themselves constitute "rereadings" of the text, but they rarely limit the possibilities of individual re-perusals of the printed pages.

In 1980, traveling in China, I encountered a young Chinese woman who spoke excellent English. She revealed that she had read many English novels. What was her favorite? I inquired. The immediate response: Jane Austen. She read all Austen's novels, she said, over and over.

I was astonished. Austen's world seemed as far as possible from the one that the self-declared rereader inhabited, in a society in which the Cultural Revolution had only recently ended, a land where men and women alike still dressed in drab pajama-like garments and the people we met seemed to recite from some manual of the politically acceptable. Did it feel like extravagant fantasizing, in such an environment, to enjoy accounts of manners and morals in Regency England? I inquired further: Why did she like Austen? "Oh," came the reply, "the irony, the wit, the grace!"

Back in New Haven, where I lived at the time, I met other rereaders of Austen: a group composed of female Holocaust survivors. They convened at regular intervals, year after year, to read Jane Austen aloud to one another. When they finished a novel, they'd go on to the next one; when they finished them all, they'd start over. Why Austen? I asked one of them. Because, my informant said, she represents civilization.

Civilization: the opposite of the barbarity that members of the group had experienced; in one of its meanings, "refinement of thought, manners, or taste." Austen's novel represented civilization to the Chinese woman, too: verbal civilization, the mastery of style that declares order and control, opposition to the barbarous in all its forms, the importance of appearances that reflect truth. We may plausibly surmise that a considerable proportion of Austen's many rereaders, from adoring members of the Jane Austen Society to casual pleasure-seekers, find comfort in civilized discourse: carefully formed plots that end predictably in satisfactory marriages, style that reflects the author's dominion over her material, characters rewarded and punished according to their deserts. Such readers will discover and rediscover a world that in its details and in its rendering speaks of a structure of social rules, generally obeyed, conveyed through disciplined plot and style. This is not our world, nor is it likely to be one that we realistically long for, but its evocation answers a need for mastery of circumstance that novels can richly fulfill.

We return to a beloved book partly to find what we loved in the first place, and most of the time the book delivers just that. There are, of course, exceptions: the book from our adolescence that proves impossibly thin when revisited in adulthood; the bestseller that at its moment thrilled readers with its innovative style, but that ten years later has lost its immediacy. Most of the time, though, we know in advance, at some level, what we want to find in a specific piece of rereading, and our expectation helps to shape our experience. The Austen novel reread in search of emblematic civilization delivers just that.

The most familiar of Austen's novels itself testifies to rereading's power and importance. At the center of *Pride and Prejudice* lies an extended scene of rereading. Elizabeth Bennet, initially outraged by a letter from Darcy that purports to explain and justify behavior she abhors, finds herself compelled to read it again and again, almost against her will. (After her first reading, she puts the letter "hastily away, protesting that she would not regard it, that she would never look in it again," yet "in half a minute the letter was unfolded again.") Every time she reads it, its meanings change. At first she rejects its explanations as self-interested, arrogant, and false. In rereading, she checks each of Darcy's claims against her factual knowledge. She consults her memory—and her memory, prodded by Darcy's words, provides information previously forgotten. Evaluating the letter's assertions in relation to her sense of logic and probability, she considers the problem of interpretation in new terms. She wanders the lane for two hours, reading and pondering, "giving way to every variety of thought; reconsidering events, determining probabilities, and reconciling herself as well as she could, to a change so sudden and so important."

The sudden and important change occurs only as a result of Elizabeth's willingness to engage with the crucial text again and again. Gradually she realizes what she could not absorb at first; gradually she takes in what she feels reluctant to accept; gradually she comes to acknowledge how wrong she has been. The rereading of the letter becomes an adventure in self-knowledge.

Such a result is not inevitable. In the final proposal scene, during which Darcy and Elizabeth come to an understanding about more than their plans for marriage, Darcy suggests an alternate possibility. "I hope you have destroyed the letter," he says. "There was one part especially, the opening of it, which I should dread your having the power of reading again. I can remember some expressions which might justly make you hate me." Tacitly suggesting that the novel's reader should also reread the letter, these sentences sketch a different plot scenario: Elizabeth might have read and reread the letter and rejected Darcy forever.

The difference between this hypothetical outcome and the one reported by the novel depends on what Elizabeth as rereader brings to the text. She comes to her reading with a set of prejudices and resentments, but also a set of principles, including justice. Despite her desire to have her views reinforced, she strives to be and succeeds in being fair in her ultimate assessment. We may suspect also that positive feelings toward Darcy of which she is yet unaware play some part in her self-realization. Inasmuch as this crucial moment in the plot of *Pride and Prejudice* constitutes a parable of rereading, it reminds us of the important fact that a text exists only in its interpretations. *Pride and Prejudice*, like the letter whose fate it narrates, holds new pleasures and new meanings not only for different readers but in different readings.

As Dr. Johnson and many others have pointed out, endurance is the test of literary greatness. Endurance implies the capacity to offer different meanings to different generations, different meanings at different times, even within a single life span. Like many others, I read Austen novels again and again, for professional and for personal reasons. Invariably, even after so many rereadings that I know the shape and substance of most sentences before I read them yet once more, I find something new. In my last rereading of *Emma,* gratified as usual by the civilized discourse I encountered, I also discovered new aspects of the novel's celebration of the civilized.

I can't remember my first reading of *Emma.* It was too long ago, and too many subsequent readings have intervened. I'm sure, though, that I noticed, as every reader must notice, Emma's gratuitous insult of Miss Bates, a poverty-stricken woman, warm and good-humored, but so voluble about trivialities that her company proves tedious to quick-witted Emma. From her first appearance in the novel, Miss Bates becomes a subject for jokes among other residents of Highbury, and the narrator makes her a joke for the reader by brilliant comic renditions of her stream-of-consciousness patter. Yet Emma, until the crucial event, behaves toward her with unfailing courtesy.

My recent reading made me attend to new aspects of Emma's behavior. On her first reported visit to Miss Bates and her mother, timed, by Emma's calculation, to avoid a letter from their adored relative, Jane Fairfax, Emma is immediately told that a letter has in fact arrived. Austen's narrator observes that her "politeness was at hand directly." She speaks not only promptly, but "with smiling interest," apparently eager to know more about the letter. Frank Churchill observes later, in the course of one of his customary sequences of dissimulation, that Miss Bates "is a woman that one may, that one *must* laugh at; but that one would not wish to slight." All the evidence prior to the Box Hill episode suggests that Emma entirely shares this view. In her strong sense of propriety and her carefulness about her responsibility to others, she embodies civilized values.

Nor does Emma behave with unfailing politeness only to Miss Bates. This protagonist's self-indulgent behavior often becomes conspicuous, but Austen emphasizes her habits of kindness and courtesy in describing Emma's sensitivity to the needs of the poor family she visits, for example; her patience and ingenuity in dealing with her self-absorbed father; her self-control on at least one occasion with Jane Fairfax, when she feels "quite determined not to utter a word that should hurt Jane Fairfax's feelings," despite her impulse to tease; as well as her customary behavior with Miss Bates. She may not visit as often as her mentor, Knightley, would wish, but she tries hard to conduct herself properly when in Miss Bates's company, as in all other company.

Well before the insult, though, Austen hints that, civilized though she may be (and propriety, for this novelist a rich word, here supplies the index for civilization), her protagonist has flaws. Before clumsy Mr. Elton's proposal opens her eyes, Emma finds his behavior irritating, but she does not rebuke him—because, as the text puts it, "For her own sake she could not be rude." It is a curious formulation—one that had previously escaped my notice, despite its importance. At first glance, it suggests that Emma possesses a strong sense of integrity. It also hints, however, that class imperatives lie at that integrity's root. She cannot be rude because rudeness would violate her sense of herself as a person who is not rude, a person of the gentry who behaves on the basis of established standards. Eighteenth-century treatises on conduct unanimously insist that good manners only codify principles of consideration for one's fellow human beings. Yet Emma, her remark indicates, adopts good manners for her own sake, not for that of others. She practices civilized forms but has lost sight of their assumed content. The insult to Miss Bates will make that fact yet more apparent.

Austen does not clearly suggest there is anything wrong about Emma's acute consciousness of social status. After all, some such awareness must ground an ordered, hierarchical society. Just that consciousness, however, helps make Emma vulnerable to temptation. It also enables her more readily to separate form from content. The novel provides abundant evidence of her snobbery. Her avowed reason for not visiting Miss Bates and her mother more often is her "horror"—that's Austen's word for her feeling—at the possibility of encountering at their residence "the second rate and third rate of Highbury, who were calling on them for ever." Her appalled reaction to Mr. Elton's unforeseen proposal of marriage derives partly from her concern about Harriet, the younger, more naïve woman whom she has led to believe that Elton loves her. Her mind dwells more fully, however, on Elton's presumption in believing himself socially fit for alliance with the Woodhouse family. Her customary assessment of others on the basis of their "elegance" reminds us repeatedly that social level matters to Emma, and that she considers those beneath her in position to be in some real sense lesser beings, as a locution like "second rate and third rate" suggests. Accordingly, her concern about "the degradation of being said to be of Mrs. Elton's party" makes her reluctant from the start to join the Box Hill expedition, which takes place after Elton, piqued, has found someone else to marry (someone else satisfactorily inferior to his first object of courtship, in status and in substance—or so Emma thinks).

At the gathering itself, issues of status, and the concerns about power that underlie them, dominate the social exchange. That was apparent to me long ago. Frank Churchill declares that Emma presides wherever she is; Mrs. Elton predictably takes offense. Giddy

with her assigned power, thoughtless about her social responsibility, infected by Frank's false wit, carried away by her own quick
wit, Emma makes her fatal joke about Miss Bates's propensity for
foolish observations, only to be rebuked by Knightley and by her
own feelings. Much has contributed to the event, and much will
come of it.

This textual moment is a crucial one for rereading because it
tests the reader's social and moral alertness. In a first reading of
Emma, I suspect, most readers would respond initially to the comedy of Emma's comment and—at least until the declaration of
Miss Bates's pain, only a sentence later—think it no more than
garrulous Miss Bates deserved. We have been invited to laugh at
Miss Bates before. In the habit of enjoying jokes about Miss Bates,
as Emma herself is, we may respond to Emma's wit before we realize how deeply it violates social standards that she herself holds
and that we may share: standards of civilized discourse. Austen
has led us on, involving us in the comedy of endless chatter and
encouraging us to believe that such chatter constitutes the whole
of Miss Bates.

Mr. Knightley's little disquisition on pronouns, one of *Emma*'s
best small moments, states precisely what is at issue in Emma's insult. Speaking of the relation between Mrs. Elton and Jane Fairfax,
in the context of Emma's wonder that Jane willingly allows herself to be obligated to Mrs. Elton, Knightley calls attention to "the
difference between the pronouns he or she and thou," making the
point that we do not talk *to* people in the same way that we speak *of*
them. His remarks occur some time before the Box Hill episode, in
which Emma's lapse of manners involves ignoring the distinction
Knightley has made: she talks to Miss Bates as she might talk of
her. She is thinking of herself, of her conversational dominance,
of what she "owes to herself" as queen of the gathering. She is
not thinking of what she owes to others.

As for the reader—although not the rereader—she has been trapped. We thought Austen was calling on our sense of the ludicrous, when she in fact demanded of us sudden moral acuity. Even in repeated readings, having experienced through the novel's renditions the tedium of Miss Bates's repetitive discourse, we're likely to feel that moment of pleasure in Emma's joke about it—a moment that Austen has carefully prepared for us. And then we may experience, immediately afterward, a faint sense of guilt. Like Emma, we have been led into temptation, and we have succumbed to it.

If we laugh at Miss Bates, we of course have done nothing wrong. We are not on the scene; we do not insult anybody. But we have briefly let amusement trump judgment, failing to make the kind of discrimination that Austen advocates and by subtle plot intricacies inculcates. Rereading, we are more likely to realize that even a smile involves us imaginatively in Emma's error. A crucial episode in Emma's moral education thus becomes an element in ours—and our education will continue through many rereadings. It is an education, one might say, in the substance of civilization: the feelings and attitudes necessary to support the behavior of civilized human beings, who avoid the barbarity of willfully hurting others.

These observations derive from my most recent reading of a familiar novel. Perhaps because I'd been thinking about my New Haven friends, I discovered that *Emma* generated reflections on the workings of civilization, as an idea and as a practice. My textual citations, however, and my extended argument, issue from what I might call *re*-rereading. Enjoying *Emma* once more, having enjoyed it many times before, I found myself, for the first time, wondering about the Miss Bates episode—thinking about how uncharacteristic of Emma her behavior actually was. In many ways, this heroine reveals herself as full of what we now call enti-

tlement. Undergraduate students often complain about her, saying
that they don't like the book because they don't like the character.
Her aura of privilege can conceal the aspect that I've been emphasizing, her general concern with behaving properly. Once one realizes that concern, though, it's not immediately easy to account
for her insult of Miss Bates. Thinking about that made me consider the episode's effect on the reader, and that in turn sent me
back through the novel seeking evidence to support my hypothesis
that Austen's project includes the reader's as well as the character's
education in the ways of civilized behavior. My rereading thus
assumed a kind of retrospective structure: it made a new kind of
sense once I had seized on a new clue.

Civilization as we understand it includes social organization, and
Austen, like novelists before and after her, interests herself particularly in the social institution of marriage. She understands marriage as a social fact, as well as, or rather than, primarily a romantic fulfillment. Thus her romantic plots and subplots also serve
educative purposes. Any rereader will have noticed how many
false clues the novel supplies, mostly about who loves whom. Like
Emma, we must sort through them.

Some of the indications that lead Emma to believe Elton in love
with Harriet are likely also to misguide the first-time reader, at
least briefly. We will probably prove somewhat more astute than
Emma, though, even on first reading, and realize before she does
where Elton's fantasies are leading him. Possibly more skeptical
about the signs of a second putative romance, we may yet be persuaded by Frank's insistent flirting, tempted to believe, as Emma
does, that he feels romantically interested in her. Indeed, for a time
Frank's maneuvers confuse even Knightley, although he perceives
the truth long before Emma does. I remember asking a class of
Wellesley students, halfway through their first reading of *Emma*,

whom they thought Emma would marry. Fully half the class voted for Frank. Knightley's behavior offers ambiguous signals about what woman, if any, attracts him. As for Emma—surely it's only on a second, or later, reading that we're likely to notice that when Harriet reminisces about a past episode with Elton, Emma remembers Knightley's physical position in the scene, even as Harriet remembers only where Elton sat. Austen's heroine provides the reader with clues about her affections that she fails to interpret herself.

Even by the standards of "chick lit," an extraordinary number of ambiguous romantic situations figure in Austen's plot. They can readily deceive us on first reading, partly, no doubt, because of other books we've read. We keep looking for plausible pairings because we know, from years of encountering various versions of the romance plot, that marriage provides the happy ending for women and that plots are engineered to bring it about. *Emma* complicates this view.

More insistently even than *Pride and Prejudice,* this novel reminds us of the economic and social pressures urging women toward marriage. Knightley's comments on "poor Miss Taylor" and her match, for instance, emphasize her need for economic and personal security—for what he calls "independence," as opposed to the financial dependency of a governess's position. Harriet's dimwittedness, both Knightley and Emma perceive, makes her marriage urgent: she can't possibly take care of herself. Emma, proclaiming her own intention never to marry, makes the proclamation into a boast: she has enough money; therefore she doesn't have to submit to a man.

Not even Emma, discussing Mrs. Weston, "poor Miss Taylor" that was, mentions "love" as an element in her marriage. Practical considerations appear to have dictated the governess's choice: at any rate, we learn nothing to the contrary. Practical considerations also dictate Harriet's marriage, yet Emma as much as Harriet assumes the paramount importance of romantic love as a means to the desired end. When the young women think about love's possibility, however, the feeling comes to seem an end in itself.

The belief that romantic love constitutes an end in itself is hardly unfamiliar; readers, too, may feel its pull. The predictive errors we make in first readings of *Emma* perhaps come, like Emma's, from undisciplined imaginations, formed partly by our reading of other books. We are not likely to be thinking of marriage as an institution, nor does the novel consistently encourage us to think this way, although it reminds us of economic and social components in personal choices. The narrator plays fair as she misleads us: the clues we misinterpret are ambiguous, not false. But this is *not* chick lit: it is not just about romance. It is, at least in part, a lesson about the difference between romance developed from fantasy and love based on experience. Emma has looked in the wrong places to find happy endings. As readers, we may at least briefly have done the same thing.

As rereaders, we know better. The plot, however, familiar though it becomes, continues to remind us of the danger and the fallacy of trying to ordain where others should find happiness—in fact, of believing that we know the location of happiness even for ourselves. Bad novels, Austen suggests, novels that pander to our desire for romance, don't provide an adequate guide to good ones. Although her plots, too, lead to satisfactory happy endings, she demands that those endings take more into account than typical romances do. The question of who will inherit Knightley's property obviously does not motivate the marriage of Knightley and Emma, but neither is it altogether irrelevant. Harriet should marry according to her social status, precisely calculated. Readers, like characters, should concern themselves about more than love when pondering possibilities of marriage.

Perhaps especially acute readers can parse all the ambiguities correctly the first time around and feel faintly superior to Emma because of her persistent mistakes. All readers achieve this sense of superiority by the second reading—and in it, I now realize, lies another trap. The feeling of superiority—to both "her" Mr. Knightley and his brother, when they offer observations about other men that she thinks wrong; to Harriet at all times; to Miss Bates; to the other residents of Highbury—constitutes Emma's chief moral error; it lies behind her cataclysmic insult to Miss Bates. Inasmuch as we duplicate it, we commit the same error.

We bear no direct moral responsibility to characters in a novel, who are, after all, composed of printed words: we have no power to harm or help them, no conceivable obligation toward them as people. Yet Austen's novel, like all great novels, involves its readers in moral questions, causing us to reflect about our own attitudes in the light of what we learn about its characters. It cannot be morally wrong to condescend to Emma, or, for that matter, to Miss Bates, but it *is* morally wrong for any real person to condescend to another: we feel that as we participate in judging Emma's mistakes. The moral reflexiveness that *Emma* induces probably intensifies with successive rereadings, as we become increasingly imbued with Austen's fine discriminations. If the novel speaks to us of civilization, it does not take civilization for granted. It tells us that civilization—even if civilization means only propriety—depends on the self-knowledge and discipline of its participants, and it invites us to participate.

Maybe, though, we hear no such invitation. Perhaps a reader simply fails to notice any analogies between her own weaknesses and Emma's. Failure to notice is always a possibility—but the more one rereads, the more difficult it becomes not to notice. If a special pleasure of rereading derives from the balance between the familiar and the new in our experience of a book, we can anticipate that even as successive rereadings make everything in *Emma* increasingly familiar, new things will strike us. Without trying to discover anything at all, we find ourselves experiencing fresh illuminations. Sometimes it's simply a matter of noticing random words or phrases for the first time—and of finding, perhaps, that they are not random at all.

Here are some examples from my most recent encounter with *Emma.* The word *heroine* jumped out at me. Emma, convinced of Jane Fairfax's secret romance with Colonel Dixon and of his status as donor of the new pianoforte, reads "in the fair heroine's countenance" her reluctance to have the instrument discussed. For Austen and her contemporaries, *heroine* often means the central character of a romance. Thus Catherine Morland, in *Northanger Abbey,* fancies herself a heroine, and that's a joke. When Emma sees Jane as a fair heroine, she calls attention to the fact that she has made the other woman into a character in a romance of her contriving. The word itself suggests a judgment of Emma. Because she understands Jane Fairfax as a fair heroine, an understanding that implies a fiction for the other woman to inhabit, Emma has skewed her own perceptions.

This insight has only remote bearing on my thesis about the novel as education in civilization. It points more directly to the complex matter of the imagination as an issue in *Emma;* thus it might, in some future rereading, lead to a new argument altogether.

Then there is Frank Churchill, who arrives at Randall's, the narrator tells us, "in all the certainty of his own self." This locution occurs at the beginning of Volume 3, before Frank has been at all exposed. It may faintly remind us of Emma's belief that she owes it to herself not to be rude: Frank, like Emma, has a perhaps excessive regard for himself. Mr. Knightley has much earlier suggested this possibility, even before meeting Frank for the first time. The young man's going to London ostensibly for a haircut brings up the possibility once more. But the narrator speaks from an omniscient point of view in alluding at this point to the character's certainty, and the statement undermines Frank's characteristic posture of compliance. Emma has already noticed, in the debate about where the ball should take place, his tendency to agree verbally with others while insistently pursuing his own way. His certainty about himself duplicates hers about herself: we may notice that fact although she fails to. Now the narrator informs us in effect that Knightley was right in imagining Frank as a "conceited puppy."

One more word that can sneak by unnoticed: *meant*, in this sentence: "Mr. Elton was proving himself, in many respects, the very reverse of what she had meant and believed him." This occurs in a sequence of Austen's free indirect discourse, a passage that reflects Emma's thoughts although it does not directly quote her. Inasmuch as Emma realizes that she has *meant* Elton to be something he was not, she has discovered something important about herself. Her intention as well as her interpretation was involved in her version of him; indeed, her intention has shaped her interpretation. She has made him, like Jane Fairfax, into a character. To be sure, she doesn't remember this self-discovery when it comes to Frank Churchill; but the reader who has noticed the word and attended to its implications will remember, and will thus come closer to understanding precisely what is wrong with Emma's construction of entertaining fictions. Another clue to the novel's attitude toward imagination, perhaps. . . .

The random examples I've cited epitomize for me the special satisfactions of the reader's new insights in late encounters with an often-read book. They are genuinely random, in the sense that they are words that just happened to strike me during one particular reading, but they fit together, and fit with much else in the novel. Each of the words I mentioned bears on the matter of self-absorption and the degree to which it distorts behavior. Emma's *meaning* Mr. Elton to be a certain kind of person is of a piece with her construing rudeness as a problem of self-image, and of a piece also with her making Jane into a heroine, and with Frank's oblivious self-satisfaction. The delights of unexpected small discoveries often turn out to underline Austen's use of every detail for consistent purpose.

That purpose, as I have already suggested, becomes fully available to the reader only after repeated readings. It is unlikely, for example, that a first-time reader would notice the single paragraph in which the narrator slides into Mr. Knightley's point of view, a paragraph unique in the novel. We are accustomed to seeing inside Emma's mind. Suddenly, briefly, we see inside Knightley's—and in his mind is Emma! The moment, equivalent to the one when Emma remembers Knightley's precise physical position in a scene recalled to her by Harriet, though more emphatic, comes well before the romantic dénouement, at the juncture when Knightley feels impelled to warn Emma of the possibility that Frank and Jane Fairfax have some secret relationship. Here is why he speaks, in Austen's words: "He owed it to her, to risk any thing that might be involved in an unwelcome interference, rather than her welfare; to encounter any thing, rather than the remembrance of neglect in such a cause." Noticing this passionate declaration, after we already know how everything turns out, we think, Of course: he loves her. But it would take a remarkably percipient reader to arrive at that idea even as a hypothesis on first reading.

Part of the thrill of rereading comes from such noticings that we don't seek. No urgency attends our reading. But we are likely to develop a sense, rereading beloved books, of infinite possibilities, countless tiny discoveries to be made. The novel will, alas, come to an end, but its riches remain endless, waiting for us to return.

What, specifically, we notice in a given rereading hardly matters. It matters, though, that there is always *something* to notice: the heavy weight that attaches to the word *sensible*, for instance; the fact that the word *must* frequently means that Emma has made up her mind that something should be the case—for example, "how very happy a summer must be before her!"—rather than that something will inevitably happen; the subtly varying meanings of *elegance;* the brilliance with which Austen makes entertainment out of utterly boring conversation. If we adopt a version of what Wordsworth called "wise passiveness," enlightenment will stream in upon us.

Willingness to yield oneself to the text in a way impossible the first time through is, I think, the crucial element in rereading. As denunciations of television customarily point out, reading, unlike TV watching, is an active process. The reader engages in constant judgment and interpretation, involved in a sequence of challenge and response. The rereader customarily feels less pressure. She can allow herself a state of suspended attention comparable to Keats's "negative capability," a condition of receptivity devoid, as the poet says, of irritable reaching after fact and reason—of irritable reaching after anything at all. To be sure, it's possible to reread because you remain puzzled by a text and obliged to tackle it again in order to figure it out. Most rereading, though, is undertaken for reasons other than exegesis, and it doesn't involve conscious, purposeful work.

We find books that we reread both familiar and forever new partly because they change as we change: a truth that applies not only to the rereading of children's books. The experience we bring alters what we see. It's not just that Austen teaches us about life— life teaches us about Austen. The delicate interplay between literary and life experience can manifest itself anywhere. Mr. Knightley on the difference between speaking to and speaking of, for example: every day confirms the point. We casually assess others—students, colleagues, acquaintances—trying to figure out their attitudes, motives, and feelings. We have occasion to reflect on the apparent strangeness of other people's behavior, to realize how little we know of that behavior's dynamics, and to notice, in ourselves and in others, the difference between the ways we talk to and of our acquaintances—even, on occasion, our friends. (There's nothing like an e-mail mistakenly sent to the wrong recipient to make that point emphatic.) Whether or not we think of *Emma* when such reflections and such conversations occur, their presence must influence our responses to repeated readings of the Knightley sequence. Our lives abound in episodes on the basis of which we can evaluate the cogency of Knightley's remarks, which we may read slightly differently every time, depending on recent happenings. Knightley's wisdom becomes ours, but ours also reshapes the meaning of his.

Maybe a larger, vaguer example will make the point better. Consider the patterns of analogy and difference that unite Emma, Mrs. Elton, and Frank Churchill. Austen reveals her protagonist's similarity to characters of whom we are invited to disapprove. All three conspicuously want their own way; each condescends to others; each has a rather exalted sense of self. Mrs. Elton and Emma in addition share a concern with social class, a belief in their own inner resources, and a desire to control social situations. As we perceive these shared characteristics, sometimes on the basis of successive readings, we must work for the principle of differentiation that will rescue Emma from bad company. We find it, perhaps, in her capacity to learn, which Mrs. Elton clearly lacks and which remains dubious in Frank. Emma need learn no new principles—she already believes in good manners, thoughtfulness, and "elegance"—but she must learn her own fallibility, as the means to a saving humility. We figure that out partly on the basis of our life experience.

Our knowledge of other human beings informs our comprehension of literary characters. Reading Jane Austen may help us discriminate among characters, but, again, the reverse principle also applies. The superficiality of Frank Churchill's charm becomes more obvious as we encounter versions of him in life.

Of course we also encounter other versions of Frank Churchill in literature, in books by writers other than Austen. Our experience of other books—which, like our experience of life, increases over the years—participates in our reading and rereading. I've already referred to ways in which romances may distort our expectations. It is equally true that the mind of a reader habituated to serious fiction will bring to *Emma* a more complicated set of expectations, which Austen's novel may confirm or modify or contradict. Our understanding of *Emma* will subtly change as our store of other reading enlarges. Frank Churchill, for example, is a distant relative of Lovelace, the villain of Samuel Richardson's *Clarissa*, another charming, attractive, seductive man, whose wiles produce far more serious consequences than Frank's do. If we think of Lovelace as we read about Frank, we'll feel less forgiving of Frank's trickery. If, instead, we recall Mirabel, the dashing protagonist of William Congreve's play *The Way of the World*, we may have more sympathy for the charming rascal. If both these predecessors of Frank inhabit our minds—well, perhaps that gives us exactly the proper sense of complexity.

To put more economically the effect of the kind of connections I've been pondering, let me suggest that the experience of rereading creates a palimpsest of consciousness. A manuscript that has been written on over and over, retaining traces of each earlier stage: that's what our minds become in relation to *Emma*, or to any other literary work repeatedly encountered. Our past readings inform our present ones; our past experiences inform our interpretations. We need not try to decipher the earlier layers; they lend their richness to what we perceive in the present. Even if we have changed our minds completely about the meaning of an event or a character, our earlier views invisibly inform our present ones. Hemingway reputedly said that you have to know everything about a character before writing about him—where he was born, what kind of shirts he fancied, where he went to school. Then you don't need to put any of that data into your story—the fact that you know it is enough; it will enrich the texture of your fiction. In reading as in writing, the more you know, the richer the experience.

What a twenty-first–century reader knows about civilization necessarily differs from what Austen knew. Our reading as well as our life experience may have taught us, for instance, more about civilization's fragility than Emma or her creator could have known. *Emma* suggests that individuals must constantly reenact civilization in order to preserve it. The threats that the novel imagines come not from totalitarian governments or religious fanatics but from inattentive men and women who satisfy themselves with forms, neglecting their meanings. To preserve the values essential to civilized life must never become automatic or even easy, the novel suggests. It remains always a vital obligation.

Embodying and celebrating civilization, Austen also redefines it. Rereading can reveal how expansive her redefinition may prove. The thought leads me back to *Pride and Prejudice,* the first Austen novel most readers encounter in their youth. Its heroine, Elizabeth Bennet, who triumphs by stretching her society's boundaries, demonstrates how the content of civilized behavior may dispense with some of its established forms. I've read this novel probably forty times and taught it in introductory courses, surveys of the novel, senior seminars, graduate seminars, and one memorable seminar for college and university teachers (in which the men and the women in the group argued passionately about whether Darcy was or was not sexy, the men saying no, the women yes). It belongs, for me, to the category of works so frequently reread that its continuing pleasure derives largely from its utter familiarity. Surely here the balance between stability and change no longer applies. All is stability: there can be nothing left to learn.

Moreover, memory operates in a different way when reading something so utterly familiar. Not only am I unable to remember my first reading (it occurred when I was very young; I recall that the book delighted me, but I've no idea why); I also fail to remember any subsequent reading in any detail. The separate experiences blur together in my mind. Rereading brings no specific memories, only that pervasive sense of familiarity.

Rereading *Pride and Prejudice* yet again a few weeks ago, though, not with the intention of discussing it in this book, yet with awareness of the book-in-progress, I realized for the first time that this delightful romance, which Austen herself suspected of being rather too light and bright and sparkling, this fairy tale about finding one's prince, has something unexpected to say on the subject of civilization. Coming back to it after my recent reading of *Emma*, I naturally looked for the same preoccupation I had found in that other Austen novel. Bearing out my own thesis that one finds what one seeks, I indeed discerned the familiar concern with civilized behavior. But I also found, contrary to my expectation, a surprise: an apparent interest also in the workings of passion.

Passion, unruly and dangerous, seems an unlikely concomitant of civilization. Indeed, *Pride and Prejudice* contains passionate characters—Mrs. Bennet, Lady Catherine—who operate outside the rules of civilized decorum, preserving on occasion its forms but not its content. It also contains, however, a hero and heroine who long conceal their passionate natures but who enable Austen to celebrate civilization and passion alike and to investigate ways in which the large principles of social control can interact productively with the extravagant feelings of individuals.

Readers of *Pride and Prejudice*—including me—tend to remember its heroine, Elizabeth Bennet, as a laugher, like her father. Father and daughter share lively wit and a capacity to take pleasure in the ridiculous. In our first extended encounter with Elizabeth, we find her turning into a joke Darcy's snub of her at a dance—a snub that might condemn a lesser woman to paroxysms of self-doubt. The novel repeatedly tells us that her normal state is one of cheerfulness. Favorite daughter of her father, superior to her sisters and her mother in astuteness as well as in wit, popular in her neighborhood, apparently free of anxieties about class and social standing, Elizabeth seems to have achieved relative imperviousness to fortune's slings and arrows.

Elizabeth's laughter, however, proves largely defensive. (Her father's mockery reveals a larger component of aggression.) It defends not only against onslaughts from without but also against the intensity of her own feelings, feelings that, subtly suggested early in the novel, become increasingly manifest toward the end. At the beginning, Jane seems the sister dominated by feeling. Lydia and Kitty and Mary, all singularly devoid of capacity for sympathy, focus entirely on their own concerns; Jane worries about other people and tries always to interpret them generously. She must often struggle to make Elizabeth speak seriously about serious matters. Elizabeth makes her laugh, but Jane doesn't necessarily want to laugh; she prefers to ponder emotional issues. Elizabeth praises her sister's generosity of spirit, but, as she confesses toward the novel's end, she often finds it naïve and considers herself far more cognizant of the ways of the world. She believes herself sufficiently knowing to be well defended.

I long ago noticed the defensiveness in Elizabeth's laughter, but I did not notice its connection to her intense emotions. Nor, for that matter, was I aware of the intensity. The character's wit and grace defined her for me, and despite my many readings I never thought much about feelings beyond those she announces herself. It must be acknowledged that multiple readings of a book run the risk of deadening rather than heightening perception. I've noticed this phenomenon often in connection with familiar poems: it's difficult even to think about what's going on in a piece as well-worn as "Elegy in a Country Church-Yard," for example. Its words trace established grooves; its rhythms seem to obviate the need for meaning. Just so, for me, with *Pride and Prejudice,* whose words and rhythms feel as though they have always existed in my consciousness. I experience no need to see something new, since what I have already seen is so satisfactory. To perceive suddenly how much more goes on in Elizabeth's heart than she ever openly confesses comes as a wonderful shock.

If we notice, we get a clue quite early that Elizabeth's character entails more than a female version of her father. In a scene during her stay at Netherfield to care for her ailing sister, she participates in a conversation with Bingley and Darcy about whether a person should yield to a friend's persuasions. Bingley jokingly claims that his deference to Darcy comes partly from the fact that the other man is so much taller than he. "I declare," he says, "I do not know a more aweful [that is, awe-inspiring] object than Darcy." Elizabeth at this time has not the slightest romantic interest in Darcy. Indeed, she doesn't even like him. A few paragraphs after Bingley's remark, she notices that Darcy watches her a good deal and wonders why. She decides that he thinks her "more wrong and reprehensible" than anyone else, but this idea does not trouble her, since "she liked him too little to care for his approbation." Her reaction to Bingley's comment, in this context, is striking. Here is the sentence that follows the designation of Darcy as "aweful object": "Mr. Darcy smiled; but Elizabeth thought she could perceive that he was rather offended; and therefore checked her laugh."

A trivial episode, to be sure, but it suggests Elizabeth's sensitivity to the feelings of others. That sensitivity does not depend on her relation to a specific person. It answers, rather, to the sense of common humanity that Elizabeth preserves: she would not willingly hurt even a man she dislikes. Mr. Bennet declares himself desirous only of having ridiculous people to laugh at. In contrast Elizabeth, although she responds to the ridiculous, responds also to an entire spectrum of possibility. Her responsiveness makes her vulnerable. It also indicates that she understands civilization's obligations: in particular, the imperative to consider the feelings of others as the basis for courteous behavior. This is a matter of propriety, but it suggests a vision of civilization as founded on a deep sense of the human community.

Elizabeth makes no parade of her own feelings, but her emotional responses are intense. Austen heavily emphasizes this point. (But I never noticed before!) Forced to hear her mother's inappropriate remarks at supper, Elizabeth "blushed and blushed again with shame and vexation." Her sister Mary's equally inappropriate insistence on self-display leaves her "in agonies." No other character in the novel reacts so strongly to emotional stimuli. By the time we know Elizabeth to be in love—sooner, perhaps, than she knows it herself—we should not be surprised to find her riding an emotional roller coaster, lurching from one extreme of feeling to another, and experiencing conspicuous self-doubt. She feels "anguish" at the thought that Lydia's errors must separate Elizabeth herself permanently from Darcy and is "cruelly mortified" by her father's suggestion of Darcy's indifference. When her not-yet-acknowledged lover visits the family, she finds it impossible to speak with him after dinner: "She followed him with her eyes, envied every one to whom he spoke, had scarcely patience enough to help anybody to coffee; and then was enraged against herself for being so silly!" This does not sound like the self-possessed young woman who defeats Lady Catherine in verbal contest. It sounds, rather, like a woman of passionate nature.

Such a nature expresses itself not only in responses to a lover but in reactions to situations and people quite unrelated to the erotic. Even in love, even when she knows herself to love, Elizabeth does not lose her ardent reactions to and about men and women beyond the object of her devotion. Her acute feelings when she learns of Lydia's misbehavior and disgrace extend both to the sister too irresponsible to grasp her own misdoing and to the sister at home bearing the immediate emotional weight of Mrs. Bennet's hysteria and the terrible knowledge of family shame. She is "wild to be at home." *Wild:* not the sort of word one expects of Austen in this context. When her uncle promises to help the Bennet family in every way he can, Elizabeth responds with "tears of gratitude." Her tears and blushes, in the final quarter of *Pride and Prejudice,* recur as often as those of any eighteenth-century sentimental heroine—an unlikely comparison indeed.

Despite the analogy, Elizabeth is by no means a sentimental heroine. No sentimental heroine laughs at herself: Elizabeth does. Capable also of a mocking stance toward others, she has her father's eye for the ridiculous as well as a propensity to make firm judgments—some of them wrong. As for her intensities of feeling, unlike her younger sisters' displays, or her mother's, they are rarely inappropriate and rarely conspicuous: as far as we are told, no one notices her blushes. In matters of love, she, like most of us, proves frequently irrational, and the narrator gently teases her as a consequence. Thus Elizabeth, having lost all hope of Darcy's returning to her, convinces herself that theirs would have been an ideal marriage, and the narrator comments, with a dig at the vanity involved in such fantasy, "But no such happy marriage could now teach the admiring multitude what connubial felicity really was." Later, before the clarification between her and Darcy, her mother's ill-judged rudeness makes Elizabeth decide in despair "that years of happiness could not make Jane or herself amends, for moments of such painful confusion." Once more the narrator mocks her extravagance, observing, "Yet the misery, for which years of happiness were to offer no compensation, received soon afterwards material relief, from observing how much the beauty of her sister re-kindled the admiration of her former lover." The narrator always retains the poise that Elizabeth sometimes loses, but Elizabeth's moments of emotional instability call attention to her depth of feeling and her human complexity.

She exceeds her admirable sister Jane in both respects. Jane is unfailingly *good*, behaving always in adherence to the principles of civilized society as she understands them. She too feels intensely, about the man she will eventually marry and about her sister Lydia and those who suffer by Lydia's behavior. As a logical consequence of her years of impeccable conduct, though, she is accustomed to repressing her feelings. She lets Elizabeth, but no one else, perceive them, and she does not consider them sufficient justification to act. Feelings, in her view, are to be controlled. Elizabeth, brasher and more opinionated, acknowledging her own feelings and the conflicts they entail, less flawless in conduct, more tumultuous in expression, has less obvious virtues than her sister. Yet Austen rewards her with the richest man: a sure sign of authorial endorsement.

Although I have been emphasizing feeling and virtue, I by no means wish to occlude the sharpness with which *Pride and Prejudice* treats moral and, indeed, social failings—the two being, in Austen's view, closely related. Both, in fact, bear on the matter of feeling. Lady Catherine and Mrs. Bennet share with Elizabeth their passionate intensity, not directed erotically (certainly Mrs. Bennet's marriage seems one with all sexual passion spent), but closely linked to their purposes. Lady Catherine wants, simply and universally, to exert her will, to control all around her. Mrs. Bennet, more focused, wants to engineer good (that is, financially sound and socially distinguished) marriages for her five daughters. The passionate energy with which the two women pursue their goals contributes to the comedy of their successes and failures. Both characters, however, remain reprehensible. In sharp contrast with Elizabeth, they share with Mr. Collins a moral imperviousness for which Austen shows no sympathy. The three figures emerge from the text with comic vigor, but with no ambiguity about the moral insufficiency of their self-absorbed lives. None of them is purposefully evil; they differ in this respect from Wickham, whom Austen never represents in comic terms. But all share an inability to see outside themselves. This fatal myopia, manifest also in Bingley's sisters, reveals itself in Lady Catherine's futile efforts to sway Elizabeth and in Mr. Collins's unsuccessful wooing, but Austen does not suggest that myopia necessarily guarantees failure. Mrs. Bennet, after all, gets exactly what she wants (at least three-fifths of it), and Mr. Collins ends up with a woman better suited to him than Elizabeth is.

Pride and Prejudice sharply and mockingly criticizes such figures, calling attention to their real moral failings, but it also treats them with a large tolerance. Austen gives Mr. Collins a little life history that helps to explain if not to excuse his insufficiencies. The man's folly inheres in his character, but circumstances have increased it. Mrs. Bennet, we learn in the first chapter, has as her "business" getting her daughters married. The word reverberates through the text. Gradually we realize its accuracy: this is indeed the business, the expected and socially supported occupation, of the middle-aged mother. With five daughters and limited financial and social resources, she faces demands in excess of her capacities. A silly woman, limited, erratic, and irritating, Mrs. Bennet hardly wins the reader's heart. Yet Austen makes us realize how difficult life is for her. As for Lady Catherine, I'm inclined to think that the novelist takes surreptitious pleasure in the sheer gusto of her self-assertion. She too is limited and wrong-headed; her social status gives her the power, moreover, to be tyrannical. Her boundless belief in her own rightness makes her a menace, but like Elizabeth's verve, it also testifies to female energy.

Austen demonstrates capacious understanding of her characters and invites her readers to enjoy the same kind of understanding, while urging them also to participate in significant acts of moral discrimination. She insists on the necessity of feeling as well as reason, reason as well as feeling, and a proper balance between the two. I use the word *proper* advisedly, and with full seriousness. Through her central characters, Elizabeth and Darcy, Austen suggests that propriety, richly understood, allows room for, indeed depends on, powerful feeling. The implications differ from those of *Emma*, but the argument inhabits a continuum with that of the later novel. *Emma* mandates broad human sympathy as the central emotion of true civilization. *Pride and Prejudice* implies that capacity for sympathy depends partly on the ability to experience and to deal with more tumultuous emotions. Dealing with them appropriately involves willingness both to control and to express them, and skill in discriminating the right occasions for following one course or the other. Jane controls too much; Mrs. Bennet and Lady Catherine express too much. Elizabeth expresses more than she controls, but unlike her mother she never loses the governing principle of sympathy.

Elizabeth is a woman of passion, Darcy her male counterpart. When Elizabeth reproaches her lover for having talked so little when he first returned to her, he replies that a man who felt less might have been able to talk more. If Elizabeth errs on the side of expressivity, he may tend to the other extreme. Yet Darcy is hardly a male equivalent of Jane, as his intemperate letter to Elizabeth and his undisguised contempt for those he considers badly behaved demonstrate. Like the woman he comes to love, he feels deeply, acts compassionately, and sometimes fails to control his emotions. His depth of feeling, and hers, will ground their marriage.

That depth of feeling causes the characters to expand their human connections—to enlarge their sympathies. I find myself moved, now that I've paid attention to feeling, by the final sentence of *Pride and Prejudice*. Less memorable in formulation than the novel's famous opening sentence, it importantly modifies that sentence. It refers to Elizabeth's aunt and uncle, the Gardiners: "Darcy, as well as Elizabeth, really loved them; and they were both ever sensible of the warmest gratitude towards the persons who, by bringing her into Derbyshire, had been the means of uniting them." The truth universally acknowledged, that a single man of good fortune must be in want of a wife, has now received a very individual kind of acknowledgment. United in emotion as well as in role, Darcy and Elizabeth join in gratitude and love for a wider circle and remind us at last that a single man, whatever his fortune, should want not only a wife but the *right* wife: one whose heart enlarges and is enlarged by his.

Such emotional enlargement, it appears, provides the ground for civilization as Austen conveys it. Elizabeth makes an explicit case for a connection between romantic love and moral principle while discussing with Jane the marriage between Charlotte Lucas and Mr. Collins, a marriage entered on both sides for reasons of expediency. The novel has allowed Charlotte to make her own argument in favor of such a marriage (before she herself has the opportunity of entering into it) and has enabled the reader to understand the justifiable desperation of an unmarried woman with no money and no prospects. Emma's smugness about having the privilege of remaining single because she has enough money to provide for herself supports the same point. Charlotte marries, as we understand, and as Jane explains, because such a marriage seems the best she can do. Elizabeth understands, too, but she cannot accept. Her sister, she says, *must* feel that anyone who marries foolish Mr. Collins "cannot have a proper way of thinking" and should not be defended. "You shall not," Elizabeth continues, "for the sake of one individual, change the meaning of principle and integrity, nor endeavour to persuade yourself or me, that selfishness is prudence, and insensibility of danger, security for happiness."

Jane replies that her sister's language is too strong, and perhaps it is. Elizabeth is, as usual, passionate, and she is here passionate in the cause of emotion. A woman should not marry without genuine feeling for the man she chooses. Erotic feeling is not sufficient as a motive for marriage: Lydia has pursued that course. It must combine with other kinds of emotion, such as respect and gratitude, both of which Elizabeth develops before her rapprochement with Darcy. "Principle and integrity," the markers of civilization, demand that marriage be founded on emotional commitment. *Pride and Prejudice* elaborately supports that position.

I reread *Emma* and *Pride and Prejudice* in close proximity to each other, *Emma* first. Understanding it anew as a gloss on the idea of civilization, I was obviously predisposed to discover the same issues in the earlier novel. But if we tend to find what we seek in rereading, that is not to say that what we find isn't really there. Under the influence of what I have discovered in my latest readings of familiar novels, I strongly suspect that I could see in every Austen text some discussion of the relation between civilization and feeling. This is surely one of the issues that interest the novelist. In speaking of Austen as a novelist of the heart, or a novelist of civilization, or both, I do not mean to suggest that Elizabeth Bennet's emotional range is necessarily the character's most crucial aspect or that civilization is Austen's only subject. Rereading does not lend itself to imperialistic interpretations that assume command of textual territory in the name of some overriding truth. On the contrary, rereading insists on multiplicity of meaning, predicated as it is on awareness of the different revelations implicit in different encounters with a single book. To understand *Emma* as concerned with the reader's moral education as well as that of the protagonist does not preclude seeing the novel as, like *Midsummer Night's Dream*, a ballet of romantic mistakes. To see Elizabeth as intense and vulnerable, well before her participation in romantic love suggests such qualities, need not interfere with understanding her affinities to her father or her often astute social observation. To see her thus may, however, remind us that Austen, despite her notorious stinting of proposal scenes, values the life of the heart as fully as that of the mind. The romance between Elizabeth and Darcy not only provides a fairy-tale ending for *Pride and Prejudice*. It also reflects the fact that the novelist has depicted her protagonists as possessing an emotional capacity far in excess of that available to—for example—Charlotte Lucas and Mr. Collins, and well beyond even that of the more moderate Jane Bennet and her Bingley. To own Pemberley is a glorious thing, but to feel widely and deeply matters more: matters for society, as well as for the individual.

4

Other Times: The 1950s

THE NEXT THREE SHORT chapters cumulatively record an ambitious, if not altogether successful, experiment. I have been wondering how far it's possible to disentangle personal and social history when we try to understand apparent changes in a text that emerge through rereading. We know that we personally have changed over the years, and we know that the world has changed. Rarely, however, can we allocate precisely the relative influence of self and world on the mutating forms of the books we read, or assess the extent to which vast alterations that we associate with the public realm shape smaller personal changes.

Rereading complicates the reader's relation to both social and individual history. Reading a novel at the time of its publication, we may hardly register how it has been shaped by its specific location in time, unless the work deliberately reminds us. Because we share the author's historical moment, that location may remain largely invisible, as it does in daily life. Reading the same book again fifteen or twenty years later, we sometimes perceive—often with a sense of shock—that it belongs to a bygone era. Such a realization need not discredit the work, but the new perspective it provides must affect our response. The entwined issues of stability and change become more perplexing, given the realization that apparent changes in an unchanging text register the passing of historical as well as personal time.

86 ·   Perhaps, I thought, I could deliberately return to a series of works that seem rooted in their historical moment, works that I read with enthusiasm at the time they first saw print. Would they continue to move me, decades after I first encountered them? I decided to choose one or more novels from each of three decades, novels that seemed in retrospect firmly grounded in their era, and to reread them to see if I could discern how changes in the broad cultural context affected my responses. All would be works that my friends and I had read and discussed and thought important. I would begin with the decade during which I first considered myself a grown-up, the decade in which I received my Ph.D. and began full-time teaching, and go on from there. That meant the 1950s, 1960s, and 1970s. The succeeding pages report the results.

For the 1950s, I picked one British and one American novel. Both seemed obvious choices, wildly popular when first published and now largely vanished from my memory. I read Kingsley Amis's *Lucky Jim* (1954) toward the end of the decade and J. D. Salinger's *Catcher in the Rye* shortly after its publication in 1951, and then taught it to enthusiastic freshmen during my first year at Wellesley College, in 1959. When I initially encountered these works, they seemed radically different from each other. Now, eerily, they share a good deal.

To someone newly embarked on a teaching career, *Lucky Jim*, focused on the career of a hapless (although ultimately triumphant) academic, seemed uproariously funny in 1957 or '58. Amis, often considered one of the Angry Young Men then engaged in mocking the Establishment, wastes no opportunity to make fun of professors and their wives. His protagonist, a would-be historian in a probationary junior appointment, feels no enthusiasm for his profession and finds its demands unfathomable. The article he finally manages to write, in an effort to improve his academic position, seems meaningless to him, but it proves good enough for someone else to steal, thus destroying Jim's sole tenuous claim to an ongoing appointment. Jim burns holes in sheets and a blanket at his professor's house and makes matters worse by cutting around the burns. He gets drunk at inappropriate times. He displays no ambition, little energy, and much self-defeating impulse. His girlfriend, whom he doesn't much like, is unattractive in body and spirit. Jim seems, by any definition, a loser.

By authorial edict, however, he ends up with a lovely, charming young woman and a promising job as private secretary to an eccentric rich man—a job that will remove him from the provinces to glamorous London and from the frustrations of academic life to the unknown possibilities of a larger world. The reader, I assume, is supposed to delight in this triumph of individual ineptitude over institutional vapidity. This reader, however, experienced outrage and disgust (Jim-like emotions), the culmination of feelings that had been building throughout my long-delayed second reading.

Fifty years ago I enjoyed each episode in which Jim Dixon—usually inadvertently—confused or defeated adversaries who embodied the might of institutionalized higher education. The most highly elaborated instance of this pattern is the public lecture that the protagonist must give, with nothing to say and no desire to say it. Having contrived a series of more or less plausible truisms, he fails to practice their oral delivery before the event and finds himself, to his horror, imitating the distinctive diction and mannerisms of the professor who has introduced him. Because he is drunk, having been plied with alcohol by his future employer, he cannot exert control. Finally, he passes out before a baffled, concerned audience that includes the professors who will determine his academic fate.

By now, I am one who has herself helped to determine many an academic fate. I embody the enemy: the forces of the Establishment. I believe in such notions as scholarly rigor and think that academics should fulfill their responsibilities. My position in life has changed since I first read *Lucky Jim:* from insecure and frightened instructor to chaired professor emerita.

Yet I find it hard to believe that my position entirely explains my current judgment of Amis's novel as a culpably indulgent piece of writing. The book no longer seems very funny, with its slapstick humor repetitious in form and lacking in wit. To be sure, Jim's verbal alertness sometimes produces genuine comedy, as when his professor's obnoxious son remarks, "I'm naturally anxious to strike while the iron's hot, if you'll pardon the expression." Jim's reaction (like other reactions he has) calls attention to the meaninglessness of much that we say: "Why shouldn't they pardon the expression? Dixon thought. Why?" He might equally well have wondered why they *should* pardon the expression: the point would be the same. Such moments remind us of the protagonist's sharp mind, despite his apparent stupidity at times, and of his irritation with the company he is forced to keep, his powerlessness to remedy his situation, and the ways that he keeps rebellion alive in his consciousness.

That consciousness, however, grows monotonous, its content mainly frustrated aggression. A characteristic bit: "He pretended to himself that he'd pick up his professor round the waist, squeeze the furry grey-blue waistcoat against him to expel the breath, run heavily with him up the steps, along the corridor to the Staff Cloakroom, and plunge the too-small feet in their capless shoes into a lavatory basin, pulling the plug once, twice, and again,

stuffing the mouth with toilet-paper." I assume that one is supposed to laugh, or at least smile, at the carefully specified fantasy
of dumping the professor down the toilet. I am not amused. When
Jim sees the departmental timetable Professor Welch has drawn
up, executed in five colors of ink corresponding to the five teaching members of the department, "for the first time since arriving
at the College he thought he felt real, over-mastering, orgiastic
boredom, and its companion, real hatred." This may be his first
"real" experience of the specified emotions, but the reader has already been subjected to the record of many plausible facsimiles.
Jim spends much of his time making bizarre faces (when he thinks
no one will see) or planning the faces he is going to make or might
make to express boredom and hatred. Like such "accidents" as the
mutilation of his bedclothes or the drunken lecture, the faces he
makes and imagines convey aggression.

· 89

Amis peoples his novel with a cast of unlikely grotesques, sufficiently peculiar and distasteful to justify Jim's hostility. *Lucky Jim*
does not pursue realism. It aspires, rather, to the status of satire,
exaggerating human possibility in order to convey the distastefulness and lack of meaning in social convention and institutional arrangements. The facile writing, however, fails to generate the uncomfortable sense of recognition that marks successful satire. The
professors I know—and I know many—rarely exhibit "attention,
like a squadron of slow old battleships," that begins slowly wheel-
ing to face each new phenomenon. If they drive like maniacs,
they're generally aware that they're doing so, even proud of their
prowess. They seldom prove unable to follow the simplest train of
thought. Amis's Professor Welch is a ludicrous figure, but his relation to academic life seems more or less accidental: he might happen to be a professor, but he could equally well be a mailman or a
CEO. The conception of *Lucky Jim*, the book's characterizations,

its animus: all seem childish to me now, and I find the endless aggression offensive. In all these aspects, the novel lacks complexity—and, consequently, lasting interest.

Once I thought it funny, and my interest didn't flag. My husband enjoyed it too, and so did our friends. Of course my husband and our friends and I were all roughly the same age, and at comparable stages in our mostly academic careers. My conviction that "everyone" read and admired *Lucky Jim* depends on a limited sample.

Since I can readily adduce evidence for what I now see as the literary inadequacies of Amis's novel, I feel tempted to believe that my current disillusionment testifies to my increased critical acumen fifty years after my first reading. But I believed in my acumen fifty years ago, too: recently out of graduate school, I considered myself a highly trained and expert reader. Increased critical dexterity might nonetheless be relevant: I'm five decades older, hence less likely to find a novel about a hapless young man appealing; but I've also read and thought about a great many novels, hence I know more and have more complicated standards. This is a matter of personal history, but just as personal and social history determined the onetime popularity of this group of texts, both presumably contribute as well to the disappointment with which I read most of them now. The times are different, and so am I.

Lucky Jim still pleases some readers. Amazon reports seventy-eight reader reviews of one paperback edition, of which fifty-one assigned the novel the highest possible rating—invariably on the ground of its alleged humor. Only three give it a bottom ranking, and two assign it the second lowest. One of the more negative readers, from 2008, complains about feeling no personal connection with the book—a view that I would emphatically echo now and would have emphatically denied in the past. But we appear to be in a minority, that negative reader and my present self.

I feel surprised by the extremity of my reaction. Although I compulsively finish almost every book I start, I disliked *Lucky Jim* so much this second time that I felt tempted to abandon it part way through. From my first reading, I remembered such episodes as the blanket burning and its aftermath and the catastrophic lecture and its consequences—remembered them as hilarious. Their humor appears to have vanished. I remembered the novel as full of wit. I find little now. Moreover, my judgment coincides with my taste in this instance, though that is by no means the case in all episodes of rereading. Whereas my reading of other Amis novels tells me that the writer was very clever indeed, *Lucky Jim* seems to me fairly simple-minded, ringing changes on a single joke; its characterization amounts to caricature; its tone quickly becomes monotonous; its standards of judgment (vital to satire) are vapid. I find little to like and little to approve.

So how is it that I enjoyed it so much, thinking it penetrating satire the first time I read it? The historical moment, as well as my personal history, must have contributed. A period of cultural repression inevitably breeds rebellion, even if that rebellion long remains covert. The spirit of the novel, its eagerness to tip over sacred cows, would have appealed to—*did* appeal to—many. *Lucky Jim* makes defiance seem cost-free. Despite the suffering that Jim allegedly endures, the novel that contains him rests on an optimistic fantasy of rebellion involving only positive consequences for the protagonist. It conveyed in the 1950s hopes that would find fuller expression in the 1960s.

In the twenty-first century, such hopes no longer seem viable, even at the level of fantasy. The book, accordingly, no longer gratifies me. As for the pleasure of rereading: it's dim. *Everything* about *Lucky Jim* appears to have changed, except for salient facts of plot. Stability has vanished, with laughter converted to boredom, delight to irritation. Only the satisfactions of critical activity and of new knowledge (about the meretriciousness of a work I once thought important) remain: not enough. Rereading, it turns out once again, does not invariably provide enjoyment.

The Catcher in the Rye resembles *Lucky Jim* both in import and in its early and later effects on me. A work that has never lacked an admiring audience, it had trade sales of 425,314 copies in 2010 alone, my editor tells me—along with who knows how many sales for high school and college courses. Salinger's death generated an outpouring of testimonials about how much the book had meant to individuals. As for me, I loved it when I first read it and taught it with enthusiasm at Wellesley. And I loathed it when I reread it.

A much older female colleague, a devout Episcopalian, re-marked to me at a Wellesley dormitory gathering where students and faculty together were discussing *Catcher in the Rye,* "I just don't see how he can be a Christ figure when he uses such bad lan-guage." I found the remark ludicrous. Discovering Christ figures was never one of my literary activities, but in the 1950s the criti-cal industry throve on doing that sort of thing. "Bad language"— by which my colleague presumably meant Holden's frequent mild swearing—obviously (to me) had nothing to do with whether or not someone could serve as a Christ figure.

Rereading the novel now, I find myself appalled by bad lan-guage in quite a different sense: the impoverished vocabulary to which Salinger limits himself in order to approximate the diction of a prep school boy. Holden Caulfield has some large ideas but a limited expressive range. "I really do," he says over and over, until I think I can't stand another iteration. To get through the text it's necessary to endure page after page of puerile and meaningless swearing (the "bad language" that my colleague complained of is less shocking than boring), verbal tics, and vacuous anecdotes, ob-viously or obscurely self-serving. This is a first-person narrative, so we are confined to Holden's consciousness, a consciousness less full of aggression than Jim Dixon's, but no less distasteful, in my current view.

The important link between *Lucky Jim* and *The Catcher in the Rye*, however, is not the distastefulness of their protagonists. The two novels actually tell the same story, *Lucky Jim* in comic-satiric mode, *The Catcher in the Rye* with sentimental-pathetic overtones. The story concerns the fate of the outsider in a hidebound, hypocritical, and fundamentally corrupt society. Jim feels alienated from virtually everyone who surrounds him; Holden has only his little sister as kindred spirit. Jim responds aggressively; Holden keeps seeking in vain to make real contact with others. Authorial intervention rescues Jim from well-deserved failure; Holden's rescue exists mainly in his fantasy life, although the novel finally hints that he may start at a new school and perform more satisfactorily than he has done previously.

I begin to see more reasons for the popularity of these books among young academics in the late 1950s. Of course—despite the fact that we felt eager to be fully socialized into the academic community—we enjoyed fictions suggesting that those who differed from their peers were pure spirits, deserving reward although unlikely to receive it. Of course we liked being encouraged to think of ourselves as outsiders in either the Lucky Jim or the Holden Caulfield sense. We could pride ourselves on our literary discernment in penetrating Holden's verbal banality to reveal the noble spirit beneath: after all, he demonstrated compassion for the young and the powerless and was sympathetic to children, nuns, and unattractive contemporaries.

That sympathy, however, costs him nothing. He imagines being the "catcher in the rye" who keeps children from falling off a cliff, but virtually his only significant generous act is giving his little sister his hunting cap. He appreciates the cute ass of a girl he picks up in a bar but patronizes her and her friends for not knowing proper behavior—since they don't invite him to sit with them. Indeed, he patronizes many others: those who laugh at movies he doesn't find funny, those who admire a piano player he doesn't admire, those he can dismiss as "phony." "Phony," his term of universal disapproval, applies often to people who lack the faintest interest in him, and it implies their adherence to the hypocritical rules of the conventional society that he despises. A friend of mine, a professor of English at a good state university, was appalled to discover that most of her students loved *The Catcher in the Rye*. She told me that they admired Holden as a character devoid of "phoniness" himself, and I think—although my recollection of specific responses remains dim—that I once understood him the same way. Perhaps more cynical, or simply more experienced after a long passage of time, I now see him as a performer of his self-image, manufacturing a set of appearances that he can approve of.

A sympathetic view of Holden might focus on the fact that he has a hard time finding a place for himself, in school and in the world. The brother he loves has died. The boys he tries to cultivate obviously think him peculiar. He apparently can't, or won't, concentrate on his studies. He doesn't fit the world he inhabits. Moreover, his conviction that he doesn't belong epitomizes an anxiety of many—probably most—real-life adolescents: he speaks as representative of a difficult time of life.

Yet much about the character makes it hard to sympathize. He is enormously privileged, with his pigskin luggage and his grandmother who sends him "birthday money" four times a year. His idea of fun seems to be getting drunk in a bar; he models his behavior not on that of his idolized dead brother but on that of his older prep school friends. He is, as he says himself, a "terrific liar." Like actual adolescents, he is altogether self-centered, but he mingles his narcissism with a rather creepy interest in cuteness (for example, small children) and in perceived lack of privilege (like possession of cheap rather than expensive luggage).

Clearly, though, the reader is supposed to love and admire him: for his difficulty making meaningful contact with others (aside from his sister Phoebe); for his inability to make his intelligence work for him in academic situations; for his eye for phoniness, his outsider status, his honesty. He (or Salinger) tries to establish an alliance with the reader, addressing from time to time a "you" who may be an imagined confidant or an imagined collective audience, but who in either case is conceived as understanding.

I don't love him; I don't admire him; I suspect him of self-display rather than value his honesty. Once, though, I found him both appealing and estimable. I thought that Salinger exposed through him the corruption of urban society. I admired Salinger too, for his capacity to use a boy with conventional adolescent pre-occupations (girls, sex, alcohol, "perversions") to reveal fault lines of the adult world. Holden's language struck me as authentic, convincingly that of a sixteen-year-old, and Salinger's choice of it as the material of his narrative appeared brave. It seemed thrilling to find that a troubled kid could uncover hypocrisy, venality, and moral confinement. I concurred in these judgments with millions of others, but now I find myself out of step with the millions who continue to find *The Catcher in the Rye* a thrilling and satisfying novel.

The 1950s figure in popular mythology as a period of dreary conformity, the repressive era of Joseph McCarthy and of stay-at-home wives. As Wikipedia puts it, "Conformity and conservatism characterized the social mores of the time." I had to sign a "loyalty oath" in order to function as a teaching assistant at the University of California. I signed it because, politically naïve as I was, I couldn't imagine an alternative. This is not to say that I failed to think it horrifying that faculty members and graduate students should have to declare themselves non-Communists in order to teach. If the 1950s were the McCarthy era, they were also a period in which many deplored and protested McCarthy's attitudes and actions. Stay-at-home wives abounded, but I was hardly the only young woman intent on a career. For the young in particular, pervasive repressiveness would obviously intensify rebellious impulses. Jim Dixon, refusing to settle into fustiness; Holden Caulfield, refusing even to go to school properly: such fictional figures embodied a powerful impulse to declare oneself outside the period's conformities. I can easily understand, with half a century's perspective, why we liked these books at the time they were written.

96 ·

I can also understand why I now find Jim and Holden unattractive. Fifty years have taught me that refusal is not enough: one must say yes to something and be willing to act in support of what one affirms. The toddler's first impulse, the adolescent's automatic response, simple negation solves few problems. For me, too, though, in the 1950s a position in opposition to the status quo seemed sufficient to define one as unusual, even brave. The 1960s would diminish the possibility of such easy resolutions.

One reason for reading novels in the first place, in addition to the pleasures of language, action, and character they provide, is to grasp new psychological and moral possibilities: to enlarge consciousness. Rereading, I find, intensifies my desire for enlightenment of this sort. Neither *The Catcher in the Rye* nor *Lucky Jim* answers that desire. In both novels, the protagonist, although he broods about his situation, learns little and embodies little to admire. Minor characters, in both novels, are distinctly minor, barely differentiated, or caricatured. Jim has energy; Holden has at least theoretical compassion. Such positive qualities, however, stimulate scant moral reflection, at least in me. Holden resolves nothing for himself; good luck overtakes Jim, and that is enough. These novels no longer speak to me.

Reading them a second time proved a depressing experience, more unnerving than any other act of rereading that I undertook for this book. No desire for pleasure, no sudden impulse, impelled me to reread Amis and Salinger; I reread them, rather, in an effort to solve a problem. And I didn't solve it, I only reiterated for myself the unsatisfying conclusion that both social and personal history inform responses to rereading at a chronological distance, their proportions hard to discern and dependent on the specific book. In the cases of *Lucky Jim* and *The Catcher in the Rye*, I could assign part of my dissatisfaction to increased literary experience and more demanding standards of judgment; part to what I had learned about relations between individual human beings and their institutions, thanks to the passage of time; part to the felt difference between the mid-twentieth and the early twenty-first century. Much of my distaste derived from my sense that the novelists made it too easy for themselves by settling for a deus ex machina solution (Jim) or for facile pathos (Holden), never engaging with the enormous egotism of the characters they had created. That uncriticized egotism troubled me, I suspect, because I dimly remembered the conviction of my own interest and importance that attended me in the 1950s—a conviction often characteristic of youth, but especially so, perhaps, in an era when it seemed sufficient to speak, in private, one's opposition to institutions and their guardians.

Private rebellion no doubt seemed attractive then because it entailed no penalties and it delivered rewards of self-satisfaction. Why did it seem adequate, though? I can only speculate: because we—the "we" consisting of my group of young academic associates—were all politically naïve? Because we had no models? Fa-

· 97

bles like Amis's and Salinger's would assure us of our own rectitude. Such representations of rebellion could hardly fail to appeal, embodied in characters with whom we could identify and to whom we could also feel superior, for their social or professional ineptness, at the same time that they reassured us that ineptness didn't matter.

I sound more like a moralizer than a literary critic. Rereading seems to bring out that side of me when it causes me to see myself as I was in the distant past: a vision that stimulates self-judgment as well as judgment of the characters with whom I once imaginatively identified.

5

Other Times: The 1960s

THE NOVEL I SELECTED for the 1960s, like those from the 1950s, had a chastening effect on me, causing me to realize more about my past self. There was no question about what the novel would be. The book that absorbed, almost obsessed, me in the decade's final years, and that likewise absorbed and obsessed virtually every woman I knew, as well as some men, was Doris Lessing's *Golden Notebook*, a mammoth work touted as a story about a new kind of woman, the "free" woman. I didn't think that anyone read it now, but then I noticed that Toril Moi was teaching a summer seminar on Lessing's novel at the National Humanities Center in North Carolina. Amazon has thirty-nine customer reviews, with fifteen giving the novel a top rating ("incredibly complex and layered") and thirteen assigning it the bottom two grades ("sacrifices coherence and focus"). First published in 1962, the novel achieved American paperback publication in 1968. That must have been when I first encountered it: I still have a battered copy, heavily underlined.

Lessing was English (originally South African), her environment and her social experience not ours. Her location in history, by no means invisible at the novel's first appearance, on the contrary often proclaimed itself the fiction's subject. The central character's heavy flirtation with Communism no doubt seemed alien to most middle-class American women in the 1960s, but the protagonist's political predicaments found analogies in our own. The book, however, overwhelmed me and many of my friends less for public political reasons than by means of a politics that seemed intensely personal. Concentrating in new ways on the relations between men and women, it delivered a powerful negative verdict about the possibilities. Full of polemic about this and other matters, it made us feel that polemic was required of us. We discussed it in the "consciousness raising" groups that marked that period in American history; we discussed it over lunch; we discussed it at home. I cannot remember, in all my years of reading, another book that provoked a comparable uproar. Its central subjects, and ours, were work and love. It generated arguments: were work and love really compatible for a woman? (This, remember, was in the 1960s.) Might it be preferable to have a lover—perhaps a married lover—rather than a husband? You wouldn't have to sew on his buttons; you wouldn't have to nurse him when he had a cold. How much could properly be expected of a husband in the way of practical cooperation and support? Lessing suggested such questions without offering definitive answers to any. Hence her provocativeness.

We—a vague collective designating my intellectual and social community—had no doubt at all that this was a great novel. It concerned important questions, and it moved us powerfully. Even at the time, some of us noticed that it contained a lot of clumsy prose, but that fact didn't matter, given the passion of its utterance.

It seems strange, considering how important it once was to me, that I never reread *The Golden Notebook* until I read it in pursuit of this project. I think maybe I was scared that it would turn out not to be a great book after all. Indeed, my rereading persuaded me that this was a novel with many defects—although still, for new reasons, one containing matter of interest.

The plot—well, there's some question whether there can be said to be a plot. The novel, self-conscious about its own writing, often tells the same story in various terms, with significant alterations between one version and another. The character of a woman, Anna Wulf, exists at its center, but we cannot be altogether sure exactly what happens to her. We *can* be sure that she wants a man, a man who will love her for the long term, and that a good man is hard to find. She writes in four notebooks of different colors: one, she explains, for politics; one for fictional versions of her experience and ideas; one for Anna Wulf as a writer (she has published one novel, sufficiently successful to support her); one a diary for the factual record of her days. Sections of these notebooks constitute the narrative. The diary, however, seems far from definitively "factual," and the problem of separating fact from fiction permeates the novel. Anna suffers from writer's block, although she does not give that name to her malady until almost the concluding pages. More often, she explains or suggests that writing is impossible or futile, given the state of the world. Toward the end, she has a brief affair with a crazy American writer, falls into something like temporary psychosis herself, tells him to leave, although she "loves" him, and begins writing what we can imagine as the novel we are reading, for which the crazy American has provided the first sentence.

The book fills 666 pages in my closely printed paperback. As I started rereading it, full of contradictory expectations, I soon found myself irritated by crude sentences, repetitious patterns, political smugness. The political discussions, of which there are many, seemed distant and uninteresting. Who left the Communist party before Stalin, who was a Trotskyite, who really believed what he was saying about the state of things in the Soviet Union? Who cares? Page after page dealt with such matters, allegedly matters of passion for Anna Wulf but not for me. Although the protagonist's anxiety, depression, and outrage about the condition of the world (at the time of the first hydrogen bomb) should be easy to identify with even now, given current causes for anxiety, depression, and outrage, her feelings seem primarily aspects of her self-absorption, introspection her raison d'être. That introspection soon became tiresome. This time through, I saw no particular reason to read about one dream after another, all comparably florid and improbable, or to parse with Anna every physical and psychological manifestation of her interior state.

The novel seems strangely claustrophobic: "strangely" because it ostensibly concerns itself insistently with the affairs of a world larger than the protagonist's immediate one. Compared with *The Catcher in the Rye*, it is spacious—Anna's consciousness is much roomier than Holden's or, for that matter, Lucky Jim's. At one point, Anna (or a version of her) takes to pinning newspaper clippings about international horrors to her walls, day after day, until the walls are entirely covered. Often her notebooks record, without comment, newspaper reports about injustice, bias, or political obtuseness. Many of the reported conversations concern the course of international Communism. A good deal of action involves recollections of a wartime stretch in South Africa, the locale of Anna's single novel, and data about the operations of racism in the colony. One could hardly imagine a fiction more deeply imbued with political awareness.

Still: like *Lucky Jim* and *The Catcher in the Rye*, the book confines itself essentially to a single consciousness, although one of some complexity.

But I deeply recognize this kind of self-absorption. As I try to summon up the self that first read *The Golden Notebook*, in 1968, I recall in me and my friends patterns uncomfortably like those in Lessing's rendition of Anna. We talked all the time about national and international affairs, complaining about LBJ (we had voted for him), exercised about the Vietnam War, scared about the atom bomb. Our small children were taught to hide under their school desks when a siren sounded. We knew people who had bomb shelters built in their backyards. The 1960s provided abundant cause for agitation—civil rights marches, missile crises, assassinations—and we were duly agitated. We worried about the situation of women and declared our commitment to advanced ideas about the equality of the sexes. Nonetheless, our self-preoccupation reached astonishing levels. Those "consciousness raising" meetings: they purported to be about our politicized awareness of the female situation, but invariably they turned into proclamations of personal grievance, and most of the grievances I can recall now seem remarkably petty.

I think we considered ourselves attuned to our times, and I think we were. When we read *The Golden Notebook*, all of us could see ourselves in Anna Wulf. We understood her as courageous in her constant self-questioning, in her willingness to acknowledge the world's horrors, and in her refusal to sell out to the movies (she declines selling the rights to her published novel). She made us feel courageous for complaining about United States politics and for obsessing about the situation of women.

The Golden Notebook was a great novel, we thought, because—as each individual woman could and did testify—passion and clarity marked it; it created a strong, sympathetic, convincing central character; and it engaged powerfully with issues of its, and our, time. Most compelling of all, it passed the subjective test: reading it proved an overwhelming experience. Four decades later, I find myself with questions about its clarity (though none about its passion), misgivings about its "engagement," and dubiety about its central character. Moreover, I discovered a lot of bad writing: sometimes actual grammatical mistakes; often, clumsy sentences and ponderous paragraphs. The novel's ostentatious formal structure doesn't pay off. The large point emerges clearly enough: Anna experiences herself—and, for that matter, the world—as fragmented. But the differentiation among the notebooks wavers, the repetitions become irritating, and finally the notebooks hardly support the argument. Anna may feel fragmented, but the notebooks most of the time sound much alike. The accounts of Anna's experience include attempts at love and at politics no matter what category they are said to belong to, and her attitudes toward her experience hardly vary from one notebook to another.

I remember having trouble the first time through, trying to keep track of the alleged differences among the notebooks. I thought the trouble was my fault. It never occurred to me that Lessing might have been sloppy. I noticed some bad sentences, too, and convinced myself that they didn't matter, given the writing's passionate force. Indeed, the disjunction between the sentence-by-sentence quality of the prose and its cumulative power caused me to wonder whether good writing was actually so important after all.

I feel troubled now, as I didn't in the past, by the novel's male characters, who prove, without exception, inadequate, unattractive, malignant. I noticed that denigration of the male, too, forty years ago, but I'd heard enough extreme feminist rhetoric to make derogatory characterizations of men seem perfectly natural. The developed female characters, in contrast, all display at least courage and often energy, loyalty, and other attractive traits, although most are victimized by men. Also "perfectly natural," four decades ago. Now the characters seem literary—or perhaps political—conveniences. I seem to have become a lot less tolerant of asserted dichotomies as well as of bad prose.

Anna is assigned a gift for reading her companions' state of mind, in often complicated ways, from the set of their shoulders or the angle of their backs. Entirely too many pages report this kind of insight, which relieves the novelist from the need to explore complex communication between characters. The habit of asserting that small physical details provide sufficient basis to understand complicated emotional states is one manifestation of a larger propensity for *telling* rather than *showing* what happens. *The Golden Notebook*, unmistakably a novel of ideas, therefore inevitably does a lot of telling. But the reader can feel bullied rather than persuaded, not only about the ideas but about the happenings of the fiction. Once I was persuaded; now I feel bullied. The ideas no longer have the energy they once possessed for me.

Mine is not, however, just a story about my disillusionment, about how the once-loved book fades into mediocrity. It's not, in other words, the story I had to tell about *Lucky Jim* and *The Catcher in the Rye*. Although I had many complaints during my recent reading of *The Golden Notebook*, about three-quarters of the way through, it grabbed me. My understanding of *why* it exerted power, however, has changed.

Not at all surprisingly, I stand now in a new relation to the text, with more distance between me and Anna. At least initially, much more distance. I no longer share much with Anna Wulf. My concern with politics is, as it always was, less passionate than hers and my sense of despair less despairing. My personal history diverges radically from Anna's. (This was equally true when I first read the book—though at that time there was a lot less personal history to compare.) My social environment hardly resembles hers, and though I'm a faithful reader of newspapers, I'm not an obsessive one—certainly not one to plaster the wall with clippings.

Like all rereading, though, my recent experience of *The Golden Notebook* compelled me to look back at the self that read the novel in the first place—and as a consequence to realize that not only I but most of my friends had in fact shared with Anna the aspect of personality that I now find most irritating. Was this manifestation—the conversion of all public experience into self-indulgent introspection—uniquely characteristic of the 1960s? Surely not. It is always true, naturally, that even the most public events can only be experienced individually, thus privately. What Lessing evokes, and what I recall, though, is something beyond this self-evident fact: a culture, a female culture, in which everyone professed great concern for public matters yet concentrated on how she felt rather than on what had happened. I don't do that now, and neither do my friends, as far as I can tell.

The Golden Notebook, this is to say, has become a historical artifact. No longer can I take Anna Wulf as we took her in the past, as a heroine, an exemplar of female freedom. She seems, rather, an epitome of her moment in time, by no means altogether admirable—though it would have been hard not to admire her in the 1960s.

At one point in the novel Anna remembers a story sent to her by a Communist comrade. It concerns the experience of a man chosen as part of a teachers' delegation to Russia, and then further chosen for a visit with Stalin himself. Stalin, in the story, is rendered as benevolent, wise, and . . . comradely. Anna reflects, "What seemed to me important was that it could be read as parody, irony or seriously. It seems to me this fact is another expression of the fragmentation of everything, the painful disintegration of something that is linked with what I feel to be true about language, the thinning of language against the density of our experience."

The entire novel, now, can easily be read as parody or irony, and not so easily read seriously. I remember vividly the serious way of reading we practiced in the 1960s: the avidity with which we absorbed the idea of "free women," even while understanding the painfulness of freedom as a condition, a point *The Golden*

Notebook makes insistently. The appeal of such reading remains. The "serious" way of apprehending the novel allows women to romanticize their everyday struggles, converting them into evidence of a beleaguered position and a heroic stance within it. The possibility of seeing *The Golden Notebook* as parody depends on emphasizing the self-indulgence of its introspection and making a joke out of the self-glorification the introspection induces. The ironic reading—well, that one functions as criticism of an epoch in our history.

First of all, I should say that the possibility of reading this novel (and many others) in more than one way doesn't strike me as necessarily evidence of the thinning of language. Rather, it might attest to not only the density of experience but the capacity of language to respond to it by allowing multiple meanings: a corresponding density of language. Rereading often reveals a new way to understand a familiar text. That is one aspect of its power and its appeal. In this case, the novel's ironic aspect, like its parodic one, depends on its pervasive introspection. The first-person voice of Anna Wulf dominates throughout, anticipating a reader's sympathetic understanding. A skeptical reader, however, understands the degree to which introspection becomes Anna's substitute for action. She claims that she wants to write, but the self-described course of her days suggests, rather, that she desires the futile search for love and prefers the pleasures of obsessing to those of creating. Read thus, *The Golden Notebook* demonstrates how even a consciousness that appears engaged with issues of political and social injustice, an intelligence alert to the incongruities as well as the horrors of public life, can allow itself the easy indulgence of self-enclosure while proclaiming wider concerns.

In such a reading, made possible by history, the novel exposes not hypocrisy but self-delusion—something like what Ibsen in *The Wild Duck* calls the "life-lie": the kind of lie to the self devised to make existence possible. Unable to write in the way she wishes, Anna looks constantly within, analyzing her own political, psychological, and sexual responses. She never sees that looking within insulates her from the experience she endlessly questions. Her illusion of political engagement protects her from awareness of her self-obsession. It's not so easy, *The Golden Notebook* suggests, really to be "political."

Nor can it be easy to write about the complex ways of avoidance. Anna Wulf's sense of the impossibility of writing novels is comparable to her sense of the impossibility of achieving meaningful political action. "One novel in five hundred or a thousand," she writes, "has the quality a novel should have to make it a novel—the quality of philosophy . . . I am incapable of writing the only kind of novel which interests me: a book powered with an intellectual or moral passion strong enough to create order, to create a new way of looking at life." It is tempting to hear Lessing's own voice in such statements, and to interpret her enterprise in *The Golden Notebook* as an effort "to create a new way of looking at life."

Through Anna's musings, Lessing specifies obstacles to such an enterprise—obstacles beyond the fundamental conceptual one. A central problem, as Anna sees it, is the nature of language: "The fact is, the real experience [of insight through dreams] can't be described. I think, bitterly, that a row of asterisks, like an old-fashioned novel, might be better. Or a symbol of some kind, a circle perhaps, or a square. Anything at all, but not words." She goes on to say that people who have had comparable experience "will know what I mean." Eighteenth-century fiction is full of such assertions: narrators who say that they can't describe some emotional situation because those who haven't experienced it will not understand it and those who have will understand without description. Anna's intermittent claims of language's inadequacy differ, however, from the trope of inexpressibility in what she would call "an old-fashioned novel"—differ specifically in the undertone of pride that marks them. A few pages after her "bitter" thought about asterisks, she writes of a "timeless" illumination: "she knew she had had an experience for which there were no words—it was beyond the region where words could be made to have sense." Although Anna would certainly pay lip service to the idea that many others have had comparable experience, her sense of being "beyond" the norm signals the conviction of specialness that dominates the novel.

An ironic reading of *The Golden Notebook* exposes the arrogance underlying the protagonist's account of her life's difficulties. After plowing through some 450 pages, full of irritation with both Anna (for her self-indulgence and confusion) and her creator (bad writing, pretentious form, repetitiveness), I suddenly again found Anna a powerful character, although not at all the character I had identified with forty years ago. She seemed then forcefully representative: representative of the female dilemma as it appeared at that historical moment. Now I saw her as representative in a new sense, embodying a dangerous response to difficulty, wallowing in self-criticism without doing anything about it. Indeed, she couches her self-criticism in terms that make it impossible for her to act in response to it, interpreting all frustrating circumstance as beyond her control. Although she often deals competently with immediate problems, she impedes her progress by her ways of understanding her own story. She is a paradigmatic image of female self-defeat rather than, as I once thought, of female freedom.

The ironic interpretation thrust itself upon me as a way of making sense out of a reading experience that had previously, this time through, felt both incoherent and uninteresting. The distance that now separates me from the character and from her historical moment makes it both impossible to take her seriously on her own terms and possible to understand her in a new way. The novel, now, can stand as an indictment of its central figure and of the kind of self-enclosure she embodies. It can even inspire retrospective self-criticism.

Only the passage of time has made such a reading possible. My reinterpretation obviously contradicts the novelist's intentions and undermines the novel's strategies. Moreover, even as I try to impose an ironic reading, I'm forced to realize the instability of the ironies I claim. The famous first sentence of *Pride and Prejudice* makes its irony unavoidable. If the reader does not immediately realize the confinement of the "universe" to which the sentence alludes, by the time she reaches the novel's midpoint she must understand the ironic edge of the initial confident assertion about a truth universally recognized. Another instance: late in *Emma*, Mr. Knightley proposes. What does Emma say in response? "Just what she ought, of course. A lady always does." In another context, this evasion might seem only that: an evasion. Toward the end of *Emma*, after the heroine has suffered grief and shame precisely because, lady though she is, she has on one occasion conspicuously *not* said what she ought, we understand the narrator's formulation first of all as an ironic comment on the social expectation that a young woman can and will invariably restrict herself by considerations of propriety. The complex irony extends also to the possible reader who wants to indulge in sentiment over the details of a proposal scene and to the kind of novel that provides lavish gratification for the sentimental reader. *Emma* has trained its readers to be alert to verbal cues. It brilliantly controls its ironies.

I have digressed to Austen because her novels provide a standard for disciplined irony and suggest by comparison how undisciplined any irony claimed for *The Golden Notebook* must appear. The irony I find there declares a rereader's rescue operation, facilitated by the passage of time, rather than an author's subtlety. Lacking the third-person narrator who controls the tone of all Austen's novels, Lessing's fiction has no consistent judging eye or voice, despite the fact that one of Anna's notebooks implicitly claims to provide just that. Irony always connotes judgment; when a reader discovers irony where the author has not clearly asserted it, she inserts her own judgmental principle.

· 111

Not that there's anything wrong with that. Every author knows the impossibility of controlling what readers will do with a text. The rereader, already experienced with the words before her, possesses some knowledge of how much she contributes to the text she reads. Engaging with the words on the page, she makes patterns and enlarges meanings, with or without concern about the text's intent. Seeking to rediscover the impressive novel I remember, I find a new way of reading a work that time has hollowed out. *The Golden Notebook* seems stronger, now, as an ironic fiction than as a straightforward one; yet I cannot fail to realize that its creator has not controlled the ironies she has allowed and that she shows no evidence of knowing her protagonist's faults. My realization may measure personal growth, but it also measures literary loss: the kind of loss inevitable with books too firmly enveloped in their historical moment.

There's another thing, though, about this novel considered in relation to the two works discussed in the previous chapter. All three fictions represent characters of intense self-absorption, but *The Golden Notebook* differs in effect from the others. I accused it earlier of feeling claustrophobic, because of the way it confines the reader in a single obsessive consciousness. Holden and Jim are almost equally obsessive: Jim in his general aggression, Holden in his critical/defensive stance. The confinement feels more intense, though, in the novels that contain these male protagonists, because these works represent no world beyond their obsessions.

The "outside world," as Holden and Jim experience it, is severely limited.

The Golden Notebook, despite the limitations of Anna, its narrator, alludes constantly to national and international affairs. Although we know nothing, from the text, beyond what Anna tells us about them, filtering everything through the prism of her self-absorption, the references to a larger realm, to historical facts that we may have read about or lived through or both, allow the possibility of a wider view—the possibility, in fact, of the "ironic" reading that I sketched. *The Golden Notebook* is a larger book than the other two—and not only in its number of pages.

Thus history beyond the personal not only contributes to my disappointment with a book I once loved; it also helps to moderate that disappointment.

6

Other Times: The 1970s

I FOUND IT DIFFICULT TO pick a text for the 1970s. *Portnoy's Complaint*, I had thought, would be perfect—but it turns out it was published, and I read it, in 1968. Philip Roth produced no major books during the 1970s, except *The Ghost Writer*, the first of the Zuckerman series, and books from series present special problems for rereading, since the need to recall events narrated in previous volumes often demands partial or carefully focused rereading, a different activity from both ordinary rereading for pleasure and the kind of reading I have pursued for this book. It was not a great decade, novelistically, for John Updike, either, except for *Rabbit Redux*, the second in a series, and *Bech: A Book*, the first in a series. *Sophie's Choice* and *Humboldt's Gift*, major novels of the period, were not important to me at the time. I remember vividly the social turmoil of those years, but that's not what I was reading about then. My favorite writers during the 1970s were Iris Murdoch and Muriel Spark.

Well, then: Murdoch—a choice based on a process of elimination rather than on any specific memory of past delights. Murdoch's novel *The Sacred and Profane Love Machine*, published in

1974, and winner at that time of the Whitbread Prize, concerns twentieth-century British life but locates itself by no specific dates. I don't think it was enormously popular in the United States at the time of publication. It seemed tempting to reread precisely because I recalled so little about it. Could it measure personal change, could it tell me something about social history?

The Sacred and Profane Love Machine does not make its program transparent. It brims with irony, at the expense of human foibles. The title's final word suggests the novel's primary ironic focus. Lovers and objects of love multiply wildly as the intricate plot develops, until the book appears to represent a universal mechanical system of operation rather than, or more than, a series of individual choices. Passion—the machine's source of energy—abounds. We are left with the question of how we should react to the perception behind such representation. Murdoch's narrator offers a clue, suggesting that "an author's irony often conceals his glee. This concealment is possibly the chief function of irony." Perhaps the reader is to share the author's glee at the intricacy and diversity of human idiosyncrasy and self-deception? Certainly glee—a kind of wild and wondering pleasure—is one of the emotions I felt in this reading.

Unlike Salinger's novel or Amis's or Lessing's, Murdoch's fiction holds up well after the passage of decades, without requiring radically new ways of reading. For one thing, it possesses complexity of a kind missing in the other books. Its characters love and hate, hope and fear, with the irrationality and elaboration and self-contradiction familiar in life. The central figure—well, sort of the central figure: a psychoanalyst who pursues his profession by instinct rather than by training, with no medical degree—sometimes adores his saintly wife, sometimes much prefers his sordid mistress. He vacillates in his commitments and contradicts his own decisions. The saintly wife shifts her affections with remarkable alacrity once her husband appears to have left her.

There's a man of unfulfilled homosexual impulse, and a man grieving for his dead wife—whom, as it turns out, he killed. There's a beautiful adolescent girl eager to lose her virginity and a grown-up woman of ambiguous sexual inclinations and a troubled young man full of inchoate desire and a mysterious eight-year-old boy who wants to grow up to be a gangster and whose relation to the sacred and the profane remains obscure. There is, crucially, an astute narrator who, unlike the narrator of *Lucky Jim*, does not appear to identify with any of the characters. The plot, involving various and shifting amatory combinations, defies summary because of the sheer multiplicity of its events.

When I first read *The Sacred and Profane Love Machine* I liked it a lot: I remember that much. I probably admired it for its plot. I always take plot seriously, believing that it points to a novel's deep purposes, and I would have enjoyed Murdoch's expert manipulations of possibility in the service of her complicated enterprise. Although I knew that this novelist was also a professional philosopher, I don't think I took her novels as profound investigations. I read them avidly, one after another, but thought of them as, in the Graham Greene sense, "entertainments."

I enjoyed my recent reading for reasons different from those I dimly recollect. The new reasons supplement the old: I still admire the dexterity of plotting and take pleasure in the speed with which Murdoch manages to shift the reader's understanding of what's going on, only to shift it again a little later. Reading about sacred and profane love in close conjunction with reading about adolescent angst, post-adolescent slapstick, and adult writing blocks, however, provided a special new perspective in addition to that supplied by the passage of time. In comparison with the other works I have recently discussed, *The Sacred and Profane Love Machine* seems more resonant, concerned at a deeper level with matters that still feel important.

The novel's characters, I now see, dramatize a philosopher's pondering of the intricate relations between sacred and profane love and between self-understanding and self-deception. The saintly wife exemplifies the "sacred" side, which, in Murdoch's telling, seems as profoundly shaped as its "profane" counterpart by unconscious forces. The wife's love for her husband manifests itself in her unfailing goodness toward him. When he reveals the existence of his long-time mistress and of the child she has borne him, the wife ordains that he must spend more time with the mistress and must pay for the child to attend a better school. Selfless in her considerations, she wishes for everyone's welfare. Yet her selflessness, as she dimly and the mistress more sharply realizes, constitutes a mode of power that leaves her in control of a complex situation and its participants. Her continued operations in this mode eventuate in her death: in the wrong place at the wrong time, she is shot by terrorists. This event is narrated, or semi-narrated, in a single flat paragraph, which ends with Harriet's covering the body of Luca, child of her husband's mistress, with her own. We learn of her death only by indirection—a device emphasizing the idea that people have various notions of what counts as "important." Harriet's death, within the plot, seems almost a non-event.

Yet in fact it solves a plot problem. It allows the novel to achieve at least a semblance of resolution, saving the psychoanalyst, Blaise, from the need to choose permanently between wife and mistress. Apparently as arbitrary a narrative device as the emergence of Jim's new job at the end of *Lucky Jim*, it works in a different way. By the time the murder takes place, the reader—at least this reader, this time through—has come to realize that the operations of the cosmic "machine" imagined as regulating the intricacies and intersections of human love resemble those of novelistic plot. As a result of the machine's working, Harriet dies. The machine has no distinct operator (this is far from a theistic novel): no Novelist, as far as the book tells us, shapes the plots that develop in the world. Those plots emerge as a result of individual decisions and actions—decisions and actions issuing often from the mini-machines that people mindlessly, inevitably construct for themselves.

The novel is not altogether clear on this point, or on any other that touches on metaphysics. It raises challenging possibilities, but then it raises further contradictory possibilities. At several junctures, however, the metaphor of machinery recurs in startling fashion. Thus in a discussion of Blaise's history and his psychological state, we learn that he mourns "for his lost goodness": in other words, even sensual, self-indulgent Blaise has his "sacred" side. The account continues: "Reflection about his psychology did not help him at all. Much of the machinery was painfully clear, but irrelevant." This psychoanalyst, who has had considerable success with his patients, despite his lack of formal training, thinks of the aspects of humanity that professionally concern him as "machinery"—and as machinery irrelevant to his own problems. Perhaps he believes himself altogether different from those he treats: the machinery may be relevant to them; only goodness matters to him. But he is thinking of going to medical school to learn more about what he does, and most of the time the notion of goodness appears far from his concerns. Harriet worries about goodness; Blaise indulges himself.

· 117

Indulgence is a recurrent theme of the novels discussed in the last two chapters, especially *The Golden Notebook*. *Lucky Jim* also calls it to mind, as Jim indulges himself endlessly in the expression of childish impulse and in an equally childish sense of entitlement. (I might add that Jim's creator, by his plot resolution, further indulges his character, providing reward rather than retribution.) *The Catcher in the Rye*, a first-person narrative, exerts no control over its protagonist's conviction of his superiority to most of those he encounters. Holden's self-indulgent fantasies, indeed, constitute the novel. *The Golden Notebook*, physically a bigger novel than the other two, therefore provides more room for the extravagant self-castigation and self-justification of its narrator in all her guises—attitudes toward the self that come to seem escapist indulgence, preventing her from doing her work in the world.

In each of these instances, the source of what I'm calling indulgence is relentless focus on the self. Each novelistic protagonist is self-obsessed to a degree that makes it impossible for him or her to pay real attention to the world outside. My irritation with the characters stems predominantly from this aspect of their representation: all four of them need to grow up! (Holden may be forgiven for not having grown up yet; but fictional adolescents can be as wearing companions for grown-ups as their real-life counterparts often are.)

Self-obsession also marks every important character in *The Sacred and Profane Love Machine*, yet Murdoch's novel bears almost no resemblance to the other fictions. Murdoch's ironic, knowing narrator provides the perspective missing in those others, calling attention to the characters' evasions, indulgences, and self-absorption and criticizing the figures of the novel by tone, as well as by frequent explicit comments. The evasions, indulgences, and self-absorption are presumably objects of the author's "glee," which the reader is implicitly invited to share, but the pleasure we may take in abundant revelations of frailty hardly modifies the demand for judgment conveyed by structure and tone. This curious combination—the invitation to glee, the invitation to judgment—defines, I now think, the special quality of Murdoch's fiction. Playfulness and seriousness mysteriously coincide: such, Murdoch suggests, is the nature of things.

As the novel progresses, Blaise's character reveals further contradictions. Other characters likewise display fundamental inconsistencies. Readers cannot readily come to conclusions about the nature of any member of the large cast, or readily decide how much to approve of any of them. The problem is not, as often in life, lack of information; it is, rather, excessive information. The kinds of inconsistency that we often tend to blur in ourselves rise before us in painful exactitude as we encounter these imaginary personages.

The pervasive sense of irony in *The Sacred and Profane Love Machine* develops partly from the conjunctions of egotism. The third-person narrator dips in and out of points of view, temporarily inhabiting the consciousness of each major character. We thus experience the self-righteousness of the wife (she knows herself to be *good* but learns that she has been nonetheless betrayed), the mistress (she has suffered psychological, financial, vocational, and erotic mishaps because of her commitment to another woman's husband), and the adolescent boy (an only child, he expects his parents' undivided love; now there's a new—illegitimate—child to share their affections). Each character firmly inhabits a privileged position and feels indignant when privilege vanishes. The reader knows far more about the inhabitants of the plot, collectively, than they know about themselves. Hence the irony: the irony of knowledge with no power to enlighten, knowledge that exposes the pettiness behind grandiosity.

The characters often feel smug in their egotism. Thus Blaise, contemplating his pity for his wronged wife ("She was good and sweet and she was wronged"), reflects, "He could perhaps have stopped loving Emily [his mistress] if he could have treated her, as he sometimes pretended to himself that he did, merely as an object of duty; and he would then have made a more challenging problem out of the task of loving his wife. As it was the mysterious chemistry of the situation, the familiar strong egoism of his own mind, had sorted it out thus for his comfort." Blaise himself perceives no irony in considering his erotic arrangements sorted out—not by him, but by "chemistry"—for his comfort. The reader, however, can hardly avoid such a perception.

Occasionally the narrator's formulations call attention to an irony that has previously been dramatized through a character's point of view. "She was a woman, and perhaps there are many such, who lived, like an embryo inside an egg, upon a supporting surrounding matrix of confidence in her own virtue." Describing Harriet thus invites mockery—yet the novel takes the idea of virtue seriously and invites the reader to value what is truly virtuous in Harriet. The "matrix of confidence," however, signals what might be called "the familiar strong egoism" of her mind, which in no obvious way resembles her husband's yet operates in the same mode. Confidence, which helps one get along in the world, is, however useful, ultimately unwarranted. Again and again, *The Sacred and Profane Love Machine* reminds us of this unnerving but crucial fact.

The "glee" remains there in the background. What might be a tragic perception—human beings know little about themselves and nothing about what fate has in store for them—in the context Murdoch establishes takes on comic overtones, partly as a result of the multiplication of diverse instances. Harriet and Blaise resemble each other only in their egotism, which in Blaise justifies violation of his marriage and in his wife encourages the cultivation of goodness. The operations of the great machine reward Blaise and punish Harriet, without the slightest regard for what they deserve. Blaise feels liberated by his wife's death, and indeed Harriet's disappearance simplifies his situation. Yet we have learned enough about how life works out for individuals to feel sure that the situation as he understands it will not remain stable. He has, in fact, dimly perceived this truth himself: "There isn't—there isn't—the machinery—for me to be forgiven—by David [his adolescent son]—it doesn't exist." Blaise makes this remark, long before Harriet's death, to a neighbor who has advised him to confess to his wife the existence of his mistress and son. By the novel's end, the sinner has confessed, the wife has died, the mistress is happy—but David remains profoundly unhappy, and Blaise is quite right: the machinery doesn't exist that will make him forgive his father. The seeds of trouble will surely sprout.

This novel in which God seems only one among the many comforting fantasies that individuals construct for themselves provides its readers with a God's-eye view of the human panorama. The imaginary individuals whom the fiction has brought to life continue to fancy that they can predict at least the immediate future. Thus *The Sacred and Profane Love Machine* concludes with a minor character's meditations on what lies before him:

> he thought to himself, and now there are no less than three women, three powerful handsome women, wanting my attention, needing my help, insisting on coming to see me. . . . The heart would be touched again, not dreadfully perhaps, not divinely, but touched. There would be innocent frivolous unimportant happiness once again in the world. Three good-looking women, he thought, and all of them after *me!* And he could not help being a little bit cheered up and consoled as he got into the Bentley and set off alone for Oxford.

Such is human life, Murdoch says. People get cheered and consoled by their fantasies of the future, and then the future becomes the present, and it's never quite what was imagined. Sometimes it's not even close. Yet no amount of experience prevents individuals from continuing to imagine what will happen next, or from being cheered and consoled by their imaginings.

One might weep or laugh over this perception. Richly representing the awfulness of what can happen, Murdoch yet invites laughter. Terrible things take place in human life: still, resilience remains. The irony of *The Sacred and Profane Love Machine* is not satiric; it does not invite reform or imply belief in reform's possibility. It invites, rather, the paradoxical condition of rueful glee.

The 1970s generated this novel, but only the summarily narrated terrorist episode makes distinct allusion to the period. The book's appeal for me at the time of its writing probably had some connection with the contemporary popularity of psychoanalysis and, more generally, the continuing widespread preoccupation with introspection. The Watergate scandal and the ambiguous conclusion of the Vietnam War had left the United States enveloped in moral miasma, but focus on the self and the possibilities of improving it provided individual escape from moral discomfort.

The Sacred and Profane Love Machine narrates universal introspection that apparently serves no useful purpose and individual moral concerns that lead in the long run to no good effects. It concerned the kind of people we knew in the 1970s—possibly the kind of people we were. It hardly ratified our self-preoccupation; on the contrary, it challenged us, to bracing effect. My reading then was naïve, but even so I could find in Murdoch's novel a perspective that encouraged me not to take myself quite so seriously.

I realize now that Murdoch provides insight into more than the self. Her technique invites distance and urges the reader's skepticism, in spite of the fact that the novelist repeatedly enters the consciousness of individual characters. The sentences about the three good-looking women, which conclude the novel, demonstrate how the narrator operates. These sentences plausibly convey the reflections of Edgar Demarnay, who has appeared late upon the scene and done nothing of great moment, but they simultaneously expose him. We participate intimately in his private thoughts, amused or sympathetic or both, yet compelled, given the knowledge Murdoch has imparted, to recognize Edgar's folly: "The heart would be touched again, not dreadfully perhaps, not divinely, but touched. There would be innocent frivolous unimportant happiness once again in the world." *The* heart, not *my* heart—as though his is the only heart in existence. Happiness *in the world*, not *my* happiness. Like most of the other characters we have encountered, this one sees himself not merely as the center of the universe but as a universe in himself. He recognizes the possibility of sacred love, dreadful and divine, but he's happy to settle for the innocent, frivolous, and unimportant.

As the novel's last word, this passage raises the possibility that no one in the lavish cast of characters we have encountered actually wishes to experience the rigors of sacred love—whatever that means. It goes almost without saying that Murdoch never explicates her key term. Certainly it does not mean love of the sacred, love of God. Rather, it seems to designate an exalted kind of feeling between individual human beings. Although Harriet perhaps considers herself to experience it, the reader is given cause to doubt the justification of her implicit claim. Perhaps it is only another fantasy. At any rate, for most of the novel's population profane love is quite enough—not always satisfactory, perhaps never satisfactory, but always conceivable in human terms.

Few readers themselves, I would imagine, truly yearn for sacred love. Perhaps *The Sacred and Profane Love Machine* disabuses those who think they do. At any rate, it does not attempt to establish cozy relations between the narrator and the reader. That's partly what I mean by "distance": the reader is offered no comfortable resting place. We are not invited to love the narrator or any of the characters; we are invited, rather, to think: to think especially about what novelists of the past would have called "human nature." With its large array of characters, Murdoch's novel insists that human beings, entertainingly different from one another, nonetheless share a great deal. The spectacle, perceived at a distance, of the various tactics by which men and women get through the world and protect themselves from too much knowledge of themselves and others provides cause for "glee." It also provides chastening illumination.

Unlike *The Golden Notebook*, *The Sacred and Profane Love Machine* does not traffic in direct statement of large ideas. Rather, it provokes readers to generate their own ideas. The pleasure it offers, beyond sheer entertainment, is that of provocation. I found rereading it not the experience of relaxation that I posited earlier as a typical element of rereading's pleasure, but rather an occasion of increased alertness—another kind of pleasure, and one that I had not previously connected with rereading. My vagueness about what my earlier experience of the book had been probably helped open me to the stimulation Murdoch provides, but the intensity of my enjoyment was a large and wonderful surprise.

The Sacred and Profane Love Machine is, in my view, a very good novel. I think so partly because it has successfully survived the passage of time. I would not confidently make the same judgment of the other works discussed in these three chapters. Murdoch's intricacies of plot, which I appreciated more than thirty years ago, correspond to intricacies of conception that I then failed to notice. The book does not, however, reflect the 1970s in the clear way that *The Golden Notebook* declares its origin in the 1960s or *The Catcher in the Rye* speaks of the 1940s while reminding one of its reception in the 1950s. Much identifies Murdoch's novel as belonging to the late twentieth century, from trivial details of home décor to speech patterns and the nature of the professional lives sketched for its characters. To claim that it unmistakably issues from a specific decade, though, would require stretching the evidence.

Perhaps the nature of the decade accounts for the fact that the novel, forty years later, does not speak specifically for its period. Maybe the 1970s lack the special flavor of the 1950s and 1960s, so that the decade provides no distinctive material for fiction—but I'm suspicious of such a convenient explanation. Alternatively, and more provocatively, and more temptingly, considering my experience of the other works I have discussed: perhaps only relatively weak fiction connects itself strongly with a given ten-year period. Nothing clearly identifies *Pride and Prejudice* with a specific decade, although much in the novel indicates its origins in the late eighteenth and early nineteenth century. The enormous readership of Austen's work over the course of two centuries suggests that many people have found in it a record of experience that they can recognize and even identify with. *The Sacred and Profane Love Machine* can hardly claim the stature of *Pride and Prejudice* (for one thing, it hasn't survived as long). It too, though, aspires to speak of universal, or at least widespread, experience. Despite its often acerbic tone, the tone of twentieth-century skepticism, it ponders life and love, the miseries and the exhilarations of civilized existence.

Murdoch's novel complicates my understanding of how social history contributes to the changes produced by rereading. I also find myself worrying about those university students who in the twenty-first century love *The Catcher in the Rye*. My friend said that the three best students in her class, a class composed of advanced English majors, hated the book; all the others seemed to find it especially authentic and especially enjoyable. If the novel belonged peculiarly to its historic moment, would twenty-first-century young people—and, for that matter, apparently many older people—still consider it meaningful? Is my disenchantment with it produced entirely by my personal history?

I don't have to think so. *The Catcher in the Rye* may indeed emerge from a sensibility imbued with the values and assumptions of its decade. Adolescents in every decade, however, feel rebellious and resentful of the institutions of authority. My friend's students, except for the critically adept among them, identified with Holden Caulfield, despite the passage of time, and made that identification the basis for judgment. In 1951, when *The Catcher in the Rye* first appeared, enthusiasm about the book was widespread. Within two weeks of publication, the novel had reached the number one spot on the *New York Times Book Review* bestseller list. In other words, it wasn't just my friends and I, and those of our generation, who read it; it spoke to the mood of the times. The book still sells hundreds of thousands of copies a year, some of which end up in high school and college English classes. Moreover, the novel still attracts the attention of many adults. Do they consider it a period piece? Are they rereaders, recalling earlier experience? Personal history, the history of their progress toward maturity, probably accounts for young people's high evaluation of Salinger's work, whereas social history, the changes in the cultural environment over the last sixty years, perhaps requires more complicated evaluations from their elders.

As for *The Sacred and Profane Love Machine*, personal history —the fact that I am now an older, more experienced reader than I was when I first encountered the novel—partly explains my taking the book more seriously now. I'm inclined to suspect, though, that the present historical moment makes it easier than it was thirty-five years ago to grasp the richness of Murdoch's novel. The intervening decades have generated widespread skepticism about psychoanalysis, increasingly public revelations about the diversities of amorous behavior, many works of fiction that manipulate the reader's relation to text and narrator. The material and methods of *The Sacred and Profane Love Machine* seem more familiar now than they did originally, as does the possibility of a novel's inviting not "identification" with its characters but dispassionate contemplation of them.

The Sacred and Profane Love Machine, then, may have been in advance of its time. Perhaps, though, it was only in advance of me—I had not yet attained the critical sophistication to understand its achievement. I am quite unable to disentwine these two possibilities, and my experiment leads me to suspect that they are necessarily and permanently entangled. We change as individuals because of our cultural surroundings, but also because of our families, our friends, and our DNA. The same forces affect our reading and rereading. To ascertain the precise quantity of their individual contributions is as manifestly impossible for reading as it is for other aspects of life.

In the 1950s, 1960s, and 1970s, I read these novels for pleasure and gained from them the pleasure I sought. Now, in the twenty-first century, I reread them to discover what I think about them and as a way to ponder a specific intellectual problem, the relationship of personal to social history. These are two very different ways of reading—guaranteed to produce different results.

My experiment, intended to tell me something about the contribution of social context to writing and to reading, has left that matter indeterminate and has reminded me once more of another variable: the reader's immediate state of consciousness. Larry McMurtry writes about the delight of discovering in a familiar text just what he has encountered there before. To achieve that comforting experience, I now would surmise, he must induce in himself a kind of emotional and intellectual regression in order to recapture something approaching the state of mind he earlier brought to the book. I, on the other hand, rereading works that I originally read, for pleasure, in the excited atmosphere of their contemporaneity, have reread them purposefully to assess their power, given the passage of time. My state of mind was far from the suspended attention that in the first chapter I declared the characteristic condition of rereading, and far from the quasi-regression I posit for McMurtry. I did not achieve the sense of security Mc-

Murtry seeks. If I had originally read *The Catcher in the Rye* with the sense of purpose I bring to it now, my assessment of it might have been more measured fifty years ago, but there would still be no way of controlling the immediate ramifications of consciousness that affect every reading.

Is reading (or, for that matter, writing) ever dispassionate? Should it be? One might rather ask, *can* it be? It can't. Reading and writing alike call on feeling as well as on thought. Given that fact, acts of reading and rereading produce outcomes as various and as unpredictable as human thought and emotion. Rereading without the kind of regression that ensures sameness, I find endless change. I offer suggestions about the import of texts I read with increasing awareness that my discoveries depend partly on the diverse circumstances of my life.

7

The Pleasure Principle

REREADING'S ABUNDANT PLEASURES often prove unpredictable. By definition, rereading reacquaints us with the familiar. It does so, often, by defamiliarizing. The book we thought we knew challenges us to incorporate fresh elements in our understanding. The book we loved in childhood provides delights we never anticipated. We thought we already knew what it was about, but now it tells us that it is about something else. As our memories inform our understanding, that understanding changes. We who love rereading love it for its surprises as well as for its stability.

Much of my current investigation of rereading concerns pleasure: sometimes a goal, sometimes a byproduct of efforts to confront various aspects of the activity. In this chapter, I attempt to think specifically about a few kinds of pleasure that I typically seek in recreational rereading—and also to think at least briefly about situations in which I have found, instead, conspicuous lack of pleasure. Both the surprises and the other gratifications of rereading typically come in bits and pieces: not grand new interpretations so often as glimpses of possibility. Here are some examples from recent experience.

*

Sometimes pleasure begins with, even centers on, the book itself. I'm thinking of an old Penguin edition, from before the era of shiny covers with pictures. It resembles others of its kind, with its thick, matte cover, dull orange; a broad white band in the middle; author and title in severe capital letters; a Penguin Books logo above, a black and white penguin image below. Inside, the yellowed pages remain strong and flexible. With a copyright date of 1938, this printing dates from 1956. On the back cover, beneath a photograph of the author and a brief summary of his life, consisting mainly of the titles of his many books, small capitals spell out "Not for sale in the U.S.A."

That phrase makes the book feel special: how many other readers in the United States own it? We must have acquired it during our first extended stay in England, in 1957, in a period of fairly indiscriminate book buying. Books were inexpensive: this one cost 2/6 new, at the time equivalent to thirty-five cents. Second-hand volumes often went for even less. We stocked up on the British classics, poetry and fiction mostly, but some drama as well, and items like Jonathan Swift's miscellaneous prose works. This, though, was a twentieth-century novel, not yet with secure status as a classic: Graham Greene's *Brighton Rock*, a fiction that the author labeled "An Entertainment."

It's not heavy, the little book—only 250 pages. It's of a size to fit into a big pocket or a medium-sized purse. Like many other passionate readers, I always carry a book. What if there's a traffic jam? What if the dentist is running late? This Penguin prepares me for emergencies that make the reassurance of rereading especially gratifying. A talisman, safety against the unexpected, it's a *comfortable* book, the more so for being dog-eared and slightly faded.

Merely to handle it delights me. The look of the book recalls a time of youthful happiness, when the ability to buy books and the plenitude of books available for buying seemed great gifts of fortune. The orange cover reminds me of all the other Penguins we acquired and of the orgies of reading that would succeed each buying spree. Moreover, the name Graham Greene virtually guaranteed pleasure back in 1957. As it turns out, it seems to guarantee pleasure still.

And pleasure matters. A lot. Dr. Johnson knew this; he brings it up in every assessment he offers in *Lives of the Poets*. "Nothing can please many and please long," he wrote, "but just representations of general nature." The authoritative-sounding pronouncement comes from his discussion of Shakespeare, which ponders why the Renaissance playwright had already remained popular for more than 200 years. Such popularity, Johnson believed, constituted the most important evidence of a work's merit. If a book did not please its readers, it could not survive, even if filled with wisdom. "Just representations of general nature," as distinct from depictions focused on unique particulars, may not conform to our notions of the pleasing, but the pleasure gained from reading—and rereading—remains as vital now as it was in Johnson's time.

As for *Brighton Rock*, my second reading of it differed conspicuously from the first. I don't mean that I now interpret the book differently. Rather, the entire process of reading feels different. Back when I had just discovered Graham Greene, I devoured novels, not stopping for reflection. Now, enjoying the physical being of the volume, taking my time, I read more thoughtfully. I find weaknesses that I didn't notice before—but that fact hardly qualifies my enjoyment. *Brighton Rock* still provides a delicious experience—and not just by its nature as an artifact.

It's strange to say so, for the dark novel contains no entirely attractive characters and several despicable ones, and it ends on a dismal note ("She walked rapidly in the thin June sunlight towards the worst horror of all"). Narrating the operations of a mob with obscure criminal objectives, the book focuses largely on the consciousness of the mob's sociopathic seventeen-year-old leader. Although several people get killed in the course of the narrative, no excitement attends the murders, nor does much suspense build around the ultimately successful efforts of an unlikely detective—a blowzy, self-indulgent middle-aged woman—to assign blame and to rescue an innocent young woman victimized by the sociopath, often referred to as the Boy. The novel's interest inheres almost entirely in its investigation of individual psychologies, particularly the Boy's.

To reread such a book is in some respects a peculiar enterprise. What suspense the plot offers of course vanishes in a second reading: I know from the outset how everything will turn out. I was previously enlightened about the psyches of the various unattractive characters; why should I wish to encounter them again? Nothing in the sordid setting (the English resort town of Brighton, as experienced by those at the bottom of the social order) invites pleasurable contemplation. Yet I found *Brighton Rock* as compelling the second time as I did in the first place.

Reading it more slowly, less avidly, I could admire the daring of Greene's enterprise. The author exerts little effort to make the Boy (his name is Pinkie) "sympathetic"; the character's consciousness remains unremittingly ugly. By a prolonged, slow process, the reader comes to realize that Pinkie embodies evil, in contrast to the girl he marries, for reasons of expediency, who exemplifies good. The girl, Rose, is uneducated, unaware, perhaps even stupid (although with an excellent memory for faces and a capacity to reach accurate conclusions)—but good. She is not attractive; she is foolish in her devotion to Pinkie; she thinks herself damned for all eternity—but she is good. Good and evil have little to do with right and wrong, the preoccupations of Ida, the amateur detective. Yet they matter enormously, and the novel makes one feel this truth. Greene has taken on a daunting challenge—making insignificant and unattractive characters important—and has brought it off.

In other words, *Brighton Rock* is a *metaphysical* entertainment, almost a metaphysical thriller. It captivates its readers by manipulating their awareness into a growing realization of how much can be at stake in the trivial and sordid concerns of a bunch of unattractive people. I come to take Pinkie seriously not because he kills people but because of the fatal confinement of his imagination. Like Milton's Satan, he carries hell around with him. He cannot escape himself; he cannot imagine solutions other than murder for his problems. The horror of his nature far exceeds that of his deeds. The process by which the reader achieves that perception creates the novel's fascination.

And fascination, in its root sense of enchantment, provides a potent form of pleasure. Graham Greene routinely supplies exactly such pleasure, in his "entertainments" and in the novels he evidently considered more serious. I've read *Brighton Rock* twice, but I suspect that I could read it several more times and find myself, each time, caught up in an agon of the soul, couched in terms of mundane actualities. This agon does not demand the reader's theological conviction. Its function as entertainment depends partly on the fact that it causes one to admire, to take pleasure in, the author's ingenuity in generating high drama out of characters who would ordinarily seem uninteresting. *Paradise Lost,* with a similar plot, announces its high seriousness by its pace and its rhetoric. *Brighton Rock,* in contrast, moves briskly along, reporting much conversation in the language of thugs and of working-class men and women. It appears to make no large claims for itself—until, in fact, it does.

"Fascination," one important source of rereading's pleasure, is a mysterious quality. How can we generalize the power of enchantment? How do we account for the possibility of its repetition from one reading to another? Sometimes, of course, the repetition fails to take place: a book that fascinated in its first reading fails to exert its power in subsequent perusals. Readers, however, may persistently seek the magic they once found. They can find it in books of many sorts: in children's books often, in fantasy and science fiction, but also in the most mundane of realistic novels. To find a book fascinating entails subjective response: fascination belongs, after all, to the reader, discovered in the interchange between reader and text. Yet it feels like an attribute of words read. I know theoretically that others might not find *Brighton Rock* fascinating in repeated readings, but that's hard for me to believe.

The fascination I feel now resembles that which I remember from my first reading. *Brighton Rock,* in fact, offered few surprises, except for the crucial surprise that it still absorbed me despite my knowledge of the plot. I admired it more than I had originally, principally, I think, because I didn't need to rush to find how things turn out, and I had time to savor the author's narrative skill. The experience of reading the novel seemed new, although the book itself did not. This distinction is vital to rereading's pleasures. Even given perfect memory of a text from previous reading, I would posit (certainly I can't make this claim from any experience of perfect memory!), the act of rereading under new circumstances, at a new moment, virtually guarantees new thoughts and feelings. After many rereadings, some texts wear out, no longer stimulating fresh reactions, as I discovered in my most recent readings of C. S. Lewis's Narnia books. I am happy that such erosion has rarely occurred for me.

I read and reread, in part, in search of new knowledge; and the acquisition of knowledge provides a dependable source of pleasure. Novels, as many before me have pointed out, offer special knowledge about the nature of the human and about the ways that men and women (and, on occasion, children) deal with life's contingencies. Realistic novels provide as one of their gifts insight into the workings of ordinary human minds and hearts. The almost universal interest in gossip, with its implicit promise of revealing domestic, political, or social secrets, testifies to widespread desire to know what *really* goes on behind the scenes—behind any scenes at all. Realistic novels supply the illusion of offering exactly such knowledge. We know that they don't purport to tell the truth; we may believe nonetheless in the kind of truth only they can tell.

These are the novels that I return to most often. *Brighton Rock* has its fascinations, but nineteenth-century English novels, to my mind, offer more solid satisfactions, no matter how many times I read them. George Eliot, Trollope, even Wilkie Collins—they can focus attention on details of everyday life and in the process uncover psychic operations that dazzle me by their rightness. By this I mean that the invented characters enacting often elaborate plots in nineteenth-century fictions steadily persuade me that they react to circumstance exactly as they would if they had real existence. The excitement—the dazzling effect, the persistent pleasure—comes from the fact that I didn't know in advance how they would respond, but once their response is recorded, it seems inevitable.

The recognitions induced by these narratives generate deep pleasure, even when little seems at stake in them. A case in point is Elizabeth Gaskell's *Wives and Daughters* (1864–1866), the author's last, and in my view her best, novel. Left unfinished at Gaskell's death, the narrative nonetheless achieves shapely form and surprising substance.

When I first heard her name, in college, Gaskell was "Mrs. Gaskell," accorded no first name, invariably cited as a "minor novelist," and not at all studied. Her *Cranford* was sometimes, patronizingly, assigned the status of "minor masterpiece." She has ascended in the literary firmament since then, partly because of her sharp awareness of contemporary social actualities, revealed in such novels as *Ruth* and *North and South*. *Wives and Daughters* acknowledges the Victorian interest in science but locates its action in a rural village dominated by the local lord, where people value the past and hardly think about changes the future might bring. It does not tell a momentous story or make grand claims of significance. Molly Gibson, the protagonist, first encountered as a twelve-year-old, grows up, falls in love, faces ethical problems and disappointments, but eventually comes out well. The narrative proceeds at a leisurely pace. Imbued with Victorian moral sentiment, it has an old-fashioned tone.

I find it utterly captivating.

Rereading such a novel exerts a special kind of charm. I've read *Wives and Daughters* at least three or four times, probably more. My copy is less well-thumbed than, say, *Pride and Prejudice*, but I've read it often enough that, as with Austen novels, I find it impossible to remember my first experience of it. When rereading a specific work becomes a recurrent activity, the processes and rewards of each individual instance of it tend to blur with those of other rereadings. I always know, though, when I have found something new.

Paying special attention to my reactions this time through *Wives and Daughters,* I noted that I was getting a bit teary only a few pages in (the book is more than 700 pages long in my Penguin edition). I frequently weep over nineteenth-century novels, but nothing sad had happened yet. The problem was that, like every rereader, I knew what was going to happen. The words on the page were telling me about Molly's close relationship with her father (her mother is dead), and I knew that Mr. Gibson, the doctor for the village and its environs, was going to marry again, largely out of a mistaken belief that his marriage would improve his daughter's situation. Molly, trusting in their closeness, assumes the permanence of father-daughter intimacy. Her ignorance of what I know will happen makes her seem pathetic; her happiness feels sad to me as a rereader.

Rereading dependably supplies the pleasure of foreknowledge. Even if the rereader fails to recall plot details, she probably retains at least a vague memory of how events develop or of how at least one strand of events works out. Such shadowy recollections often suffice to generate the kind of effect that elicited my tears early in *Wives and Daughters*. The pleasure of weeping over a big realistic novel should not be underestimated, but foreknowledge also produces emotion of other kinds. In general, it enriches the reading experience. The excitement of rereading differs from that of reading for the first time. It stems from a process of accretion: knowledge of what is to come changes speculation about outcomes to speculation about meanings—a deeper form of excitement.

Back to Gaskell's plot. Mr. Gibson's marriage will fuel much of the succeeding narrative, but it will also bring Molly misery— which she will confront by means of concerted moral effort, making herself into a heroine and, since this is a Victorian novel, thus guaranteeing her own ultimate happiness. The presence of a beautiful stepsister of her own age, a young woman who lacks Molly's moral stamina and also lacks scruples, complicates matters and for a time threatens Molly's growing love for Roger Hamley, son of one of her father's friends. Such situations obviously present ample opportunity for psychological as well as moral investigation, and Gaskell vigorously pursues both.

Molly has had an early encounter with the woman her father marries. At the age of twelve, she attends a social event at the Towers, residence of the local lord, and is accidentally left behind by the people who brought her. Mrs. Kirkpatrick, a former governess in the household, is assigned to look after her. Although she operates behind a façade of constant sweetness, the ex-governess reveals to her charge a selfish, deceitful, and conniving nature.

When Mr. Gibson tells his daughter of his plan to marry Mrs. Kirkpatrick, "She did not answer. She could not tell what words to use. She was afraid of saying anything, lest the passion of anger, dislike, indignation—whatever it was that was boiling up in her breast—should find vent in cries and screams, or worse, in raging words that could never be forgotten. It was if the piece of solid ground on which she stood had broken from the shore, and she was drifting out to the infinite sea alone."

Molly's father has provided the solid ground of her life. Her sense of dangerous drift, of having lost her moorings, has considerable justification. The brilliance of Gaskell's perceptions, however, emerges sharply in the clause set off by dashes: "whatever it was that was boiling up in her breast." Molly doesn't know what she's feeling; she only knows that she feels passionately and painfully. Gaskell's capacity to rest in uncertainties, not to spell out every emotion but to specify both the presence of feeling and the impossibility of grasping it, authenticates her account of Molly's development. The girl's emotional life—along with her moral progress—creates a powerful focus of interest.

The novel dwells convincingly on the emotions of even its more unattractive characters. Thus we encounter Mrs. Kirkpatrick, before Gibson has proposed to her, meditating on the drapery of a mirror in her guest room on the lord's estate. She has tried to create a comparable effect in her own home, only to find that muslin gets dirty, and ribbons fade, and money to remedy such conditions is not readily available. "Now here," she thinks, "money is like the air they breathe. No one even asks or knows how much the washing costs, or what pink ribbon is a yard. Ah! it would be different if they had to earn every penny as I have! . . . I wonder if I am to go on all my life toiling and moiling for money? It's not natural. Marriage is the natural thing; then the husband has all that kind of dirty work to do, and his wife sits in the drawing-room like a lady. I did, when poor Kirkpatrick was alive. Heigho! it's a sad thing to be a widow." The widow's reasons for thinking marriage "the natural thing" expose her nature and prepare the reader for the demanding wife she will prove to be. Yet her meditations also reveal the pathos of poverty for a woman with social aspirations.

Mrs. Kirkpatrick is not vicious, but she's annoying (to the reader, at least this reader, as well as to Molly and her father), self-preoccupied, incapable of empathy, interested in the superficial and vigorous in rejecting all beyond it. Trying to fulfill Roger Hamley's injunction that she think of others rather than herself, Molly strives, often successfully, to accept her stepmother and conform to her mandates. Yet she retains and develops her own sense of right and wrong.

The special intensity of *Wives and Daughters* depends on its insistence that the emotional as well as the moral life matters. Molly's father has trained himself in repression. He deplores any expression of "sentiment" and considers it best to leave feeling unspoken. Her beautiful stepsister, Cynthia, effortlessly attracts men but seems incapable of deep feeling; she tells Molly that she has never loved anyone, of either sex. Cynthia at least is able to admire what she cannot attain: she values Molly. Her mother, Molly's stepmother, shows no capacity for feeling beyond petulance.

Inhabiting this human environment, Molly nonetheless acknowledges and sustains her own intense feelings. She controls their expression when she thinks she should, but she values emotion as the very principle of life. In an early conversation with Roger, she evinces skepticism about the idea of subordinating herself to the desires of others. "It will be very dull," she says, "when I shall have killed myself, as it were, and live only in trying to do, and to be, as other people like. I don't see any end to it. I might as well never have lived." Such insight into the emotional danger implicit in a life of self-sacrifice is uncommon in late nineteenth-century fiction, which often attaches high value to female self-abnegation. Molly's struggle to retain both her emotional vitality and her integrity is sometimes painful, sometimes exhilarating, and always compelling. It provides the kind of revelation about the inner workings of human nature that I spoke of earlier as a source of pleasure in the realistic novel.

Such pleasure may recall the classical dictum that literature should delight and instruct—instruction justifying delight, delight sweetening instruction. Dr. Johnson, with his talk about just representations of general nature, assumes exactly such a conjunction. Without assuming it, I find it in such novels as *Wives and Daughters*, where instruction concerns the workings of human nature and pleasure derives from the identical source. Pleasure of this kind does not constitute "escape" from day-to-day life. Rather, it invites the reader to appreciate such life as a result of being enabled to contemplate its fictional counterpart.

The pleasure of psychological insight becomes available to any reader the first time through the novel. Second and subsequent readings can intensify the delight by diminishing concern for how the plot will work out. True, the plot of this and other novels exerts surprising force even after one knows its outcome and its ways of getting there. Yet the choice to reread implies interest in more than what will eventuate. We want to see more clearly the steps by which the plot achieves its intricacies, or we look forward to re-encountering a delightful character, or we hope to revel in the language of a narrative when we no longer need to pay such close attention to events. If a novel's penetration into the interior workings of the mind and heart has struck us in first reading, we may seek to reinforce our original impression or to incorporate more firmly the insight we have achieved.

Wives and Daughters, reread, gives me more of what I found there in the first place: the dependable pleasure of psychological and moral insight. I admire the restraint with which Gaskell handles Molly's romantic life. The girl realizes her love for Roger at approximately the time when he becomes engaged to Cynthia, who, in Molly's view, does not sufficiently value him or his love. After Cynthia breaks the engagement, Roger gradually comes to love Molly. He is obligated, however, to spend six months more in Africa, where he has been making great, if unspecified, scientific discoveries. Because there is scarlet fever at Roger's home, Molly's doctor father forbids him to come to the Gibson household. The lovers, therefore, cannot meet. Roger never acknowledges his love to Molly (although he confesses it to her father), and he must depart for Africa. She achieves only an imperfect view of him, impeded by the physical obstacle of her stepmother's insistent efforts to attract the young man's attention, as well as by driving rain. The fact that the novel ends at this point, before its projected final chapter, intensifies the reader's sense of authorial reticence. Again, this is not what one would expect of a Victorian novel.

In my previous readings, I had been struck by the book's evasions of Victorian mores. Although Molly acts like a conventional "good girl," albeit with occasional flashes of temper, her capacity to follow her own lights even in the face of community disapproval marks her singularity. In a successful effort to help Cynthia, she compromises her own reputation. Not even to her father will she explain what she has done.

But rereadings, as I have said, often reveal the unexpected. This time I noticed with real surprise how successfully Gaskell manages to have it both ways. Molly, early in the novel, speaks of the cost of self-sacrifice, the probability that one will lose oneself in thinking only of others. In fact, though, she willingly sacrifices herself to Cynthia's needs, although she recognizes her stepsister's moral flaws. If she preserves her emotional vitality—and this, I repeat, is an unfamiliar concern in the period—she also intensifies her moral discipline. She cannot be faulted for any significant deviations from Victorian orthodoxy, the orthodoxy of the community: if she refuses her father's request for information, she does so in the service of a higher moral obligation. Yet she declares to him the importance of her autonomy: "Perhaps I've been foolish; but what I did, I did of my own self. It was not suggested to me." She both conforms to conventional ethical standards and asserts her independence.

Gaskell's treatment of Cynthia, the frivolous and superficial beauty, evinces the same double pattern. Cynthia gets into complicated trouble as a result of her vanity and lack of foresight; she uses her virtuous stepsister for her own ends; she cannot live up to the good opinion of the admirable man to whom she engages herself. She realizes her own moral and emotional inadequacies and suffers shame and guilt. Her realistic view of herself enables her to know that she cannot live without the admiration of those around her. She consequently attracts and marries a well-to-do but superficial Londoner who thinks highly of her and who removes her from the company of those who understand and reprehend her nature. Although the novel makes Cynthia's deviations from rectitude clear, it does not punish her for them. She gets exactly what she wants. Moreover, the narrator solicits sympathy for her: the girl's self-awareness pains her, yet she cannot discover in herself the resources to combat faults she deplores. *Wives and Daughters* conveys the conventional moral message: good girls are more admirable than bad girls and deserve greater rewards. It also, however, suggests that even the morally weak may have admirable human traits; even they can be loved.

The quiet pleasures of rereading *Wives and Daughters* epitomize the emotional tone of much rereading. The excitement of initial encounters with an imaginative work fades in repeated assignations, replaced by the serenity of knowledge and the mild stimulation of confident expectation, as well as by the new kind of excitement involved in more complicated speculations than a first reading allows. Something has been lost, to be sure: the intellectual and emotional challenges of a plot and characters encountered for the first time. Inasmuch as each repeated reading entails for the reader the remaking of the text, informed by the sum total of previous experiences with it, a new and more personal drama of individual discovery replaces the original relation with the plot as discovery of events and meanings. Like multiple meetings with an old friend, multiple engagements with a familiar text deepen a relationship.

I cannot specify the nature of my original relationship with *Wives and Daughters,* beyond saying that it involved a sense of intimacy, with story and with characters, that has grown steadily in successive readings. Comparable feelings of intimacy mark my experience of many fictions of particular power. It is as difficult to describe such feelings in detail as it is to delineate the contours of intimacy with another person. Like intimacy with a person, intimacy with a book adds value to the revelations that relationship involves. Its intensification is one of rereading's great pleasures.

Rereading, it must be said, can supply antipleasures as well as pleasures. Rereading oneself is especially dangerous. I'm thinking in particular about the experience of coming upon old notes in works long ago read for the first time. "Symbol!" I find in the margin of a novel read in college, and cringe. I've sometimes seen other people's marginalia in books borrowed from the library. When the notes and exclamation points and underlinings obviously issue from undergraduates, they generally irritate; but many marginal comments strike me as wonderfully revealing. Not my own, though; never, that I can remember, my own.

Still, I can muster some indulgence for the products of my youth, even the college essays, marked "A," that I as a teacher would have graded far less leniently. It's harder to find excuses for books that, once treasured, seem in reiteration altogether vapid—although here, too, some tolerance for a younger self, the self that did the treasuring, may be required. The books that I discussed in the last three chapters as disappointing me, *The Catcher in the Rye*, *Lucky Jim*, and *The Golden Notebook*, didn't make me unhappy or indignant when I reread them, perhaps because I was too greatly interested in the explanation for their falls from grace. Often, though, I've felt emotions varying from disappointment to outrage at discovering that a book no longer provides the nourishment I expect from it.

You never know what book it's going to be. I set out, writing this chapter, to find a book that would deliver negative emotions, so that I could talk with more immediacy about what such feelings—the feelings of un-pleasure—are like. With some confidence, I decided on *The Wizard of Oz*, a book that I loved as a little girl and haven't read again since my childhood. I had encountered in some critical work the observation that bad prose marked Frank Baum's story; I knew, therefore, that I wouldn't like it.

But I thought the prose was exactly what it should be: simple, straightforward, emphatic—what one might call a Kansas sort of prose. A random example: "They walked along listening to the singing of the bright-colored birds and looking at the lovely flowers which now became so thick that the ground was carpeted with them. There were big yellow and white and blue and purple blossoms, besides great clusters of scarlet poppies, which were so brilliant in color they almost dazzled Dorothy's eyes." Baum does not tell us what kind of birds or flowers: their kind doesn't matter. He specifies only the poppies, which will soon put the lion and Dorothy and the dog Toto to sleep, dwelling mainly on what a child would see: bright colors, brilliance. Then he makes comedy out of the responses of the Scarecrow and the Tin Woodman. When Dorothy asks, about the flowers, "Aren't they beautiful?" the Scarecrow responds, "I suppose so. . . . When I have brains I shall probably like them better," and the Woodman observes, "If I only had a heart I should love them." Like other moments in *The Wizard of Oz*, this one can (though it need not) stir speculation about the nature of thought and feeling. Why would brains make one like flowers better? Why does the Woodman keep postponing his capacity for love, despite the fact that he clearly loves his companions?

And how does this repeated trope—everything would be different if only I had a . . . whatever—work in the text? The reader, even a very young reader, quickly realizes that the characters already have what they seek. An adult reader may begin to suspect that, far from naïve about language, Baum is calling attention to language's power. The Scarecrow, the Woodman, and the Lion all name themselves as lacking; the naming intensifies, indeed creates, the lack. The Wizard eventually solves their problems by giving them inanimate objects and naming those objects as the desired powers. That naming heals, making it possible for the Lion to feel courageous, the Scarecrow intelligent, and the Woodman loving.

The suspicious adult reader, however, will probably acquire her suspicions only toward the end of the first reading and will work out their meaning in second or subsequent readings. Only after she knows how the characters' problems are solved can she fully understand their nature; only then will she have the kind of consciousness that allows her to perceive and to enjoy the small dramas of words and meaning. Or so I surmise, after this, my second, reading.

I called Baum's style a Kansas sort of prose in allusion, of course, to Dorothy's origins in Kansas. A character in Gregory Maguire's *Wicked: The Life and Times of the Wicked Witch of the West* describes Dorothy as "plain and straightforward as mustard seed," and it's a good description. (A small digression about Maguire: *Wicked*, which I recently read for the first time, provides its own kind of entertainment, with its elaborate account of events from the witch's perspective; it's much scarier than Baum's book, and infinitely more complicated, full of loudly announced big ideas. To my mind, it doesn't work nearly as well. I don't think I'll ever reread it.) Kansas, in the Judy Garland movie that surely shapes responses to the book for most adult readers now, is gray and dreary; Oz, colorful and vibrant. The grayness-versus-color contrast exists in the book version of *The Wizard of Oz* as well, but Kansas also figures emphatically as *home*, a place of love and shelter, and implicitly as the source of Dorothy's unpretentious straightforwardness. Baum's prose reveals the same virtues of plainness and integrity: "They went to bed quite early and slept soundly until daylight, when they were awakened by the crowing of a green cock that lived in the back yard of the palace, and the cackling of a hen that had laid a green egg." The greenness of cock and egg, treated as ordinary detail, oddly inflects the matter-of-fact sentence.

The story relies heavily on rhetorical devices of this sort. Never does the language insist on the strangeness of characters or happenings. Even when the Wizard appears to assume the form of a disembodied head, a roaring monster, or a ball of fire, little emphasis rests on the remarkableness of the appearances. The rhetoric echoes the substance of the narrative. Things happen as they happen. When the Wizard comments that Dorothy has killed the Wicked Witch of the East, she responds—"simply"—"That just happened . . . ; I could not help it." It is Dorothy's character, her straightforward Kansas character, to deal with whatever she has to deal with and then move on.

I can't remember why I loved this book when first I read it (I was very young), but I know several reasons for admiring it now. Prose style is one of them. For this reader, at least, to encounter prose that knows what it's doing generates the purest of pleasures—pleasure instantly recognizable and unmixed. Baum's prose proceeds with modest authority, never claiming much for itself, always doing the job. It doesn't get in the way of the story. Indeed, it moves the story right along. A lot happens in any given short stretch of narrative time, and the matter-of-factness of its presentation facilitates its acceptance.

Then there are the characterizations, simple as well, to the point of being almost rudimentary, and altogether satisfactory. I belong to a generation trained in college English courses to seek and admire "complexity." The discovery that simplicity concealing no compensatory intricacy offers its own pleasures even now fills me with wonder. (*The Wizard of Oz* has over the years attracted several critical interpretations that in effect make it into an allegory, usually about economics. I don't believe a word of them.) Dorothy, like the three implausible companions she acquires in Oz, is assigned only a few qualities: the straightforwardness I've already mentioned, a tacit faith that problems can be solved, ready acceptance of whatever comes along, and underlying concern for others. (Her desire to return to Kansas is largely motivated by her worry that Aunty Em will be upset by her continued absence.) The Woodman, the Scarecrow, and the Lion react to everything on the basis of their soft-heartedness, smartness, or bravery, or else of their desire for these qualities that they don't realize they have. Dorothy confronts all situations in direct and practical ways: after she has inadvertently destroyed the Wicked Witch of the East by melting her, "Dorothy drew another bucket of water and threw it over the mess [of the Witch's melting]. She then swept it all out the door." As in other episodes, one can respond to these sentences as comedy—Dorothy's refusal to take the Witch's death as cause for emotion of course has comic aspects—or with admiration, as further evidence of Dorothy's tendency simply to get on with things.

Finally, there is the story. It's a good story, in which things happen fast and unpredictably, the constant surprises for the reader contrasting appealingly with Dorothy's characteristic lack of astonishment. A fairy-tale structure, in which questers must pass a series of tests in order to achieve their objectives, controls the narrative, with the comic twist of a wizard who turns out to have virtually no power at all. I suppose some of it might be a bit scary for a child (though I don't remember being scared), but difficulties resolve quickly. I suppose there's some suspense—will the travelers make it to the Emerald City? Will Dorothy get back to Kansas?—but certainly not a whole lot. Each individual happening, though, offers its own satisfactions.

Rereading *The Wizard of Oz* has been a peculiar experience. The book seemed so fresh to me that it felt as though I were reading it for the first time—an effect facilitated by the fact that I remember from my initial experience only the delight it induced. Perhaps the movie (which I saw in my childhood) overlaid the original reading encounter and caused it to vanish from my memory. In any case, I can say nothing about how this second reading differed from the first. It was all a surprise.

Yet I can say with some confidence how it *must* differ from the first. I was reading everything I could get my hands on at the time I first read *The Wizard*, and reading happily, without critical discrimination, taking in a store of imaginative knowledge. Now I am in a position to say what it is that I enjoy, and the formulation of what in the text provides the experience of delight constitutes its own form of pleasure: the pleasure, in miniature, of writing this book, and of the thought and self-awareness that preceded the writing. Moreover, rereading invariably supplies at least an agreeable aura of vague memory, a kind of undifferentiated pleasure. For *The Wizard of Oz*, that aura evokes for me the atmosphere of long hours, beginning when I was very young, in the window seat of a public library that inhabited a mammoth Victorian house. More grown-up books—less often banished from the realm of specific recall—also frequently recuperate a stage of life, or a physical environment, even when I don't remember my original reactions to the book in question.

The pleasures I cited earlier from my recent reading of Baum— the joys of expert prose, good characterization, and vigorous narrative—could equally enliven a first reading. But the satisfactions of rereading most obviously differ from those of initial encounters with a book because of the ways that rereading adds the pleasure (or un-pleasure) of memory to the exchange between reader and text. Memory often enriches reading, first readings as well as later ones, by recalling experiences that illuminate the page before us. The memories attached to rereading, however, also recall the particular experiences of earlier reading, often in their emotional or circumstantial context. They thus provide a special form of enrichment.

Such memories, however, delightful as they may be in themselves, only intensify the sense of disappointment and the multiple unpleasures of a book that fails to survive the second reading. *The Wizard of Oz* did not enable me to test this thesis; *Gone with the Wind* did. Indeed, I couldn't even get to the end of it, the second time through—I hadn't remembered that it was such a *big* book (1,448 pages in the Pocket Book edition). A big book full of bad prose, constructed out of clichés that it may in some cases have originated (a possibility that does nothing to make them palatable), based on a sense of history so romanticized that it seems dubiously fit even for a ten-year-old: how could it have won the Pulitzer Prize?

To my ten-year-old self, though, it seemed wonderful. I couldn't stop reading it; I read it under the covers with a flashlight—the only time I can remember flagrantly disobeying my mother's injunction to turn out the light and go to bed. (Well, technically I obeyed: I indeed turned out the light and went to bed. But not to sleep.) Although I suspected myself of resembling the good girl, Melanie, more than Scarlett, the beautiful, exciting, bad girl, I identified with Scarlett and imaginatively participated in the myth of the South. I lived in central Florida. My parents were Yankees, and I seemed unable to develop a southern accent, although I tried. (My sister, for some reason, managed this accomplishment with ease.) In school we learned a great deal about Confederate heroism and nobility, and very little about Abraham Lincoln. Robert E. Lee's birthday was a school holiday. Lincoln's was not. Being translated in spirit to the scene of the Civil War seemed a wonderful consummation.

I knew and cared nothing about prose style. Reading was like taking something in through the pores, a process of instantaneous absorption. I hardly realized that I was reading words, so completely did I live within whatever I perused. If someone had told me that the words that composed *Gone with the Wind* were carelessly chosen and clumsily put together, I would have understood neither what was meant nor why it mattered.

I treasure the memory of that kind of reading, with its capacity to remove me from the everyday. I value also, though, the kind of reading more characteristic of me now: not so mindless as my earlier passionate immersion; indeed, mindful in the extreme. Often, as with *The Wizard of Oz*, the rewards, assessed in terms of the amount of pleasure delivered, at least match and on occasion exceed those of childhood absorption. When, however, a book that once generated mindless ecstasy now produces irritation, boredom, and distaste, the sense of disillusionment is profound. This is disillusionment in the most literal sense: I feel deprived of an illusion that gave me great pleasure. The only pleasure that replaces it in the immediate experience of the disappointing book is the empty satisfaction of feeling smarter now than I was at ten.

Here lies a danger of rereading. I believe firmly in a magical theory about reading—that one mysteriously discovers, at every stage of life, just the books that one really needs at that moment. *Gone with the Wind* belonged to the ten-year-old moment when I was beginning to wonder about the relations of men and women and how they might come about. Fairy tales had long satisfied my desire for romance, for imaginative participation in a world more like Oz than like Kansas, but now I wanted something more—and Margaret Mitchell's novel gave me that more. Its crudely drawn, clearly differentiated characters; its repetitive sentiments; its historical weaknesses—none of that would have mattered even if I'd known enough to recognize such aspects of the book. So, at any rate, I surmise, looking back.

All these years later, I know enough: know enough not to enjoy something that once gave me delight. The sensation of loss coexists with the perception that I'm more astute than I used to be but far exceeds it in emotional weight. I feel affection for that little girl reading with a flashlight, but also a faint overlay of shame that I was formerly so benighted. Rereading may measure progress of various kinds. It also can measure deprivation.

I return to those dependable nineteenth-century novels, specifically to one that has provided a series of complicated pleasures over the years, through multiple rereadings: George Eliot's *Middlemarch*, a wise, intricate, mesmerizing work. I hadn't read it in—oh, probably twenty years. My recent rereading offered an unexpected initial experience of un-pleasure. I had returned to the specific book from which I last taught *Middlemarch*, expecting that the physical object would help me recall previous encounters with Eliot's masterpiece. An old Riverside paperback from Houghton Mifflin, it had not, unlike the Graham Greene Penguin, aged well. The back cover, half torn off, only partly protected crumbling pages. As I read, the book shed flakes of paper on my lap. No matter how carefully I turned the pages, they disintegrated at my touch. Usually a fast reader, I found myself, after ten days, only 200 pages into the 840-page volume and dreading the task of reading—the "task" of reading one of my favorite works. Clearly, I needed a new book. An up-to-date Penguin transformed my relation to Eliot. The new book had no special associations. It neither reinforced my memory of past reading by preserving the physical volume I once read nor suggested by its embodiment of decay that this novel's day might be over. The next 600-odd pages of *Middlemarch* took only four days and provided lavish pleasure—including the pleasures of laughter and of tears.

The novel's wisdom manifests itself to me in new ways as I age. This time, I found myself pondering the wisdom of tone in Eliot's presentation of her intricate philosophical drama. It has long been clear to me that this novelist achieves powerful effects by manipulating a tone of peculiar authority. Unlike such predecessors in the novelistic art as Henry Fielding and Laurence Sterne, she rarely flaunts her power over characters or reader, but the reader probably feels at least dimly conscious of being under the control of a narrator who can keep in mind the individual perplexities of a large cast of characters. We ponder with the narrator as she explores the subtle relations of strongly imagined persons, in a web of meaning (to use a figure that Eliot herself is fond of) that she elucidates even as she declares its mystery. The goal of the enterprise—the reader's enterprise, and the narrator's—is not to discover anything definitive. Rather, the pondering itself becomes the goal: the will and capacity to take imagined lives with utter seriousness, and thus, perhaps, to find new ways to understand one's own experience.

What strikes me most forcefully now is the interpretive force of irony in *Middlemarch*. It's not that I haven't noticed the text's ironies before: I still remember my sense of shock when I first realized that the narrator poked fun even at Dorothea. My main concern, though, has been substance rather than tone. I considered Eliot—I still consider her—a great moral educator. Although she sometimes propounds dicta, the education she provides inheres more profoundly in her delicate discriminations of character. Years ago, I engaged in a prolonged discussion (it took place over several lunches) with a colleague about whether or not human beings could change in essential ways. My friend said no, I said yes. At one point I brought up a powerful argument on my side. "George Eliot," I announced, "tells us that people can change." "Of course she does," my friend replied. "That's why you believe it."

She won the argument. I realized immediately the truth of her assertion—realized that much of what I believe about the nature of right and wrong and of moral action comes from my reading of just such books as *Middlemarch*, which engage ethical questions profoundly and subtly and which seemed at the time of the argument more concerned with issues I was pondering—quandaries about character and about human relations—than were the adults I knew directly. Yes, many of my ideas came from books. When my colleague suggested that her notions of human possibility derived from observation of real people, whereas mine depended on fiction, I felt refuted. First-hand experience, I readily assumed, must be more dependable than second-hand.

I no longer think so. I trust that if that long-ago argument had occurred this week, I would have defended Eliot as a moral authority and claimed that the evidence she offers about human nature is probably better than that we have acquired by observation. Her basis for judgment, like ours, presumably consists of actual men and women, but her observation is larger, her comprehension greater, her moral intelligence more commanding than the capacities of anyone I know—certainly more powerful than mine. Precisely because I have been so fully preoccupied with Eliot as moral authority, though, I have paid less attention to how she achieves her effects than to the nature of the effects themselves.

If we could read everything, or anything, sufficiently often, we could eventually pay attention to all its aspects. "Sufficiently often," however, is not a possibility: one never gets to all the aspects. Yet even insufficient rereading often allows the pleasure of discovering new ways to pay attention, a treat in itself. So it is with me and *Middlemarch,* as I focus on irony.

Irony, which has been at various times a fashionable term in literary criticism, at the moment has a rather bad name in popular discourse, associated as it often is with superficial airs of superiority and a tendency to dismiss opposing viewpoints as not worthy of attention. Eliot's irony, however, is anything but superficial. One of the best-known moments in *Middlemarch* epitomizes her serious use of it. Dorothea, the novel's heroine, and her much older husband, Casaubon, on their wedding trip to Rome have their first quarrel, which comes as a shock to the bride. She has inadvertently articulated to her husband his own fear that he will never manage to write the great scholarly book that he has planned. Although she does not fully understand what has happened, she realizes vaguely that he, too, has inner urgencies and that she cannot grasp them. As Eliot puts it, "To-day she had begun to see that she had been under a wild illusion in expecting a response to her feeling from Mr. Casaubon, and she had felt the waking of a presentiment that there might be a sad consciousness in his life which made as great a need on his side as on her own." Then comes the serious irony: "We are all of us born in moral stupidity, taking the world as an udder to feed our supreme selves."

The metaphor of the world as udder may bring us up short because of the wild discrepancy of its components. Any visual conception of the figure of speech will be impossibly grotesque, yet it is easy to grasp its meaning. The discrepancy is precisely the point. We—"all of us"—assume at the outset of consciousness that the world's vastness exists for our individual gratification. Moral intelligence, as opposed to moral stupidity, originates by implication in awareness that we do not hold a position of supreme importance in the universe. This abstract statement, however, lacks the force of the metaphor, which by its grotesqueness emphasizes the disproportion of self-preoccupation.

The ironic tone depends largely on another discrepancy: between the imagined supremacy and the actual stupidity of the self. Exactly this disjunction supplies a primary subject of *Middlemarch,* which repeatedly exposes the structures of illusion its characters build around themselves and the ways that their sense of importance becomes undermined. Even Dorothea Brooke, the novel's most admirable figure, has to learn that high aspirations for virtue do not suffice; even she provides an occasional target for the astute narrator.

In the early chapters of *Middlemarch,* irony abounds. The two-page "Prelude," largely concerned with Saint Theresa, preserves a straightforward serious tone, but from the beginning of Chapter 1 the narrator displays an ambiguous and slightly unsettling attitude toward her characters. We learn that Miss Brooke "was usually spoken of as being remarkably clever, but with the addition that her sister Celia had more common-sense. Nevertheless, Celia wore scarcely more trimmings." What does that "Nevertheless" mean: what controls the perceived relation between common sense and trimmings? Evidently a woman of common sense, in the view of the community, might be expected to show a certain extravagance in the matter of trimmings, but Celia defies expectation. Should we scorn or admire her for this reason? That question is apparently beside the point. "Frippery," it turns out, links firmly to class. "Young women of such birth [as Dorothea and Celia], living in a quiet country-house, and attending a village church hardly larger than a parlour, naturally regarded frippery as the ambition of a huckster's daughter." "Naturally"? If class distinctions have come to be considered natural, the society must be rigid indeed. Already we have a hint that Dorothea may find little encouragement for her impulses toward mental and spiritual expansiveness. Unable to "reconcile the anxieties of a spiritual life involving eternal consequences, with a keen interest in guimp [an underblouse intended for wear with a low-cut dress] and artificial protrusions of drapery," Dorothea, the narrator also hints, may aspire to martyrdom and find it at an unexpected juncture.

The special quality of the narrator's irony, directed often at Dorothea in the novel's early chapters, and often also at more obvious targets, depends on its generally affectionate tone. Rarely does it seem cutting. Often it is deliberately and generously inclusive, suggesting that all of us (first-person plural pronouns appear frequently) share whatever trait has attracted the narrator's gently mocking attention. The momentousness of this pervasive irony, though, may be suggested by a narratorial comment: "any one watching keenly the stealthy convergence of human lots, sees a slow preparation of effects from one life on another, which tells like a calculated irony on the indifference or the frozen stare with which we look at our unintroduced neighbour. Destiny stands by sarcastic with our *dramatis personæ* folded in her hand." "Destiny" appears to be another name for the novelist, who, without parading her godlike control of her characters, indeed folds them in her hand and cannot altogether avoid "sarcastic" perceptions of them. Her knowledge of what is to come inflects her perceptions and causes her often to mingle compassion with acuity. Only toward the sadistic miser Featherstone—an apparently unredeemable character—and his avaricious relatives is her irony unremittingly harsh. More often, she acknowledges that the faults she mocks belong to human beings in general. Thus, even Casaubon at his worst, in his jealousy of Dorothea's interest in Will, attracts the narrator's sympathy. Dorothea's husband now suspects "that he was no longer adored without criticism"; the narrator comments wryly that his suspicion rests on good reasons, including the "strong reason" that "he was not unmixedly adorable." Then she adds, "He suspected this, however, as he suspected other things, without confessing it, and like the rest of us, felt how soothing it would have been to have a companion who would never find it out." All of us, whether or not we acknowledge it, yearn to be purely adorable; all want companions who think us so—another version of the self-absorption that makes us consider the world an udder for our sole enjoyment.

The narrator's slightly astringent tone toward Dorothea and her unworldly idealism recurs. The young woman's desire for selflessness (or for egotism disguised) provides a counterpart for a more open universal focus on self. This would-be Saint Theresa, however, must live in the world and must accordingly learn the limits of personal possibility; reminders of this imperative come frequently to the reader's attention.

As the long novel approaches its end, its ironies finally almost disappear, as though the narrator's godlike perception no longer allows criticism of the book's central character. Dorothea, to be sure, learns something about limits, although, like the other characters chastened by experience, she never articulates the nature of her learning. Her new understanding allows her finally to marry her dead husband's cousin, Will Ladislaw, against her husband's explicit prohibition. In my previous readings of *Middlemarch*, I found this marriage almost as distasteful as Casaubon thought it in jealous anticipation—although not for Casaubon's reasons. I thought that Eliot had depicted Will as a romantic figure (and "romantic" is not a positive term in my personal lexicon) of much posturing, little substance: a man by no means worthy of Dorothea's devotion. Instructed anew by the novel's ironic commentary, though, I understand that Dorothea has learned to accept her own nature as well as that of others. Grasping that the world's udder exists not for ourselves alone implies such learning. Dorothea needs to devote herself; Will wants her devotion. Worthiness is irrelevant: no one, finally, is worthy. Dorothea's fate falls short of her initial aspirations, but it involves the whole-hearted acceptance that enables happiness.

Much earlier in the novel, Mrs. Bulstrode exemplified marital acceptance—if not happiness—as she stood by a husband who had been publicly exposed as a dabbler in corruption and a possible murderer. The narrator conveys only respect and admiration for the woman's fidelity and compassion. The object of her devotion may be weak and hypocritical, but her faithfulness to her marriage and to the suffering man with whom she is yoked merits praise. Similarly, the narrator's final comments about Dorothea, while acknowledging that neither of the protagonist's marriages was "ideally beautiful," hint at admiration for the qualities of character displayed within them. A tone of slightly anxious justification, a tone verging on the apologetic, replaces irony. The narrator too, it seems, has acquired a new point of view. "Certainly those determining acts of [Dorothea's] life [that is, her marriages] were not ideally beautiful. They were the mixed result of a young and noble impulse struggling amidst the conditions of an imperfect social state, in which great feelings will often take the aspect of error, and great faith the aspect of illusion." In other words, Dorothea did not fulfill her own aspirations, but she did the best she could, given the state of society.

The "mixed result[s]" of other characters' lives, however, do not receive the same kind of justification. Lydgate, under the pressure of his marriage, compromises his ideals, yields to his wife's opinions, and dies young. A touch of the narrator's irony remains in her summary of the doctor's career, and more than a touch in her account of Rosamond's success in managing her husband—although both, at least as clearly as Dorothea, also suffer from "the conditions of an imperfect social state."

Irony depends on distance (as we saw in *The Sacred and Profane Love Machine*)—in *Middlemarch* the distance from which Destiny contemplates the fates of her unaware *dramatis personæ*, the distance from which an author can on occasion consider her characters. To the novel's end, the narrator retains her ironic distance from Lydgate, despite her sympathy for his shattered hopes. Dorothea is another matter. Here are the book's final sentences:

> Her full nature, like that river of which Cyrus broke the strength, spent itself in channels which had no great name on the earth. But the effect of her being on those around her was incalculably diffusive: for the growing good of the world is partly dependent on unhistoric acts; and that things are not so ill with you and me as they might have been, is half owing to the number who lived faithfully a hidden life, and rest in unvisited tombs.

The godlike distance from which the narrator contemplates her subjects—contemplates, indeed, the universe—remains, but this is a wise and benevolent, not at all "sarcastic," observer. "We"—you and me, the multitude previously implicated in the same follies as the characters—now exist as objects of action rather than as actors. Dorothea has come to represent a human force of salvation. In tone and in substance, these sentences strike a new note, insisting on the individual and universal importance of the character who has compromised her early hopes and accepted a modest life. She has nonetheless, the novel maintains, used herself fully—unlike Lydgate, who also compromised his hopes, but willfully accepted mediocrity.

I hear some strain in the final words: they do not altogether convince me about Dorothea. They do, however, persuade me that Eliot has modified her own views as she has tried to educate her readers, bringing herself to believe that self-subordination can constitute female triumph. (She arrives at a similar position in *The Mill on the Floss*.) Her pattern of irony resolves itself in irony's rejection, as if to say that the storyteller must celebrate as well as question the contours of human nature. Yet the irony has done its work, at once distancing and implicating narrator and readers alike in the confused responses of imagined mortals to the intricacies of their condition.

These comments on irony and its novelistic resolution barely touch the complexities of Eliot's novel. They call attention, however, to a particular pleasure of rereading that first readings can hardly approach: that of seeing a new facet of a large work illuminated. In first readings one wants and needs to grasp a novel as a whole. Questions often remain in the reader's mind after the initial encounter; certainty even about the book's contours may require several readings to achieve. But successive readings, attended with diminishing anxiety about taking in the nature of the whole, allow attention to smaller matters. To see something new, to take hold afresh of even a single aspect of the work, provides a special joy: one of the multifarious pleasures of rereading and its surprises.

My training as a literary critic of course inflects the "smaller matters" that attract my attention. I take particular pleasure in teasing out the ways that a piece of fiction works on me, how it creates its effects—not just superficial effects, but profound influences on me as a reader. *Middlemarch,* which I have long loved and often read (read too often to recall my initial experience of it), is also a novel that I greatly admire: for its wisdom about human beings and for its dexterity in creating an imaginative structure that can convey that wisdom. My love and admiration, however, only encourage my effort to figure out how Eliot accomplishes so much.

But I do not urge others necessarily to pursue the same activities, nor do I believe that my literary pleasures should constitute a model for other readers. I urge that rereaders, rather, note and value their own forms of pleasure as they engage and re-engage with favorite books—and that those who have not previously indulged in rereading allow themselves to experience its multifarious delights.

8

Professional Rereading

M ANY—SURELY, MOST—readers and rereaders consciously or unconsciously seek pleasure in their activity, in both the ways specified and the many ways neglected in the previous chapter. Those who pursue advanced degrees in literature, those who teach literature in colleges and universities, typically begin on their path with delight in and love for the books they study and teach. Yet their study and eventually their own teaching rarely emphasize delight.

As one of those university teachers of literature, I must confess that I infrequently (although not never!) talk about the pleasure of reading in my classes. Even when I recently taught a freshman seminar called Rereading Jane Austen, in which we read three novels twice in the course of a semester, we didn't much discuss enjoyment, although students occasionally mentioned their pleasure in reading, say, *Pride and Prejudice* for the third time. Our focus lay elsewhere. I want to think about that "elsewhere": about how what I call "professional rereading" works, how it differs from recreational rereading, and what some of its values are. My purpose is twofold. I want first to speculate about the nature of this "professional rereading." Beyond that, I plan to ponder the possible relation of such rereading to canon formation and to what we call "the rise of the novel," in order to convey a large sense of what purposeful rereading can accomplish.

By professional rereading, I mean the kind of rereading that I engage in as a profession. People who teach literature reread the same texts again and again, and get paid for it. That, after all, is their—our—vocation. We reread in order to teach and in order to write literary criticism or literary history. We annotate and underline and turn down corners in our battered paperback texts, and when the time comes to replace old copies with new ones, it seems a disaster. To throw away the record of year after year of response risks the loss of much that we have thought and felt and of the process through which understanding developed.

Rereading of this sort, the kind we do for the sake of teaching or writing, may feel at times merely routine, yet it can also come to seem an index of literary quality. Every literature teacher knows that some books endlessly offer fresh delights and insight, while others wear out after a few iterations. Teaching modern drama every year for several years, I repeatedly read Shaw and Chekhov. After a few years, Shaw bored me. Chekhov became better and better. I concluded that Chekhov was a great playwright and Shaw considerably less great.

That was a judgment forced on me, or so it seemed, by experience. The repetitions of rereading—and this goes for "frivolous" rereading as well as for its professional counterpart—carry peculiar authority. As we encounter the same text again and again, it comes to inhabit the deep reaches of the brain. Repetition generates belief. Rereading, by virtue of its repetitions, can provide its practitioner with the illusion that she has total possession of a text, and thus is winning the subtle contest between writer and reader that always coexists with their implicit collaboration.

Professional rereading, however, does not depend on repetition alone. The most important difference between rereading as self-indulgence and rereading as professional discipline concerns purpose. The pleasure of rereading something just because you feel like it derives partly from the absence of any conscious goal beyond pleasure. Enjoying familiar cadences ("During the whole of a dull, dark, and soundless day in the autumn of the year . . ."), tracing familiar plots (girl meets boy and likes him a lot, boy prefers someone else, boy sees the light . . .), looking for nothing in particular, you can discover new things and relish the old, without seeking enlightenment. Rereading in order to teach a class or to write a paper, you look for something. Perhaps that "something" takes no specific shape in advance: maybe you're seeking anything at all in the way of a unifying idea that will give coherence to your account of *Roderick Random*. Or possibly you already have a hypothesis: you're looking, say, for examples to support your notion that illness in the eighteenth-century novel customarily signifies emotional instability. In either case, your attention is focused. You will probably find what you're looking for; you may miss many serendipitous possibilities.

The value of recreational rereading inheres largely in its unpredictable results. The philosopher John Kaag called my attention to a phrase of Immanuel Kant's in the *Critique of Aesthetic Judgment*. Kant writes of "a purposiveness without a definite purpose"; Kaag suggested that the phrase might characterize the state of mind in which one engages with a book for the second or fifth or eighth time, just for the sake of enjoyment. Free from anxiety about outcomes, the reader feels uncompelled by the need for resolution, unfocused on any particular goal. The general purpose of achieving delight governs the act of reading, but little urgency attends it.

Professional rereading, in contrast, directing itself toward some specific end, can feel both pointed and urgent. Although it, too, can reveal unpredictable possibilities, it can also be channeled. Whether we seek to find an argument—a thesis around which to organize a class or an essay—or look for confirmation or elaboration of an idea dimly apprehended, we direct the text to our purposes rather than give ourselves over to its intents. The results are often valuable. Less open to random possibility than the impulsive rereader, the professional rereader finds instead the excitement of opening or developing a line of thought—another kind of discovery.

The sheer bulk of the professional rereader's reading helps to direct her purpose and to protect her against error. Looking for a fresh hypothesis about *Roderick Random,* she not only rereads that novel. Ideally, she will have reread also Smollett's other novels, and Fielding's, and Richardson's. She will have immersed herself in eighteenth-century culture. She knows the shape of the period's plots; she understands its assumptions about character. Even if she has not mastered everything she needs to know—and who has?— she has wide-ranging expertise derived from reading and rereading, and that expertise contributes to the value she derives from each individual textual exploration and re-exploration.

Like all thought processes, though, the kind associated with rereading has its pitfalls. I remember vividly my graduate school experience with a long eighteenth-century poem by James Thomson, *The Seasons,* about which I eventually wrote my dissertation. I encountered this poem initially in a graduate seminar and found it heavy going. Only in a theoretical way did it interest me: that is, I found some of its ideas worth pondering, but I had virtually no response at all to its quality as a poem. Once I had decided on the dissertation, my feelings changed dramatically. I read *The Seasons* over and over again. The more I read it, the better I liked it. I read other poems, too, but all subordinated themselves in my mind to that central text. By the time I had written the dissertation, I found it bewildering that not everyone considered Thomson at least the equal of, say, Chaucer.

166 · That frame of mind was perhaps valuable for the purpose of getting a Ph.D., but it has yielded over the years to a more measured view of Thomson, the result, partly, of reading and rereading many other poets from a less myopic perspective. Rereading may correct reading; it may also correct previous rereading. Yet it doesn't guarantee insight. As my experience with Thomson suggests, it can create a kind of obsession that obscures rather than illuminates. Or professional rereading, particularly the kind that prepares for teaching, can become listless, yielding only reiterations of what the reader has thought before. As a teacher, especially, to some extent even as a critic, one encounters the same texts over and over. On occasion, they go dead: rereading becomes automatic and superficial, gliding over familiar surfaces. Sometimes it is difficult really to pay attention.

In the form of multiple rereadings, however, rereading guards against other critical faults, such as allowing oneself to be excessively influenced by the last critic read or by the brilliant idea struck off in class one day. An inherently conservative practice, valuing the reader's past and present experience and seeking the wisdom of accretion, it yet allows the eruption of new insights, while guarding against the temptation of unsubstantiated idea-spinning. Rereading with a critic's eye, one constantly assesses not only the quality of a piece of writing but the quality of the evidence it produces. Ideally, that critic's eye serves as a check to dubious interpretation and false memory.

I don't mean to suggest an absolute division between "recreational" and "professional" rereading. Pleasure plays its part in both, whether or not we speak of it: pleasure provides a starting point for perception. And perception abounds, for rereaders of every kind. The professional, however, will probably push her perception further, in order to construct or to support a thesis. She will discipline her insights, as the recreational rereader need not, in the process perhaps eliminating potentially fruitful ideas, but creating orderly argument for the sake of transmission. The professional rereader constantly assesses what she discovers; the recreational reader can simply embrace it. Both, however, engage in and value the reassurance and the discovery that rereading provides.

Professional rereaders operate within a conscious community and engage in professional conversation, written and oral, about their rereading. They have collective effects on widespread views. Collective rereading—rereadings by individual critics in close chronological conjunction—is largely responsible, I'll venture, for what we call the literary canon. Collective rereading, moreover, has the power to change the canon.

Let me be more specific; let me turn, in fact, to the rise of the novel. That phrase, "the rise of the novel," gained widespread currency after the publication, in 1957, of Ian Watt's book with the phrase as title. Watt argued that the significant rise of the novel took place in the early eighteenth century, exemplified by the writing of Daniel Defoe, Samuel Richardson, and Henry Fielding, the only novelists he seriously discusses. His view exercised a powerful influence, and his book inaugurated an extended period in which the novel occupied a conspicuous place in the consciousness of critics, teachers, and students.

The conviction that the novel "rose" between 1720 and 1750—rose in importance as a way of articulating cultural truths and rose in sophistication as a form—is an altogether retrospective notion. Those living through the eighteenth century in England were, by and large, conscious of no such rise, although they noted, and frequently deplored, the ever enlarging number of novels published. If many critics were willing to grant the moral and stylistic excellence of certain specific works of fiction—not without debate about what specific works these might be—virtually no one took the novel seriously as a genre of comparable importance to drama or poetry. Sarah Reeve, in her 1785 book *The Progress of Romance*, made the strongest overall case for the form, but her work had little immediate influence. Throughout the eighteenth century, circumstantial evidence suggests, people tended to apologize if they were caught reading a novel. Jane Austen's famous defense of the novel, in *Northanger Abbey*, includes a little scene in which a young lady, asked what she is reading, responds "with affected indifference, or momentary shame," "Oh! it is only a novel!" The narrator, decrying this reply, characterizes the generic novel as "some work in which the greatest powers of the mind are displayed, the happiest delineation of its varieties, the liveliest effusions of wit and humour are conveyed to the world in the best chosen language." Such a view, however, remained a minority opinion.

The current high status of the novel as genre, then, is a relatively recent development, as is the concern with tracing its rise to its present state of critical significance. The rise of the novel as a fact of literary history is actually a phenomenon occurring most importantly in the minds of critics. Not that the novel didn't begin at some point—of course it did, and of course its examples became increasingly abundant over time, and it became increasingly popular with increasing numbers of readers: in all those senses, it certainly rose. But its alleged starting point varies according to the views of individual critics, asserted to be just about every time from the great days of Rome and Greece to the early eighteenth century, and its rise can accordingly be located in equally diverse periods. What interests me is how it happens that critics decide to announce the rise of the novel, or the lyric, or the tragic drama— or, for that matter, the death of the novel, or whatever—and at some point their announcement becomes received opinion.

Looking back on a series of such announcements, we can see them as cyclic. Critical attention focuses for a time on the novel and then shifts to—oh, say, narrative poetry. We can be pretty sure that after a generation or so (and critical generations don't last long), it will turn back to the novel again. I suspect that these shifts take place as inevitable results of the process of professional rereading, and I think that the process deserves attention.

Not that it's easy to study. Every individual act of rereading differs from every other, from other acts by the same reader, and even more emphatically from rereadings by other persons. The shifts of critical focus that I've alluded to derive from what I have called *collective* rereading: from the cumulative effect of many individual acts, all different from one another, but all at least in some ways tending in the same direction. I've had the experience, and many others must have shared it, of suddenly noticing that several critical essays that I've read in different places over a period of weeks or months manifest a common attitude or assumption that I haven't attended to before. Such a new common assumption may well portend a general shift.

To say so, however, tells us nothing about how rereading has produced the new manifestation. I want to speculate about just that: about how collective rereading might generate changes in ways of thinking about the canon and changes in the canon itself. Since evidence is hard to come by, I'll start, as usual, with myself as guinea pig: I propose to think about two recent rereadings of my own, hoping that such thought might lead at least to useful surmises about how assumptions change, and literary canons with them.

Tom Jones, an uncontested classic of the English novel, has survived many critical shifts, because Henry Fielding's work, like Shakespeare's, offers fodder for diverse approaches and satisfaction for diverse desires. I read *Tom Jones* as a student; I have read it many times as a teacher; I have written about it more than once. Now I have reread it again; in a moment I'll describe what I found. The other novel I've looked at once more, Elizabeth Inchbald's *Simple Story,* is less firmly canonical. To be more precise: at the moment it is widely accepted as an important work, but that status extends back only thirty or forty years, resulting from the fact that many critics have recently turned their attention to previously neglected novels by women. I did not encounter this novel as a student, but it, too, has provided a subject for my writing and teaching.

I reread these books most recently as a professional, for the specific purpose of writing this chapter. Because I had previously published critical treatments of both—I have written about *Tom Jones* in three books of my own and about *A Simple Story* in at least two—I had a special professional problem: I wanted my rereading to produce something in the way of new insight, without duplicating what I had said earlier. It's sometimes hard to get out from under your own earlier reactions, but this time something struck me immediately that I had not noticed before.

I have long been interested in the ways plot functions to generate meaning in fiction. Plot, which can be taken as a superficial organizing system, can also be understood as reflecting the deep structure of a novel. Two great critics—Samuel Taylor Coleridge in the nineteenth century, Ronald Crane in the twentieth—have declared that *Tom Jones* has a "perfect plot." That plot can be simply summarized, a version of the fairy-tale pattern by which a young man goes through various trials in order to win a princess. Tom, a foundling, loves a wealthy young woman, daughter of a squire; after various temptations, mistakes, and mishaps, he learns his true parentage and wins his beloved. The details of his adventures and an enormous cast of characters complicate this formal scheme. The plot might be considered perfect because it has, as

Aristotle demanded of tragedy, a distinct beginning (a detailed account of Tom's advent and of illuminating episodes in his boyhood), middle (Tom's eventful journey from Paradise Hall, the home of his adoptive father, to London), and end (the youthful rake's convincing reformation, his discovery of his true parentage, and his marriage to his beloved Sophia). The plot is also symmetrical: the novel consists of three parts, each containing six books; one part devoted to Paradise Hall, one to the journey through England, and one to London. Most important, the plot deploys an intricate arrangement of events, rich in surprises, yet with everything prepared for. Chekhov said that if the audience sees a gun hanging on the wall in the first act, that gun must be fired by the third act. In *Tom Jones*, every gun is fired.

But so what? Such aspects of plot sound trivial, not clearly contributing to the emotional power or the psychological, moral, and social wisdom that we seek when we read novels. To be sure, plot ingenuity and symmetry play their parts in achieving a novel's aesthetic effect, as they generate a pleasing sense of order; and it's agreeable to trace the intricate arrangements by which fictional happenings are made to occur. Still, it's not immediately apparent why a perfect plot should be grounds for high praise. Amazon.com currently offers a list of ten works of fiction with "perfect" plots. They include such titles as *The Chocolate Cat Caper* and *Thief of Hearts*. I haven't read either of these books; still, I somehow doubt that they would meet the standards of critics who understand plot as a deep structure of undeniable import.

Plot, seriously considered, raises many questions. Crane, for instance, considers plot the very essence of every novel, involving action, character, and thought. To understand it, in his view, is to grasp the whole fictional enterprise. I'm inclined to agree. Reading *Tom Jones* yet again, I came up with a new question about how its plot works. My puzzlement concerned the novel's conspicuous narrator and his relation to the novelistic action. To what extent, and how, could the plot be said to include him? Fielding's interfering narrator provides one of the most distinctive aspects of *Tom Jones*. Chapter 1 consists of the narrator's explanation of his role as resembling that of an innkeeper, offering travelers a menu of delights that might lure them to stay. Each of the novel's subsequent seventeen books begins with a chapter in which the narrator reflects, sometimes at considerable length, on a matter that interests him. Moreover, he intrudes in the story at will, calling attention to his own cleverness, urging readers to go back and notice something they have presumably missed the first time through, offering moral judgments of his characters, pointing out similarities among the various innkeepers and doctors Tom encounters along his way.

The narrator's interventions are miscellaneous but not random. As many critics have noted, this figure—who comes to seem as much a "character" as anyone involved in more conventional ways with Tom's career—demonstrates a preoccupation with control, flaunting his control of the reader as well as of the characters he has invented. This preoccupation, I began to think, as I tried to answer my own question, provides a key to the plot's workings. All plots in conventional novels derive from their characters' desires—desires that typically conflict with one another or that resist fulfillment because of the laws of nature or the strictures of society. In a tight-knit plot, major characters duplicate one another's desires, sometimes clashing by virtue of their competition for a single goal, sometimes constructing alliances or enmities on the basis of their differing understandings of the same purpose. In *Tom Jones,* the major characters share with the narrator a desire for control. They seek control of various sorts, for various reasons, in various ways, dramatizing by their procedures the nature of their imagined beings.

Let me outline a few manifestations of Fielding's intricate pattern, to suggest how that pattern adumbrates a fiction of moral and psychological depth. Apart from the narrator, the character most obviously concerned with control, and the only one who grasps the possibility of exercising different kinds of mastery to his own advantage, is Blifil, the novel's villain. Initially introduced as Tom's foster brother, finally revealed as his half-brother, Blifil in every aspect appears as Tom's opposite. Unlike Tom, he always knows exactly what he's doing and why. Desire for control of wealth shapes many of his actions and interpretations. Yet his manifest pleasure simply in controlling others by manipulation often dominates: this activity confirms for him his own superior cleverness and wisdom. His apparent success in every endeavor, which persists almost to the novel's end, stems from his skill at such manipulation. He controls the good opinion of his tutors and even that of his benevolent and wise uncle, Squire Allworthy, shaping their correspondingly negative views of Tom. Blifil's delight in control soon reveals its sadistic edge: he woos and almost wins Tom's beloved Sophia, knowing that she despises him, but imagining with glee the prospect of possessing her although—really *because*—she hates him.

Tom, in contrast, desires merely control of his own life. That proves difficult to achieve because of his lack of self-awareness and his tendency to respond without forethought to immediate situations. When Squire Allworthy expels him from Paradise Hall (on the basis of Blifil's misleading claims about him), Tom feels utterly out of control, with little money, no clear goal, and no prospect of gaining the woman he loves. Matters get worse before they get better, as the young man tumbles from one catastrophe to another. Squire Allworthy has given him a five hundred pound note—a very large sum of money. Before Tom has even looked at this note, he loses it. He goes to bed with a woman he rescues from another man, and thus fails to encounter Sophia when she comes to the inn he briefly inhabits. He manages to get hit over the head by a soldier; the doctor claims the wound will probably prove mortal. He keeps finding himself in uncomfortable situations as a result of no conscious choice. Thus, in London, his heart still belonging to Sophia, he serves as gigolo to a rich and self-indulgent woman. He ends up in prison for allegedly killing a man without provocation. While in prison, threatened with hanging, he is informed that the woman he slept with at the inn was in fact his mother. Despite these and other mishaps, however, he achieves his happy ending, making a series of conscious, willed decisions that indicate his achievement of self-control, and winning Sophia as an indirect result.

Several of the novel's figures manifest their determination to exercise parental control, most importantly Squire Western, Sophia's father. At least two minor characters duplicate his will to control a daughter; they prove as unsuccessful as he in their endeavors. Indeed, efforts to control money or to control other people rarely achieve what they attempt in this novel. Two significant exceptions to this generalization are the king of the gypsies and the presiding narrator, both of whom exemplify the power of benevolent control.

The king of the gypsies appears to inhabit *Tom Jones* in order to demonstrate the principles of good governance: control on a large scale. Tom and his traveling companion, Partridge, encounter him and his band. A short time in their company reveals that the king rules with absolute power, on principles of wisdom and justice, and that his people consequently live in happiness. The narrator comments that benevolent dictatorship produces the most satisfying human situations. The only objection to absolute rule, he continues, is the extreme difficulty of finding a human being capable of exercising it properly.

As for the narrator—well, I'll get to him in a minute, after a brief digression about the status of women in Fielding's novel, which represents females as always subject to male authority, a force that they may try to elude but can never wield. Sophia demands for herself only sufficient control to exercise a negative: to refuse a suitor she loathes. She willingly contracts never to marry against her father's wishes. Squire Allworthy's highest praise of her centers on her refusal even to offer an opinion when appealed to by male disputants. She demonstrates wisdom, fortitude, courage, and ingenuity, but she never seeks control beyond her minimal demand; this lack of interest in possessing authority constitutes an aspect of her excellence. Women more assertive than she—Squire Western's sister, who wrongly believes herself able to control Sophia, and Lady Bellaston, who wishes to control Tom—prove conspicuously unsuccessful.

If the desire for control is socially unacceptable for women, the scheme of Fielding's novel suggests that in all its manifestations but the aspiration to self-control, it finally possesses little value for men—except, perhaps, for the narrator, another benevolent dictator, who acknowledges his interest in money; whose manipulations, more conspicuous even than Blifil's, create the plot's intricacies; who professes parental feelings toward the characters he successfully controls; and who seems triumphantly at ease with his own opinions and convictions, a model, in this respect, of self-possession. Unlike Blifil, Squire Western, or Lady Bellaston, he never fails. Unlike benevolent Squire Allworthy, who allows everyone room to be him- or herself until he finds fundamental standards of decency violated, the narrator never makes mistakes of judgment. His sense of control extends to appropriating literary material from his classic predecessors—and he freely confesses and justifies the habit.

The reader's experience of Fielding's novel includes being bullied, teased, and enticed by the narrator: in other words, being at least partially controlled by him. Such an experience may provide reading pleasure partly because it's always escapable: we can close the book. Indeed, the narrator seems quite aware of this fact, expressing occasional uneasiness at his knowledge that he cannot, after all, ultimately control the reader, despite his many manipulations. Inasmuch as readers feel themselves within the narrator's power, though, they at least peripherally participate in the large plot of control. The novel provides a dynamic map of society as a chaotic arrangement of struggles for dominance. If divine Providence compensates—as in Fielding's world it does—for the problems such struggle creates, it does not diminish the immediate difficulties of living through the strains those problems produce. A vivid case in point is the young man, a minor character, who takes to the road as a highwayman in an effort to feed his starving wife and children. He exemplifies both the passion and energy that mortals bring to their struggle to control circumstance and the moral, social, and physical obstacles they may face in their endeavors.

Like most of Fielding's characters, the reluctant highwayman reveals few details of his psychic life. The plot rewards him because he, like Tom, Allworthy, and Sophia (and conspicuously unlike Blifil), has strong and generous feelings. The recipient of benevolence from Tom and others, he eventually can feel at least partly in control of his life: perhaps the most that anyone should hope for.

To understand that the narrator inhabits the same plot as the other characters, playing out the same drama of control, and that not even the reader can escape involvement, raises the possibility that the plot of *Tom Jones* aspires to be the plot of life itself. In some form or other, the desire for control appears everywhere—as do the forces that frustrate it. Like *The Divine Comedy*, although confined to a densely realized version of mortal existence, Fielding's novel offers the story of humankind.

Such a claim suggests Fielding's daring and his abundant innovations. Even at the beginning of the novel's "rise," the fertility, inventiveness, and sophistication manifested in such works as Fielding's imply that the genre required no long process of rising: it sprang full-grown, as it were, from the head of Jove. Focusing attention on the plot of control calls attention to the comprehensiveness and subtlety with which Fielding engaged the issues implicit in the fact of a universal desire for mastery—including, through the reader's relation with the narrator, hints about the experience of being controlled.

I turn now to *A Simple Story,* not because I've exhausted *Tom Jones,* but because I think it's worth pondering a late-century novel of female authorship in conjunction with the better-known mid-century story of a male career. Inchbald's novel is much shorter than its predecessor. It makes few claims for itself: the author's preface asserts that only financial necessity caused her to write it. Its plot, far from "perfect," seems slightly haphazard, and critics often treat it as just that, since the book was written in two disjunctive sections composed at different times, one concerning the career of a mother and the other that of her daughter. I thought of rereading it in conjunction with Fielding because of the clear contrasts it presented, because of its female authorship, and because it's a novel I particularly enjoy, no matter how often I read it. My most recent rereading has shed further light on the functions of plot and on the importance of control as a thematic issue.

Unlike *Tom Jones, A Simple Story,* with its ironic title, does not have the kind of plot that falls into a familiar pattern. It tells of a spoiled, beautiful, rich, orphaned young woman, Miss Milner, who falls in love with her guardian, a Catholic priest named Dorriforth. When circumstances free him from his religious vows, he becomes Lord Elmwood and marries his ward, at the insistence of another priest, his former tutor, although he has previously sworn not to do so because of her willful disobedience. They live in great happiness for four years, with an infant daughter, until Lord Elmwood has to go away for an extended period. During his protracted absence, his wife commits adultery. When he returns, she flees, to die, repentant, in her thirties, leaving behind a seventeen-year-old daughter, Matilda. Although Lord Elmwood has rejected his daughter as well as his wife, at his dying wife's request he permits the girl to live in one of his houses, so long as she never crosses his sight. Accidentally, she sees him and is expelled, to the deep regret of her cousin, Rushbrook, now Lord Elmwood's heir, who has fallen in love with her. A dissolute nobleman abducts her and threatens rape; her father rescues her, restores her to his love, and condones Rushbrook's love for her. The narrator appends a moral: Miss Milner would have been better off with an education in adversity, like Matilda's, which has made the daughter, unlike her mother, into a compliant, emotional young woman. The details of narration make all this seem less improbable than it may appear in summary.

Rereading this novel immediately after *Tom Jones*, I—perhaps predictably—saw not contrast but similarity. *A Simple Story*, too, turns out to center on control, with a plot more strongly unified than many critics have allowed by virtue of its continuing focus on obsessive desire for dominance. The novel opens with Miss Milner's father on his deathbed, pondering the choice of a guardian for his daughter who will in time make her good "by choice rather than by constraint." He implicitly wishes this guardian (who turns out to be Dorriforth) to constrain the young woman—to keep her under control—until she internalizes the desired condition of "goodness." Dorriforth, the priest who subsequently acquires the title of "Lord Elmwood," agonizes over his ward's frivolities and exercises his authority in, for example, forbidding her to go to a masquerade—a prohibition that she ignores. Once she and Lord Elmwood declare their love for each other, she openly asserts that she wants to test her power over him and deliberately engages in one provocation after another. Meanwhile, a subsidiary battle for control rages between Miss Milner and Sandford, Elmwood's former tutor.

In her remorse for having asserted her power through infidelity to her husband, the former Miss Milner explicitly abdicates all will of her own, dying without making any provision for her daughter. After his wife's betrayal, Lord Elmwood, we are told, becomes "a hard-hearted tyrant." As he says to Sandford, "I am not to be controlled as formerly." Matilda accepts the necessity of complete subservience to her father; Rushbrook and Sandford fear to cross him. The last section of the novel dwells on Lord Elmwood's control of all around him and on its failure to bring him happiness. Only when he relaxes that control does he gain the satisfactions of familial harmony. In the novel's final sequence, he cedes control to Matilda, who has never sought it, telling her she can decide whether to grant Rushbrook's request: a request, although Matilda does not know this, to marry her.

The novel does not tell us what happens after Rushbrook proposes. Instead, the narrator explicitly calls on the reader to decide how Matilda would answer, thus alerting us to the fact that here, too, the narrator, as well as the characters, participates in a plot of control. Her role is strikingly different from that of Fielding's narrator. Instead of claiming authority, she frequently calls attention to her own lack of knowledge about the thoughts and feelings of characters in tense situations. In a final display of uncertainty, after allowing the reader to "surmise" Matilda's response, she points out that even if the reader chooses for Matilda an affirmative answer, room for doubt remains about whether the couple's "wedded life was a life of happiness." Then, suddenly claiming ultimate control of meaning, she appends her moral, rich in subjunctive constructions: "And Mr. Milner, Matilda's grandfather, had better have given his fortune to a distant branch of his family—as Matilda's father once meant to do—so he had bestowed upon his daughter a proper education."

The subjunctives call attention to the uncertainty enveloping this firm final statement: all its possibilities are contrary to fact. Moreover, the nature of "a proper education" remains undefined. Matilda's education in suffering has made her docile, overwhelmed with remorse each time she momentarily asserts her feelings. Is this the kind of education the narrator recommends as more valuable than money for Miss Milner? Given such training, Miss Milner would not have allowed herself to fall in love with a priest: there would be no novel. Ending her novel with moral repudiation of her first protagonist, Inchbald in effect abdicates narrative control.

At a superficial level, the plot of control seems obvious in *A Simple Story*. The battle for authority between Miss Milner and Lord Elmwood occupies most of the space in the first part, and the struggle between Miss Milner and Sandford is equally conspicuous. Lady Elmwood's deathbed claim to have no will of her own, a claim dramatized by her refusal to compose the document called a will, receives great emphasis, as do Lord Elmwood's insistence on his own absolute authority and Matilda's ardent compliance. Less obvious are the narrator's and the reader's participation in the pattern. Long before she invites the reader to decide how Matilda answered Rushbrook, the narrator has shaped her discourse from time to time to call attention to possible differences of opinion. "Who shall say?" she inquires, when she suggests the possibility that Lord Elmwood's feelings over a newspaper notice of his wife's death might match Lady Elmwood's on her deathbed. As she seems to struggle for adequate interpretation of her characters' behavior, she tacitly calls on the reader to participate in the same struggle. Unlike Fielding, she expresses implicit interest in the psychological roots of dominance and submission. Inasmuch as she gives her readers moments of control, she hints that their psychologies too are involved. The struggle for control, the novel demonstrates, is both futile and destructive—but also inevitable, given the nature of human beings.

How did it happen that, rereading two familiar novels, I perceived a pattern that I'd never seen before? It's quite typical of rereading's discoveries that they seem to come out of nowhere. They don't, of course: fundamentally, the text controls the possibilities. Other forces also contribute. Like recreational rereading, professional rereading responds to circumstance. My physical surroundings now differ from those in which I previously read these novels; I've been reading different things and doing different things, seeing different people, thinking different thoughts. Moreover, the world has changed, as it continually changes, and critical discourse has changed. The issue of control comes up in the popular press; it comes up in conversations between parents. All these extraneous circumstances presumably bear on what I saw in my recent readings. If I cannot precisely parse the individual influences, my vague sense of the possibilities at any rate contributes to my awareness of the complexity entailed in any act of rereading.

The particular rereading I have reported does not begin to engage all the issues these novels present, but its discovery of a common plot of control in two apparently dissimilar novels suggests the new insight that rereading may offer and the unexpected affinities it can discover. I have outlined an argument that might be elaborated at considerable length—but what has it to do with the rise of the novel?

In one sense, nothing at all. But we are in the realm of speculation here, and, at least speculatively, bringing *Tom Jones* and *A Simple Story* together as I have done itself implies an important argument. Received opinion, the general understanding of what constitutes the canon and of how its books should be assessed, declares the significance of *Tom Jones* as a monument of the early novel. The stature of *A Simple Story* remains comparatively indeterminate. To demonstrate that the two works share a sophisticated understanding of the possibilities of plot as enlightenment implicitly claims the necessity of taking Inchbald's novel seriously, not because of its female authorship, but because of its formal dexterity. To understand *A Simple Story* thus constitutes one tiny step in its ascendance toward secure canonical status.

I said earlier that rereading is inherently conservative. It holds on to the individual reader's past. It rests on the assumption that a past experience, revisited, may yield fresh knowledge and understanding. Even if the new discoveries of rereading are small ones, they carry their own delight. To note that the narrator, by declaring his parental feelings toward his characters, connects himself with Squire Western, with his bafflement over the fact that his daughter won't do as he wishes—to note this is to see a little joke, as well as to be reminded of the close connections that govern Fielding's fictional world. Rereading, however, may also generate far-reaching insights.

Small or large, a series of perceptions can add up to an important realization. The happy experience of discovering that fact is familiar to most critics, as well as to rereaders who aren't looking for anything in particular. Those cumulative perceptions, however, need not belong to a single critic. Shifts in the canon do not customarily occur as cataclysms. They arise gradually, as the result of multiple tremors of opinion. Nuances of evaluation change, one critic at a time, and eventually so do assumptions about where individual works belong in the hierarchy.

Not that we talk much about hierarchy these days. The very notion of evaluation raises hackles, and few willingly negotiate the minefields involved in declaring one work better than another. By what standards? For what purposes? The concept of the rise of the novel, however, imports a system of evaluation in disguise. If the novel as genre increases in importance over a given span of time, that fact suggests that individual novels become more compelling than novels have been in the past. The traditional story about eighteenth-century developments has been that the novel "rose" with Defoe, Richardson, and Fielding, then declined, in importance if not in the number of its examples, as ever more women presented themselves as writers of fiction and as, toward the end of the century, the novel became sensationalized by the incursion of Gothic and was also used as an instrument of political propaganda. Then, the familiar story has it, it began rising again, with Jane Austen and, after her, the Brontës, and finally the great age of the Victorian novel.

But let me sketch the scenario for a new story. Say a critic, maybe me, rereading familiar and less familiar texts alike, discovers that Elizabeth Inchbald, long considered rather cavalier in her fictional constructions, in fact employs a formal design of considerable subtlety in her best-known novel. Then imagine that more critics find further aspects of excellence in *A Simple Story,* and others start rereading my favorite late-century political novel, which has the unlikely title of *Hermsprong,* and think that it offers a distinctive and exciting mode of characterization. And that leads them to take a fresh look at other political novels, and to reevaluate them. Before long, we have a new story, in which the eighteenth-century novel doesn't decline at all: it just keeps right on rising.

I'm not trying to promulgate that particular story, exactly. In a recent book of mine, though, *Novel Beginnings,* I argued strongly for a new way of considering eighteenth-century developments in fiction, as a pattern of experimentation. Even as I constructed this argument, I reflected that its efficacy would depend on the contributions of many succeeding critics, who might affirm it in different ways. Critical change, change in the stories we tell ourselves about literature, occurs only by slow accretion. That accretion rests on a foundation of multiple rereadings, one of our most dependable inlets to fresh insight.

The specialness and the value of professional rereading do not inhere solely in the possibility of its changing the canon. Like its nonprofessional counterpart, it thrives by virtue of its individual insights and of the patterns those insights create. Written down, though, it doesn't sound quite the same as a record of recreational reading. Nor does it originate in the same way as this book's other accounts of novels. Its motivation began with the desire to say something different from what I have said before in print, a desire emanating from my role as critic rather than primarily as enjoyer. The new aspects I discovered in the novels accordingly differ in kind from those I have generally written about in preceding chapters. Emphasis rests on structural elements of plot and narrator and on the pattern of the whole rather than on psychological or moral insight or individual perceptions. I felt conscious concern to write something that I could imagine as the basis for a full critical treatment. Such a treatment would engage with other critiques of Fielding and Inchbald, perhaps also with other writings by both novelists, possibly with cultural or political history of their periods, all in support of the discoveries I have made about two specific works. Its argument might be expanded to take fuller account of more characters or to consider the issue of control as eighteenth-century thinkers perceived it. It would stress not my experience of rereading but my judgment of novelistic achievement. If it did all or most of these things, it might participate in an ongoing critical conversation. Its origins in a critic's rereading would be assumed rather than seen as a matter worthy of special consideration. Its merits as argument would be paramount.

Professional rereading differs from its recreational counterpart in its purposes and in its effects, both of which involve dissemination. Professional rereading entails public action: writing for publication and teaching. Recreational rereading develops mainly in private, shared on occasion through personal conversation. Professional rereading assumes the importance of literature as artistic construct and as a way of knowledge and operates with the goal of understanding both. Recreational rereading takes place on the basis of diverse assumptions. Typically, I suspect, it is more open-minded than its professional equivalent. Both, however, are vital functions of cultural life and growth.

9

Books I Ought to Like

IN ITS METHOD, the experiment recorded in this chapter may appear to contradict one of my earlier claims about recreational rereading: that lack of focused purpose characterizes it. The rereading I report on here, however, does not even closely approach the recreational, although it's not "professional," either, in the sense that I have just described. It issues, however, from assumptions developed through my professional functioning—assumptions of a sort long ago mocked by David Lodge in his comic novel *Changing Places* (1975), which imagines a game played by literary academics in which participants confess to not having read some literary work that they "should" have read. The hapless protagonist acknowledges not having read *Hamlet* and is thereupon fired.

I too, it seems, believe that reading entails *should*s. I set out to reread—deliberately, carefully, purposefully—several books that most other people I know admire, whereas I disliked them intensely the first time around. Feeling that they are books I should take seriously, I thought I should give them a second chance. In the normal course of events one rarely rereads books that have initially seemed disagreeable. What would happen if, after a lapse of many years, I deliberately returned to works I recalled as providing unpleasant, or at least non-pleasant, experiences? Could I will myself into enjoyment? Did it make sense even to try, given the irrationality of taste? Perhaps my taste would have changed over the years without the intervention of will. With some eagerness, I proposed to find out.

One of the novels I chose for my investigation, *Pickwick Papers,* is a popular and valued classic of English literature. The other two, Ford Madox Ford's *Good Soldier* and Saul Bellow's *Herzog,* perhaps don't quite achieve classic status, but people with sophisticated literary sensibilities generally extol them. I had read none of the three more than once before my recent endeavor.

I wanted to find out whether I could make myself take pleasure in a book that I didn't "naturally" enjoy. Like many other readers, I have experienced (and in preceding chapters reported) the disappointment that comes from discovering that a book has somehow transformed itself in rereading from a source of delight to a nexus of tedium or irritation, but I can't recall the opposite experience of finding that a book once disliked has turned to a treasure. Now I was going to make an effort to transform previously read books in my consciousness.

First, *The Pickwick Papers.* My initial attempt at reading it occurred thirty years ago or more. I remember only two things from that experience: my resentment because the introduction to the book I read compared its achievement to that of Henry Fielding, and the powerful sense of tedium that overwhelmed me as I tried to make my way through what I thought an inconsequential and long-winded work. As it happens, the introduction to the Oxford World's Classics edition I recently perused also makes the Fielding comparison, and it still annoys me. I can see characteristics that the young Dickens shares with his predecessor—the use of inset stories, for example; the reliance on a loose scheme of travel as a principle of narrative structure; the grotesque representations of minor characters—but the differences, to my mind, greatly outweigh the similarities. Dickens may feel as strongly as Fielding does about such social ills as corrupt lawyers and incompetent doctors, but he does not appear in this work to take fiction itself seriously as a demanding genre. *Tom Jones* has a "perfect plot"; *Pickwick Papers* only gestures toward constructing a plot, although it supplies some sequences that might be said to have logical beginnings, middles, and ends. The novel as a whole proceeds through a rambling succession of "adventures" and ends arbitrarily with Pickwick's sudden decision to retire from traveling. The often flimsy connections established between one episode and another serve the author's convenience. As Dr. Johnson famously remarked of *Clarissa*, if you read this novel for the plot, you'd hang yourself.

The real reason for my irritation, though, is that I think Fielding a great novelist. I did not—and do not—think the youthful Dickens his equal. I know that Dickens did not set out to write a novel when he produced, for periodical publication, a series of popular individual sketches about members of the Pickwick Club: all the more reason not to compare him with Fielding. The novel that resulted from putting together the sketches remains, in comparison to Fielding's work, haphazard.

Again I experienced in the early sections of *Pickwick Papers* the sense of tedium I recalled. I also found a new source of annoyance in the tone of humorous condescension that the narrator employs toward Pickwick and his friends in the first quarter of the novel. Having invented the characters, Dickens, through his narrator, in effect disowns them, trying to have it both ways. Nonetheless, in the end I changed my mind, at least partly, about *Pickwick Papers*. By the time I reached its second half, I was finding a good deal to admire. My "effort to transform" my experience from negative to positive disappeared, as the narrative itself took over my consciousness.

Perhaps I should say at the outset that I have long had a high regard for the author of *Little Dorrit* and *Bleak House*, novels that I have reread with increasing pleasure, as I have reread *Great Expectations* and *Hard Times*, even (more than once) *David Copperfield*. I had read all of them at least once at the point when I first encountered *Pickwick Papers*, so I expected in my initial reading to enjoy Mr. Pickwick and his friends and was shocked as well as disappointed when I didn't. On the contrary, expecting *not* to enjoy the Pickwick Club when I reread the novel that represents it, I felt astonished to realize that I was looking forward to my daily session with Dickens.

To get to this point I had first to get over, or at least try to suspend, my conviction that plot matters greatly to most novels worth the reading. I admire the interplay and tension between openness and formal order in Fielding's fictional structures. His characters ramble about; they appear to steer themselves by happenstance; yet the narrator's guiding hand (standing in, as several critics have argued, for divine providence) makes rational structure out of what seem random happenings. The young Dickens accepts happenstance more wholeheartedly as a narrative principle. He does not traffic in the apparent coincidences that frequently operate in *Tom Jones*. His characters, seemingly left to their own devices, simply express their natures, sometimes bringing down catastrophe (of a mild sort) as a result, sometimes achieving happy endings.

The expression of their natures, however, creates the delight of the novel, especially when coupled with Dickens's verbal inventiveness—a quality that he notably assigns to Sam Weller, Mr. Pickwick's devoted servant, who interprets every experience in

terms of often bizarre comparisons and who characteristically justifies himself by claiming to quote someone else, usually someone
of higher social status than he. My favorite instance, I think (but
there are many competitors for this position), occurs when Sam is
riding on the outside of a chaise during a morning of relentless
rain. The chaise stops for a change of horses, and Bob Sawyer,
also riding outside, comments that Sam doesn't seem to mind the
weather. Sam explains that he doesn't see any use in minding it,
and Bob acknowledges that he has offered an unanswerable reason
for his coolness. "'Yes, Sir,' rejoined Mr. Weller. 'Wotever is, is
right, as the young nobleman sveetly remarked ven they put him
down in the pension list 'cos his mother's uncle's vife's grandfather vunce lit the king's pipe with a portable tinder box.'" The
elaboration and explanation of the cliché constitute a miniature
comic fable with an undertone of social criticism. This instance
of Sam's verbal behavior typifies his conversational technique,
which depends on far-fetched analogy and unpredictable elaboration. The details of that elaboration reward consideration, as with
the unexpected word "sveetly" in the rejoinder just quoted.

Sam's analogies often create pleasure by their hints at stories
untold. How did it happen, in Sam's imagining, that the young
nobleman suddenly got put on the pension list because of a long-
ago action by a remote relative? Is the young man really "sveet,"
or is his sweet response ironic? Is he a reader of Leibniz, or does
the dictum that whatever is is right come to him as a family maxim
justifying the social order? There's no way to know, but one can
hardly avoid speculation.

On another occasion, following orders from his master, Sam
guards Mr. Winkle as a preliminary to taking him back to Pickwick. Winkle, his social superior, orders him out, but Sam insists
that he will stay, announcing that if necessary he will carry the
young man away pick-a-back. "But," he continues, "allow me to

express a hope as you won't reduce me to ex-tremities: in saying vich, I merely quote wot the nobleman said to the fractious pennywinkle, ven he vouldn't come out of his shell by means of a pin, and he conseqvently began to be afeerd that he should be obliged to crack him in the parlour door." Once again Sam cites a nobleman as his authority, thus appropriating for himself the force of social prestige. "Pennywinkle" is his version of "periwinkle," a minute mollusk characteristically removed from its shell by means of a pin. Periwinkles, sold as street food, would not ordinarily feed a nobleman. Here too a story lurks. The disproportion between a parlor door and a periwinkle—the door would be a ludicrous and ineffectual means of getting at the tiny bit of meat within a little shell—suggests the nobleman's inexperience. He's not accustomed to the food of the poor. What circumstances have led him to experiment with such food? Why is he chatting with a wee shellfish? "Fractious" as an adjective for such a shellfish, like the adverb "sveetly" in the previous example, epitomizes Sam's lively imagination: he gives character to even the most negligible of beings. (Note that the "pennywinkle," in his version of things, has a sex.)

Stories figure largely in that lively imagination. Not only does Sam tell them; not only does he imply them by his analogies; he also shows himself capable of reinterpreting the most familiar tales. On one occasion, Sam's father announces that he has found a cure for gout. Mr. Pickwick eagerly takes out his notebook to write it down, as Mr. Weller explains that "the gout is a complaint as arises from too much ease and comfort"; its cure lies in marrying a widow with a good loud voice and "a decent notion of usin' it." (He himself has married a widow; his rueful reflections on the fact form a running theme of his discourse.) Pickwick asks Sam what he thinks of his father's prescription. "'Think, Sir!' replied Mr. Weller; 'why, I think he's the wictim o' connubiality, as Blue

Beard's domestic chaplain said, with a tear of pity, ven he buried him.'" This fresh perspective—Bluebeard as victim—on a well-known story exemplifies Sam's originality. The world to him looks different from the way it looks to others. Only he would link his father to Bluebeard; only he would think about the fairy tale from its villain's point of view; only he would authorize himself by citing Bluebeard's domestic chaplain. The idea of Bluebeard as victim is so far-fetched that it hints at the son's skepticism about his father's claim of victimhood, but that possibility remains but an undertone.

Stories abound elsewhere as well in the universe of this novel. They can come from anywhere and anyone. They may be incomplete or finished, improbable or plausible, told for a purpose or apparently random. Early in *Pickwick Papers,* Mr. Pickwick and his friends encounter a stranger who will turn out to be a scam artist. The stranger avoids giving himself a name, but he talks constantly and energetically, although always in fragments. His passing allusion to Spanish girls leads Mr. Tupman, one of the Pickwick group, to inquire whether he has been in Spain. After the stranger claims to have lived there for ages, Tupman inquires further: "Many conquests, Sir?" The stranger replies: "Conquests! Thousands. Don Bolaro Fizzgig—Grandee—only daughter—Donna Christina—splendid creature—loved me to distraction—jealous father—high-souled daughter—handsome Englishman—Donna Christina in despair—prussic acid—stomach pump in my portmanteau—operation performed—old Bolaro in ecstacies—consent to our union—join hands and floods of tears—romantic story—very."

This minor comic moment may amuse the reader by its narrative speed and its combination of romantic cliché with the unexpected detail of a stomach pump carried around in a traveler's portmanteau, but one hardly expects any follow-up to it. There is more to be told, though: the stranger goes on to report, in answer to a question, that Donna Christina died as a result of the stomach pump operation. He adds that her father subsequently disappeared, sought everywhere to no avail. Then a great public fountain suddenly stopped working, and eventually the father is discovered sticking head first in a pipe, having committed suicide to express his remorse at having interfered with his daughter's romance.

Two pages later, members of the Pickwick contingent comment on the stranger's various anecdotes: "Mr. Tupman said nothing; but he thought of Donna Christina, the stomach pump, and the fountain; and his eyes filled with tears." A reader who has laughed at the stomach pump and the fountain may feel startled. Mr. Tupman has responded to the stranger's spasmodic account not as a bit of comic self-characterization but as pure narrative. Tupman's reaction speaks also to his own romantic nature, which helps to blind him to the ludicrous aspects of the story, and Dickens's reader will probably see Tupman, too, as comic in his ability to make a ridiculous story serve his own emotional purposes. Yet the character calls attention to an important aspect of this apparently haphazard novel: its constant celebration of story as insight, stimulation, entertainment, and rhetoric. If *Pickwick Papers* lacks ongoing plot and displays little awareness of plot's importance, it yet provides numerous miniaturized plots that supply enjoyment and even revelation for characters within the novel and readers outside it.

Pickwick Papers thus compensates for its chaotic narrative structure by providing God's plenty of stories and story possibilities: Sam's imagination-provoking analogies; the anecdotal conversations between Sam and his father; the stories told by people the travelers meet; the things that happen to Mr. Pickwick and every member of his club. At one point, Pickwick goes voluntarily to prison rather than pay an unjust legal judgment that would enrich both corrupt lawyers and a corrupt landlady. Not to be outdone, Sam manages, with the collusion of his father, to get himself sent to prison as well. For Dickens's purposes, prison becomes a lavish new source of stories.

Social commentary often lurks in comedy's background. The injustices of law and the sufferings of poverty frequently recur as subjects in *Pickwick Papers;* so do the follies and corruption of elections and the horrors of the henpecking wife—and, occasionally, the torments suffered by the wife whose husband abuses her. Dickens even takes a moment to sympathize with partridges, mistakenly carefree on the morning of September 1, the beginning of partridge-hunting season. He introduces as minor characters two young doctors, more concerned with self-publicizing than with efforts to cure anyone, who enable him to take easy swipes at medical practices. (His best, and most subtle, attack on the medical profession, however, comes from yet another of Sam's stories, about a man fond of eating four crumpets every evening. A doctor pronounces this a lethal habit; the patient thereupon devours three shillings' worth of crumpets and shoots himself. "What did he do that for?" inquires Mr. Pickwick, confused by this tragic resolution. Sam explains that the suicide was an act defending the conviction that crumpets are wholesome.)

I keep returning to Sam's stories, which interest me more than anything else in *Pickwick Papers.* Although Sam conforms to the literary stereotype of the faithful servant, he emerges as the novel's most complicated character, by virtue of those stories—both such anecdotes as that about the doctor and the crumpets and the miniatures implied by his characteristic analogies. Even uncomplicated characters, however, create narrative interest. Just as the stories engage a reader's attention by their sheer multiplicity and variety—despite the fact that many of them are unlikely and many undeveloped—the characters demand attention because of their abundance. The novel represents, or at least sketches, dozens of named individuals. Most have only two or three recognizable traits: Joe, a servant, is fat, loves to eat, and constantly falls asleep; Mr. Winkle is physically clumsy and apparently adept at nothing; Mr. Wardle wants everyone to be happy. Even Mr. Pickwick, although we see more of him than we do of anyone else, lacks a fully defined nature. He acts consistently with generosity and compassion, although not always effectually, but we know few details about his character. Sam, with his highly individual rhetoric, stands out among the others. Yet the abundance of personalities, however vague their individual definition, helps to create the narrative's texture. At the novel's end, Mr. Pickwick proclaims, "I shall never regret having devoted the greater part of two years to mixing with different varieties and shades of human character, frivolous as my pursuit of novelty may have appeared to many." His statement in effect claims for Dickens's novel the same purpose as that of *Tom Jones*, which the narrator announces as offering a feast of human nature. The Dickensian feast is less nourishing than Fielding's—the novel does not penetrate deeply into the human condition—but it has its delicious aspects.

I'm left with a sense that I've read not a great novel but a pleasant one. I suspect now that I simply didn't take enough time to appreciate it the first time through—annoyed by the book's haphazardness, I didn't pay attention to its details. Or perhaps I was more doctrinaire when I was young, with my commitment to plot blinding me to the possibilities of loose narrative. At any rate, I've come a considerable distance from my earlier irritation and boredom. Perhaps to use rereading to its best advantage as a marker of personal change, one should make a practice of deliberately subjecting herself to new encounters with books earlier discarded from her personal canon. Such encounters will not necessarily result in reversals of opinion, but when reversal takes place it provides a dramatic measure of what we may hope is psychological, moral, or aesthetic development.

My new reaction to *The Pickwick Papers,* to be sure, hardly constitutes a reversal. I read the novel hoping to like it, and I liked it better than I had before—yet it hasn't become a book that I love, or expect to love. I would not have reread it without a special reason, and I'm unlikely ever to reread it again for pleasure: the pleasure I have found in it is fairly minimal. The novel doesn't speak to my sensibility.

Sensibility, an old-fashioned word, for a time in the eighteenth century connoted a nature in which feeling led to virtue. The *OED* defines it as "quickness and acuteness of apprehension or feeling," but the citations the dictionary offers as examples (e.g., "I have often remarked this sensibility of the common people of Spain to the charms of natural objects") suggest that a better definition might be "emotional responsiveness." The term designates a spontaneous, uncontrollable feeling, a form of sensitivity. A book that appeals to one's sensibility will feel authoritative and *right,* at a level more profound than any designated by the orthodox terms of literary criticism. As in relationships with people, we seek in relationships with books evidence of a kindred spirit. Finding it may cause the reader to announce, to herself or to others, that she *loves* the book. I have noticed my own habit of announcing just that—and on every occasion that I do so, I feel convinced that no other formulation would convey the right shade of meaning.

My experience with *Pickwick Papers* causes me to realize anew how deeply influenced I have been by studying the eighteenth century. Perhaps, though, it should, rather, make me realize why it was that the eighteenth century attracted me in the first place: it spoke to my sensibility. I seem to want in literary works, as Alexander Pope and Jonathan Swift and Samuel Johnson wanted, order, control, and rationality. The rambling of *The Pickwick Papers* alienates me. I perceive the novel's virtues, but it nonetheless continues to ramble, and I continue to find it slightly uncomfortable to read.

I took a number of fiction-writing courses in college, and in all of them, it seems to me retrospectively, the teacher praised *The Good Soldier,* by Ford Madox Ford, as a novel of consummate skill. Desiring to write a novel myself—preferably a novel of consummate skill—I read the book forthwith, not as part of an academic course, but in hope of recreation and instruction. I failed to understand what was so wonderful about it, I didn't enjoy it much, and I certainly found nothing I could imitate. I didn't even quite finish reading it. More recently, I read an essay by Jane Smiley in the *Guardian* (May 27, 2006) that referred to *The Good Soldier* as "a masterpiece, almost a perfect novel." It seemed high time to reread it, but I did nothing of the sort until my present project returned the novel to my memory.

I'm not at all sure I know the characteristics of "a perfect novel," nor am I certain that I'd recognize such a novel if I read it. I was prepared, though, to treat *The Good Soldier* with respect— as, indeed, I had done, to no avail, the first time through, or partly through: I originally lost interest a bit before the end. On the back cover of my Vintage edition of the novel, published during the 1950s (*The Good Soldier* first appeared in 1915), "fifteen distinguished critics" are said to have signed a statement about the book: "Ford's *The Good Soldier* is one of the fifteen or twenty greatest novels produced in English in our century." These critics include Conrad Aiken, Leon Edel, Louise Bogan, Graham Greene, John Crowe Ransom, Mark Schorer, and Jean Stafford. With such certification, the book must be worth reading; surely I was wrong the first time.

Well, maybe partly wrong. I still don't recognize *The Good Sol-*

dier as a perfect novel, and I always have trouble with top-ten (or -fifteen, or -twenty) lists, but the book demands serious attention. I remember nothing of the circumstances under which I read it before, beyond the provocation from my teachers, but I remember well my annoyance with the narrator, who seemed to me not worth bothering about, and my impression that the narrative was needlessly confusing and tedious. I seem to have missed, however, a great deal else in the novel. Moreover, I suspect that I'm probably still missing a lot, since this turns out to be a work of considerable density. Clearly, I was too young—probably no more than sixteen, since I went to college at an early age—the first time.

It's a problem for precocious readers that they invariably read much that they're too young for, and they don't necessarily realize that fact. My parents, strict in many ways, did not approve of literary censorship. I was allowed to read anything I wanted, and I read many novels that dealt extensively with sexual activity before I had the slightest notion what sexual activity meant. Somehow or other, I made sense of them. They couldn't corrupt me, since I didn't understand them. (That had been my mother's theory in the first place.) The mysterious pleasure that many of them provided caused me to return to several after I was old enough to grasp what they were all about, and often they pleased me again. I thought I was quite grown up already, though, when I read *The Good Soldier*, and it never occurred to me to read it a second time.

I still don't *like* it much, but I'm forced to admire some of its aspects. The narrator remains troublesome, though at least intermittently compelling. I find no kindred spirit here. I feel no natural affinity. I'm certain that Pope and Johnson would not admire this novel, yet I don't doubt its status as a work of craftsmanship and intelligence. I feel forced to realize that my theory of natural affinities, my notion that I can't enjoy a book unless I'm fundamentally in sympathy with it, demands modification. Sympathy, the engagement of my sensibility, makes it easy to respond to a literary work. Some works, however, urge me to expand my sympathies.

The subtitle of *The Good Soldier* is "A Tale of Passion." Its first sentence reads, "This is the saddest story I have heard." The novel that follows in a sense justifies both the direct statement and the implied one ("this book will tell a tale of passion"), yet both are also misleading, like so much else here. Although assertions of sexual passion abound, all allude to feelings so complicated that no single noun adequately characterizes them. The story the novel tells is sad indeed, but the narrator has not only "heard" it; he has acted in it, all the while declaring himself on the periphery. Both the subtitle and the opening sentence suggest conventional stories, but although convention figures importantly, the narrative itself is hardly conventional.

· 199

One index of its unconventionality is the place of plot. *The Good Soldier* has plenty of plot—it bears no resemblance to *Pickwick Papers*—but plot is less important than the way in which it is revealed. The plot itself is too complicated for full summary. It turns on the relations between two young-middle-age couples, the Dowells (Mr. Dowell is the narrator) and the Ashburnhams, Captain Ashburnham the obvious "good soldier" of the title, although Dowell may also have a claim to this designation. The Dowells have a sexless marriage because of Mrs. Dowell's allegedly bad heart. Mrs. Dowell ("poor dear Florence") turns out, however, to have had a prolonged affair with Captain Ashburnham, whose marriage is also sexless, although it apparently was not so at the beginning. (The reader has to figure out many ambiguities: words like *apparently* come in handy.) As for Captain Ashburnham, he, the good soldier, it develops, has had several affairs and has been more or less interested in several women other than his wife. The plot complications that I won't even try to reproduce all concern various women. Complexities of relationship result in the suicide (by poison) of Florence Dowell, the suicide (by cutting his throat with a penknife) of Captain Ashburnham, and the madness of a young woman who loves him, as well as the metaphysical despair of Dowell, the narrator.

The plot is not without absurdities. (A perfect novel, with absurdities of plot?) When Dowell decides to marry Florence, against the wishes of her family, he climbs to her room in the middle of the night on a rope ladder and finds her expecting him, although he has said nothing of his intention. Does she expect every suitor to procure a rope ladder and climb it? Or does she perceive a special kind of enterprise in Dowell? Certainly the novel offers little other evidence that he is an enterprising character. When Nancy, the girl who loves Ashburnham, learns of his suicide, she becomes instantaneously and unalterably mad, demonstrating her insanity by saying repeatedly, "Credo in unum Deum Omnipotentem." She says nothing else, except, occasionally, "Shuttlecocks!" The suicide, the instant madness, and the manifestations of her insanity all seem implausible, but occasional implausibilities hardly diminish the narrative's powerful effect, which depends on Dowell's gradual discovery of what has happened and his efforts to convert the happening into a story that will help him make sense of his own life.

The story he tells is disjointed, and the reader feels the obligation to make sense of it herself in order to understand the narrator's conclusions about his experience. Dowell calls attention to his narrative's incoherence. "I have, I am aware," he writes,

> told this story in a very rambling way so that it may be difficult for anyone to find his path through what may be a sort of maze. I cannot help it. I have stuck to my idea of being in a country cottage with a silent listener, hearing between the

gusts of the wind and amidst the noises of the distant sea the story as it comes. And, when one discusses an affair—a long, sad affair—one goes back, one goes forward. One remembers points that one has forgotten and one explains them all the more minutely since one recognizes that one has forgotten to mention them in their proper places and that one may have given, by omitting them, a false impression. I console myself with thinking that this is a real story and that, after all, real stories are probably told best in the way a person telling a story would tell them. They will then seem most real.

I've quoted this paragraph in its entirety because it contains so much of importance. In the first place, the country cottage. At the novel's outset, Dowell has worried about how to tell the story: whether to tell it "from the beginning, as if it were a story; or whether to tell it from this distance of time, as it reached me from the lips" of others. He decides to take the second course, and to imagine himself in a country cottage "with a sympathetic soul" opposite. He will tell the story as though he were telling it aloud, to a sympathetic listener who remains always silent. The silence, I think, is a crucial detail: Dowell wants no questioning of his interpretations.

The reason for his decision to tell the story this way is suggested by the early phrase "as if it were a story" and by the later assertion "They will then seem most real." It turns on a distinction between truth and fiction. Fiction, it seems, has recognizable formal order; truth does not. Dowell is greatly concerned to tell the truth, as his worry about creating "a false impression" indicates. Ford, the novelist, one may suspect, feels a similar, although not identical, concern. I surmise this on the basis of Dowell's insistence that "it's the business of a novelist to make you see things clearly." Both Ford and Dowell tell muddled stories, and for both the reason seems to be the same: the truth of life is muddle, and muddle seen clearly proves both sad and obscurely clarifying.

After my recent rereading I find this idea worth pondering. When I struggled with *The Good Soldier* as a girl, I failed to grasp that any "idea" was involved in Dowell's disorderly and difficult narrative. The disorder annoyed me and caused me to conclude that Ford Madox Ford was not after all a very good novelist. Moreover, my intellectual confidence at that early period far exceeded my confidence later in life. I was getting all A's; everyone thought I was "smart"; I considered myself an excellent judge of literary merit. Instead of trying to figure out what the fiction writer was up to, I concluded that he didn't know how to tell a story. For a judge of literary merit, I certainly didn't think very hard.

A large question lurks behind the theory of muddle that Ford and his narrator convey: does the muddle of this story actually illuminate? The story, to be sure, is not really a muddle but an artful imitation of muddle. Its apparent confusions serve at least a triple purpose: they indicate the strain Dowell is under, hint at how much is at stake for him in defining and telling the story, and help to develop the characterization of Dowell that is at the novel's heart. Thus, in the paragraph I quoted, we learn of Dowell's narrative scrupulosity and his full awareness of it. It's possible to believe in that scrupulosity, even while suspecting that the narrator uses it as a means to conceal things from himself—for Dowell, like every other person who tells fragments of this story, is an undependable narrator.

His undependability derives mainly from his ignorance about himself. He sees himself as someone whom no one cares much about. Among other things, he tells us that he has been embraced warmly only once: when he arrived from the rope ladder to elope with Florence. He claims to love, or to have loved, several people: Florence, once, although he hates her now; Mrs. Ashburnham (Leonora), once, although he dislikes her now; Nancy, the girl who goes mad and whom he patiently waits to marry when and if she regains sanity; and Captain Ashburnham, whom he greatly admires. None of them loves him back, he thinks, and the reader has no clear basis for thinking otherwise, although both Captain and Mrs. Ashburnham obviously have high regard for him. He has no sexual experience and no hope for any. He has a lot of money and nothing much to do with it.

Here is part of his summing up, just before the end:

> Yes, society must go on; it must breed, like rabbits. That is what we are here for. But then, I don't like society— much. . . . No one visits me, for I visit no one. No one is interested in me, for I have no interests. . . . So life peters out. . . . But, at any rate, there is always Leonora to cheer you up [Leonora has remarried and is pregnant]; I don't want to sadden you. Her husband is quite an economical person of so normal a figure that he can get quite a large proportion of his clothes ready-made. That is the great desideratum of life, and that is the end of my story.

The story that has begun with the narrator's characterizing it as the saddest he has ever heard thus concludes with his announcement that he doesn't "want to sadden" his imaginary listener.

But this is a lie—or yet another self-deception. Of course Dowell wants to sadden that listener—as well as the reader. His summing up suggests active hostility to his imagined "sympathetic" listener, in the brief fantasy that the idea of Leonora, who has now relapsed into utter conventionality, will cheer up the listener—a fantasy conveying only contempt for the person who might be cheered in such fashion. We may surmise, further, that the real point of the story is to express enormous self-pity: because no one loves him; no one visits him; he has no connection to "society"; the girl he claims to love goes mad; she doesn't appreciate him, and neither does anyone else, and he doesn't want anything to do with anyone. What he literally declares the end of his story is the allegation that Leonora's new husband is so ordinary that he fits into ready-made clothes—like the "perfectly normal, virtuous, and slightly deceitful husband" he is. Dowell communicates aggression and snobbery in addition to the self-pity; all contribute to his implicit claim of superiority.

His contempt for Leonora, her husband, and their unborn child (also destined, he avers, to be "perfectly normal, virtuous, slightly deceitful") issues from his startling assignment of himself, three pages before the end, to "the category of the passionate, of the headstrong, and the too-truthful," the category to which Edward Asburnham belonged. "I love him because he was just myself," Dowell concludes, sounding rather like Emily Brontë's Cathy in *Wuthering Heights* ("I *am* Heathcliff"). If only he had had Ashburnham's courage, virility, and physique, he continues, he would have behaved exactly the same way.

What a large "if"! Lacking the other man's courage and virility (whatever that means: sexual power? manliness?), to say nothing of his physique, Dowell can make only a dubious claim of identity with Ashburnham. Moreover, courage has not seemed, from the story Dowell tells, a conspicuous characteristic of his alleged counterpart, unless we are to take as a sign of courage (as well as one kind of virility) his repeated sexual overtures to various women. Since those overtures, in the version of the story that we have read, are associated with extreme sentimentality, they do not readily connect themselves in the mind with courage. Dowell misreads both himself and the man he admires. His ironic assertion of identity between them only emphasizes his covert envy and his confused sense of self.

At the novel's end, in fact, many of Dowell's assertions reflect a retreat into fantasy. The only two persons whom he has ever really loved, he now declares, are Ashburnham and Nancy, the mad girl whom Ashburnham also, and more convincingly, loved. For Dowell, this alleged love emerges more or less out of nowhere. It eventuates in his arranging for Nancy to live in his house, perhaps so that he can watch for the returning sanity that will allow him to marry her, perhaps only to torment himself further. When he acknowledges that he now dislikes Leonora—an emotion that the reader is likely to have developed long before—and is jealous of her new husband, he speculates that the jealousy might arise from the fact that he desired himself "to possess Leonora." This is the first we've heard of it, and it's little more convincing than his great love for Nancy. He concludes that he himself comes "into the category of the passionate, of the headstrong, and the too-truthful"—the terms he has just assigned to Ashburnham and Nancy, in contrast to the normal, the virtuous, and the slightly deceitful who uphold society.

Like so much else in the novel, all these assertions have ambiguous weight. I suggested that Dowell, rather than discovering truth, has retreated into fantasy in interpreting his experience, but there is another possibility. Although he has presented himself as largely an onlooker at events of passion, lacking the courage (and the "virility") even to question his wife's insistence on a sexless marriage and on keeping her bedroom door locked at all times, perhaps he is actually, as he finally claims, passionate and headstrong as those who create most of the novel's action, but more disciplined than they. Perhaps he finally discovers rather than evades the truth of his own nature. Perhaps the narrative's multiple disasters—his wife's suicide and Ashburnham's, Nancy's madness, Dowell's misery—derive indirectly from the narrator's self-control. In other words, perhaps that narrator himself is the "good soldier," patiently soldiering on, and thus causing destruction all the way.

By the story, I claimed earlier, Dowell wishes to make sense of his life. The sense he makes is the sense he can bear: that he resembles those others whom he sees as passionate and headstrong and as making things happen. But he allows readers to glimpse an entirely different sort of sense, in which the story emanates from its teller's fatal passivity. There are other possibilities as well: for example, that of seeing all the major characters as self-indulgent and irresponsible, all unaware of their own natures, all failing to find for themselves any governing motive beyond the search for pleasure. Such a description might apply even to Ashburnham, who intermittently expresses, by financial generosity, concern for others. All the major characters epitomize the corruption of a hierarchical and (Dowell is right about this at least) conventional society. They participate in an allegory of self-destruction.

Given such a range of possibilities (and there are doubtless others), the narrative's point would seem to be that making sense is a matter of finding an interpretation that satisfies—which is to say, comforts—you. Ashburnham, not loving—never having loved—his wife, longing for a woman whom his sense of rectitude forces him to send away, can discover no such interpretation. He kills himself, Dowell suggests, because he is "a sentimentalist, whose mind was compounded of indifferent poems and novels." Or perhaps, also according to Dowell, because he has suffered enough. Dowell is full of interpretations, of others as well as of himself. His air of uncertainty at the novel's beginning has given way, as he discovers or makes a story of what has happened, to a distasteful confidence in his own conclusions—"distasteful," in my view, because those conclusions covertly glorify himself (as above convention, as chance-taking; implicitly, as a survivor) and because their cynicism seems facile and inadequate to the facts.

I didn't care for the narrator when I first read *The Good Soldier*, and I don't care for him now. My older self can see, as I couldn't in the past, how artfully Ford reveals his character, how dexterously he uses a self-serving narrative to expose its constructor. I understand how deftly the novelist devises a story that appears muddled but that finally emerges as full of meaning—indeed, of so many meanings that one can hardly choose among them as a basis for judging characters and actions. Those who praise this as a well-nigh "perfect" novel no doubt respond to its superb craftsmanship, as I do, too—rather grudgingly. I now see the novel as biting commentary on a society as well as on a few of its inhabitants.

Yet I still feel the narrative's alienating coldness and its distracting and, to my mind, unnecessary intricacy. Dowell's distance from the wrenching emotional and moral implications of the events he relates, added to the self-satisfaction that seems intimately connected with his alienation at the end; the easy cynicism with which he dismisses Leonora and her new life; his lack of commitment to anything at all, except his unaccountable idealization of Ashburnham—these aspects of his character cast their shadow over the novel, since his is the only voice we hear at any length. Dowell, to be sure, is not Ford. The novelist has expertly manipulated both the events and their telling to illustrate the pains of decadence—and the difficulties of making a story. The unattractiveness of his narrator, crucial to the novel's impact, contributes to what some have declared its near perfection.

At least theoretically, I admire the novel's achievement. If I were teaching it, or writing about it in a different context, I might elaborate the interpretation I have sketched and say nothing about my feeling of distaste, which still extends, as it did in my youth, from the narrator to the fiction. But the self-conscious imbrications of the narrative scheme, creating a puzzle with little point beyond its own cleverness, alienate me. If I admire *The Good Soldier*, I still don't like it. I've been reminded by my rereading that, experientially, judgment need not affect taste—although the converse does not hold: taste tends to affect judgment. In my first reading of Ford's novel, the fact that it was not to my taste made it impossible for me to exercise my critical faculties on it. My rereading aroused those critical faculties but revealed once more my lack of affinity with *The Good Soldier*.

Herzog was the only part of this experiment that worked out as I had originally hoped. I found the novel both tedious and irritating the first time I read it, back in the 1960s: tedious because Herzog's voice, which controls the narrative, strikes only a few notes; irritating because it felt claustrophobic to be confined within a perverse, self-pitying consciousness. Now I can't fathom what was wrong with me when I felt thus. Now I find myself astonished by the variety included in the self-pitying consciousness; now I'd be happy if the book went on longer. To be sure, I sometimes feel Bellow's voice hectoring me; I occasionally feel annoyed by the novelist's apparent inability to imagine a real grown-up woman— but for the most part I can forget Bellow and cheerfully inhabit Herzog.

There's not much plot. Things happen, but nothing that happens makes a great deal of difference and there's little sense of cause and effect. Much of the significant happening has taken place in the past. Herzog, a middle-aged ex-college professor, once aspired to write a book of great importance and spent a good deal of time accumulating pages of such a book. He has, however, abandoned this project, along with his academic career, and has been abandoned by his second wife, who prefers his best friend. There are two small Herzog children, a boy from the first marriage, a girl from the second. Both live with their mothers. There is a satisfactory (from Herzog's point of view) girlfriend, Ramona, an excellent cook, and good in bed. There is a large Victorian house in the

Catskills that Herzog has bought with a $20,000 inheritance and fixed up by manual labor. For most of the novel, however, it stands deserted, scorned by the ex-wife who wants the urban academic career that her husband has rejected, and more or less forgotten by Herzog himself.

Important happenings also occur within Herzog's consciousness. The book educates its readers in ways that initially seem trivial—educates them to take Herzog with a seriousness comparable to his own. This currently unemployed man spends much of his time composing (mostly in his head, sometimes on paper) unfinished letters, to people he knows, to powerful political figures, to philosophers, writers, psychiatrists, and theorists of various kinds. At first the letters mainly express the chaos of his mind, chaos so conspicuous that even his affectionate brother thinks him insane. ("If I am out of my mind, it's all right with me, thought Moses Herzog": thus the novel begins.) Gradually, though, I realized that the letters convey Herzog's wrestling with himself, not in connection with life events so much as in an effort to understand (a modest aim!) the world and his position in it. In the course of a train ride, for instance, he composes a letter to Monsignor Hilton, the priest who brought Madeline, Herzog's second wife, into the Catholic Church. He suggests that his addressee does not understand ordinary Americans, because he lives among great concepts. There are, Herzog continues, enough Irishmen, Poles, and Croatians watching television in bars to understand the monsignor as he preaches to them. *"But I,"* the letter goes on,

> *a learned specialist in intellectual history, handicapped by emotional confusion . . . Resisting the argument that scientific thought has put into disorder all considerations based on value . . . Convinced that the extent of universal space does not destroy human value, that the realm of facts and that of values are not*

eternally separated. And the peculiar idea entered my (Jewish) mind that we'd see about this! My life would prove a different point altogether. Very tired of the modern form of historicism which sees in this civilization the defeat of the best hopes of Western religion and thought, what Heidegger calls the second Fall of Man into the quotidian or ordinary. No philosopher knows what the ordinary is, has not fallen into it deeply enough.

The letter, or the part that Herzog has composed, finally mentions its author's *"no doubt mad"* idea that his own actions have historic importance, inasmuch as he embodies the ordinary. He thus knows more than any philosopher.

Reading this at the relatively early point in the text where it occurs, I thought it indicative of Herzog's obsessive self-absorption: *his* life will prove a point that effectively refutes philosophers and historians who assert wrong views of the human condition. If this, like most of Herzog's other letters, constitutes a stream-of-consciousness utterance, the consciousness it reflects is, I thought, confused and confusing. And why should a reader care?

That was at page 133. On page 205, Herzog approaches the end of a letter he is composing to Harris Pulver—once his tutor, now the editor of a magazine—ostensibly to share a "marvelous idea" for an essay. This essay will deal, he says, with *"the inspired condition."* His concept of that condition enlarges as the letter goes on. *"Annihilation is no longer a metaphor,"* he writes. *"Good and Evil are real. The inspired condition is therefore no visionary matter. It is not reserved for gods, kings, poets, priests, shrines, but belongs to mankind and to all of existence. And therefore—"*

Here the sequence of thought breaks off, for the moment. Herzog feels the energy at work in his head, expresses his spiritual tension in his physical posture: "He wrote, *Reason exists! Reason . . .* he then heard the soft dense rumbling of falling masonry, the splintering of wood and glass" (ellipsis in text). Ignoring such phenomena, he continues, writing now about "Eisenhower's report on National Aims" and claiming that the article he has been sketching would (somehow) be a review of this report. Then "[h]e thought intensely, deeply, and wrote, *Each to change his life. To change!*"

This passage occurs at almost the exact midpoint of the novel. For the first time, I think (I'm not altogether certain, because Herzog's musings are voluminous and intricate and thus hard to remember precisely), the narrative's central consciousness, Herzog, clearly articulates the deep theme of all his meditations and anguishes: Can he change? Should he change? *How* should he and can he change? Whether he writes about Eisenhower or Kierkegaard, about the power of the Church or the inadequacies of city policing, to his ex-wife, his psychiatrist, his dead mother, or a monsignor, the subject is ultimately himself and the question of whether he can—indeed, whether he wants to—escape his quasi-madness.

But not only himself—and here is an important truth that I missed in my first reading. This is one of those rereadings that urge one to chastise a former self for obtuseness. (Perhaps one reason for rarely rereading books I disliked in the first place is reluctance to risk discovering my own past stupidities.) I find it hard to understand, hard to condone, ignoring so much the first time through. All I remember about the circumstances of my first reading is a general context of praise for Bellow: my husband, my friends, and I all considered him a master of fiction. I had taught to Wellesley freshmen *The Dangling Man*, *Seize the Day*, and (less successfully) *Henderson the Rain King*, all of which I admired. I expected to admire *Herzog*, then didn't; and as with *The Good Soldier* much earlier, I devised quasi-moral critical justification for my distaste, complaining about the protagonist's self-indulgent egotism. I begin to suspect, now, that my real complaint was what I perceived as the egotism of those around me, a complaint that I was unwilling or unable to express directly. At any rate, I disliked Herzog and *Herzog* and complained loudly about the fact.

I see now, though, how importantly the world, the twentieth-century world of noise, politics, threats, and catastrophe, figures in the novel, although entirely as filtered through Herzog's consciousness. In the back of that consciousness lies the Holocaust; in the foreground are the circumstances of his life, past and present obscurely intertwined. As awareness of different elements impinges upon him, he reacts accordingly: he writes a letter, which may in the process turn into quite a different letter from the one he seemed to be writing; or he telephones or telegraphs someone; or he paints a piano or opens a can of beans.

This sort of random behavior turns into a moral process. The behavior itself becomes increasingly outrageous. Herzog steals his father's gun, remembering how his father had once pointed it at him, although the gun never served any lethal purpose. Herzog has nothing particular in mind when he takes it, but he decides he will use it to shoot his ex-wife and her lover. With two bullets in the gun, he lurks around their house, spying on them, watching the lover give Herzog's daughter a bath. He decides not to shoot them. He takes his daughter on an outing in the car he has rented. His carelessness or aggression—it's not clear which—causes a traffic accident. The police find the loaded gun, for which he has no permit, and take him to jail. His prosperous brother bails him out, urges him to see a psychiatrist but actually takes him to a doctor who tapes up the ribs broken in the accident, and drives him to the house in the Catskills, where he settles in among the desiccated carcasses of small birds and large insects that have perished there in his absence.

I said earlier that nothing much happens in the course of the novel. The foregoing summary of events toward the end perhaps sounds like a good deal of happening, yet reading about the gun and the accident and the time in jail doesn't feel like reading about significant occurrences because no episode receives much emphasis or elaboration. Herzog finds himself in jail, then released, with remarkable speed. Everything accumulates meaning in the protagonist's mind, but the accumulation seems as chaotic as many of the events do individually. Although Herzog's meditations, and especially his letters, often seem meaningful (if hard to make sense of as a totality), his actions and reactions rarely strike me as carrying individual or cumulative weight.

Yet Herzog changes, the book changes, and toward the end I began—this time through—to feel that all the crazy letters, all the random events, added up to something important. A short Wallace Stevens poem, "Anecdote of the Jar," reports placing a jar in Tennessee—

And round it was, upon a hill.
It made the slovenly wilderness
Surround that hill.

Something makes the slovenly wilderness of Herzog's life organize itself around him. There is no round jar; there is only the totality of his experience. Late in the novel, he writes a note to God: "*How my mind has struggled to make coherent sense. I have not been too good at it. But have desired to do your unknowable will, taking it, and you, without symbols. Everything of intensest significance. Especially if divested of me.*" For such a figure to imagine the possibility of a world divested of him amounts to an enormous realization—a realization obscurely connected to his perception that his mind has struggled to make sense. Now he tacitly decides to stop struggling. He lapses into, or ascends to, a position of acceptance, in which he appreciates every moment of sensuous experience: the cold of water, the beauty of sunset, the sound of birds. In interior dialogue, perhaps with God, he imagines his interlocutor inquiring, *"But what do you want, Herzog?"* And he silently replies, *"But that's just it—not a solitary thing. I am pretty well satisfied to be, to be just as it is willed, and for as long as I may remain in occupancy."* Two pages later, the novel ends. Herzog thinks of calling an instruction to the woman who is cleaning his house. "But not just yet. At this time he had no messages for anyone. Nothing. Not a single word."

We are evidently to believe that this disappearance of the need to imagine messages for multitudes, including God, will be permanent, for less than twenty pages earlier a paragraph starts, "Thus began his final week of letters." There is no more need for letters: this self-indulgent and disorganized man has, after, and perhaps as a result of, much flailing, much suffering, and much introspection, achieved a state of equilibrium that will endure.

I observed earlier that I had noticed for the first time in this reading that the novel concerns the world as well as the workings of an individual consciousness. Despite the fact that Herzog's perceptions filter our knowledge of the larger world, his references to that world are recognizable, reminding the reader of larger scenes of chaos than the one within the eponymous character. The world, as rendered by Bellow and as known by those who live in it, abounds in aggression, vice, hypocrisy, and pretension. All these qualities existed before the twentieth century and persist after it, but *Herzog* makes vivid the enveloping sense of conflict that is their immediate consequence. Neither Herzog nor his father will shoot anyone, but the possibility of shooting or being shot remains. People fall in and out of bed with various others, and the experience rarely brings joy. Life is dangerous and confusing, and most people don't even try to understand it.

Herzog *does* try and, inevitably, fails. Inasmuch as he comes to terms with his own perceptions, he does so by accepting actualities and taking what pleasure is available. The pleasure in small things (flowers, light, temperature . . .) and small imaginings (the prospect of visiting his son at camp . . .), although it seems negligible in relation to earlier grand imaginings, is real and comforting.

I was able to write earlier of *cheerfully* inhabiting Herzog, in my role as reader. One reason that it's possible to feel cheerful in relation to a character who is usually melancholy, distraught, or acutely anxious is that Herzog reacts with such passionate intensity to everything. He seems at all times vividly alive. Although I may deplore this protagonist's tendency to overreact, it is hard not to respond positively to someone so full of vitality. So I think now: I didn't think so in the 1960s. Even when pondering death, Herzog throbs with life. All his folly testifies to his constant effort to cram every rift with ore, to make the most of every experience—by writing about it, or thinking of writing about it, or suffering over it, or imagining concomitant possibilities. He responds with his entire being to all that happens to or around him.

This intensity of reaction, to be sure, contributes largely to the chaos that envelops Herzog. Life, richly apprehended, offers more stimulus at every moment than one can possibly deal with. Protective blindness guards most of us; Herzog sees entirely too much for his own comfort. The lesson he learns, the way he changes, involves a new capacity to acknowledge and allow the workings of the world without needing at every moment to analyze them. He believes himself about to live more peacefully. Perhaps he is right; perhaps he will descend again into chaos; perhaps he will die.

Such a resolution to the novel does not imply that Herzog has been mistaken in his perception that much is wrong in the world that surrounds him and that clergymen and politicians and philosophers and literary theorists need to change their ways in order to contribute to solutions rather than to problems. It may imply error in his assumption that he possesses the knowledge and wisdom to explain to them how to change. The apparent message at the novel's end—Just relax—implies a corollary: Relax, but don't stop seeing what surrounds you.

This is not a didactic novel. It does not urge us, its readers, to relax and see. It only invites us to ponder Herzog and his curious career. I don't quite know at the end whether he's out of his mind, the possibility suggested by the novel's first sentence, and I no longer care any more than he does. *Herzog* has not compelled me to identify with its central character—only to witness. (Perhaps such a relation to a novel was impossible for me forty years ago.) The effect such witnessing can have is incalculable.

Of course we do not watch Herzog as we would watch a real person: we watch him through the medium of Bellow's language. The precision and grace of that language compel attention. Here is a random sample, from Herzog's memory of childhood train trips:

> a holiday should begin with a train ride, as it had when he was a kid in Montreal. The whole family took the streetcar to the Grand Trunk Station with a basket (frail, splintering wood) of pears, over-ripe, a bargain bought by Jonah Herzog at the Rachel Street Market, the fruit spotty, ready for wasps, just about to decay, but marvelously fragrant. And inside the train on the worn green bristle of the seats Father Herzog sat peeling the fruit with a Russian pearl-handled knife. He peeled and twirled and cut with European efficiency. Meanwhile, the locomotive cried and the iron-studded cars began to move. Sun and girders divided the soot geometrically. By the factory walls the grimy weeds grew. A smell of malt came from the breweries.

The details are those that a child would notice, but the ordering and the language belong to the expert novelist, whose rhythms and diction make Herzog's memory into a kind of poem. "He peeled and twirled and cut": a little song, interrupted by the rather jarring evocation of European efficiency. The locomotive cries instead of whistles; soot gets divided into regular spaces, as though the geometrical division belonged not to a child's perception through the windows but to the nature of the soot itself. The grimy weeds, precisely noted, seem as enchanting as the crying locomotive and the studded cars. Every detail has the value not only of nostalgia (although certainly that too) but also of exact notation (the pearl-handled knife, the green bristles of the seat). At the center of the scene, for the child once and now for the reader, Herzog's father buys the pears and peels them and allots them. Then the wonder of what the windows show removes attention from the patriarch, directing it to the journey itself.

A combination of exactness and exuberance governs the language throughout, partly registering Herzog's emotional energy, partly declaring the author's control. Delighting readers, bearing them along through the narrative, it also assures them that Herzog in his quasi-madness will not abandon them in his own chaos.

The novel delighted *me*, at any rate. It mystified me a bit, too: I can't really understand, although I can theorize, why I found it so distasteful the first time. Herzog is not Holden Caulfield. By the end of the book, he seems a real grown-up. Perhaps in the 1960s, although I had the chronological credentials, I wasn't sufficiently grown-up to understand him.

Reading *Herzog* for the second time provided the experience of discovery that I sometimes mistakenly associate only with first readings. That experience, indeed, was in some ways more thrilling than its first-reading equivalent because it not only came as a surprise but also felt oddly like a triumph. In itself it fully justified my experiment.

10

Guilty Pleasures

DURING MY PERIOD of passionate reading in early adolescence, it never occurred to me that I might feel embarrassed if other people knew about some of the books I enjoyed. After a couple of years as an English major, I knew better. For the rest of my college career, I simply stopped reading, or rereading, what might prove embarrassing. By graduate school, however, I had reverted to surreptitious self-indulgence—although not by any means to full disclosure. I was trying to establish myself as an intellectual; I could not afford to reveal that I loved, for instance, the *Ladies' Home Journal*.

That was probably my first literary vice—and it persisted, I blush to say, for many years. My mother subscribed to the *Journal*, so I started reading it when I was young, and I loved it all: stories, recipes, and especially the monthly feature called "Can This Marriage Be Saved?" The answer to that question was invariably yes, and I enjoyed speculating about and then discovering how the happy ending could be effected. I felt that by reading the monthly revelations about marital difficulties and their resolution I was storing up useful information for my future. I still remember my dismay when, just before I went to college, the title changed one month to "This Marriage Could Not Be Saved."

Gradually my enthusiasm faded; I might read the magazine if I saw it in a dentist's waiting room, but not otherwise. Now it doesn't tempt me. The need from time to time for mindless reading, though, endures. Unlike many of my colleagues, I don't enjoy detective novels or spy thrillers. I've made some attempts at "chick lit," but it doesn't hold my interest. I can't read Dan Brown. Nonetheless, I've occasionally found something that filled my need. The fact that my frivolous reading is in a sense surreptitious—I don't often tell people about it—only heightens its enjoyment, just as reading *Gone with the Wind* under the covers long ago brought special delight.

In my young adulthood, one of the somethings that filled my needs was the works—the abundant works—of P. G. Wodehouse. I liked the Jeeves stories best, but everything by Wodehouse that I read offered the same undemanding satisfactions. The book that has survived multiple purgings of my library is called *The Most of P. G. Wodehouse,* and I hadn't looked at it for many years, until, recently, I did. It provided an episode of rereading unique in my experience. For the first time, I think, I really understood what Larry McMurtry celebrated as the joy of rereading: having a book remain the same, and reveling in the fact. Usually my own second, third, and tenth encounters with a book have supplied aspects of sameness and of difference; on balance, the differences have interested me more, if only because they created for me the impression that I had changed and grown. When the Narnia books began to offer no surprises, I lost interest in them.

Everything that I recently reread by Wodehouse remained absolutely and completely the same as I remembered, and that seemed wonderful. I found nothing new, no new depths, no new insights. I wanted nothing new. I appear not to have changed at all,

although I thought I had left Wodehouse behind with other childish things. Jeeves was entertaining as ever, in precisely the ways he
was entertaining before. The prose of the stories offered familiar
delights. The plots remained cavalier, unlikely, and fun. How did I
get along without these pleasures for so long?

In a sense, a Wodehouse story or novel, always deeply forgettable, is readily forgotten. Its inconsequential plot presents itself
as a mechanism to allow both characters and narrator to perform.
There is no need to remember it; it doesn't matter. I remembered
that Jeeves always solved the problem, whatever the problem
might be; I didn't remember the nature of either problems or solutions. I remembered that the language of the stories always struck
me as perfect, but I couldn't have offered an example. I remembered a tone of invincible good humor, but not how it was
achieved. It was only in the act of rereading that I seemed to remember everything. I still couldn't necessarily have said what
would happen next, but as it happened, I would remember it, too.
Moreover, I would remember the pleasure of the past and would
re-experience it in the vivid pleasure of the present.

And now I have the further pleasure of specifying my gratifications. First of all, plot. Deep meaning is beside the point here. I
haven't felt impelled to look for any, and I don't really believe any
is to be found. Instead, Wodehouse offers insanely rapid sequences
of action for their own sake, although the characters always have
some end in view. They act like little mechanical figures: the fiction writer winds them up and sets them going, and they thereupon don false mustaches, or teach the butler how to improve his
craps game, or discover that all the rich people in the vicinity are
actually poor, or eat and eat and eat some more, all the foods that
they know will put them into agonies of dyspepsia.

I take these examples from *Quick Service,* the novel included in
The Most of P. G. Wodehouse, though it would be easy to find com-

parable instances, if not such an abundance of them, in any of the short stories. Mostly the characters, in short stories and novels alike, experience endless frustration in their efforts to fulfill a clearly defined purpose. If Jeeves inhabits the fiction, he will cause everything to work out properly in the end. If no Jeeves appears, the narrator will juggle possibilities to achieve the same outcome. Readers are not urged to care much about how things come out, only to have fun along the way.

Quick Service provides a revealing case in point because it puts on display Wodehouse's utter unconcern with plausibility. The plot's intricacies are purely and wonderfully silly. That's why they're so entertaining, but it would not be entertaining to summarize them all; it would be like trying to explain a joke. At the center of the plot, though, is a prosperous businessman who long seems to be the villain. (By the end, nobody is a villain.) Obsessed with the ham he purveys, he has long ago broken an engagement with a woman who did not take his ham seriously enough. Now he detests her (and, for that matter, all other women as well) and dreads the very possibility of seeing her. Getting wind of her intention to complain about the quality of his ham, he decides to steal (well, to have someone else steal) her portrait and to use it for advertising purposes. Then, for multiple unlikely reasons, he decides to marry her. After that, reverting, he decides not to marry her. At the novel's end, he once more concludes that he seeks marriage. His on-and-off beloved happily concurs with his plans. Then, in the novel's climactic implausibility, she comes up with a splendid idea. To express her new enthusiasm for the ham, she suggests that her fiancé reproduce her portrait for use in his advertisements. The line of copy she recommends as accompaniment precisely duplicates the one he has imagined long before.

The in-your-face unlikelihood of this development underscores Wodehouse's defiance of the notion that a reader's imaginative participation in fiction requires a willing suspension of disbelief. Wordsworth coined that phrase as a definition of "poetic faith," but it describes as well the mental state traditionally ascribed to readers of fiction and viewers of plays. No such condition lulls readers of *Quick Service*. Quite the contrary: they more likely will spend the period of their perusal in hilarity over the wild imagination that generates not only such an intricate series of improbable events but also a group of characters, each bent on his or her own purposes, who enact an interlocking pattern of crazy behavior without ever noticing its craziness. It's impossible to "believe in," much less to "identify with," the characters; it's impossible to consider the plot as having any relation to actuality. But it's quite possible, and can be engrossing, to delight in the spectacle produced by mechanical characters performing maniacal plots.

The Jeeves stories, of which there are many, when assembled amount to a one-thing-after-another novel consisting of multiple repetitions. Wodehouse, endlessly inventive in producing dire situations for inept Bertie Wooster and unexpected resolutions of them by clever Jeeves, Bertie's valet/butler, devises each story in the same pattern. A representative instance, "Jeeves and the Impending Doom": Bertie, invited by his Aunt Agatha, who dislikes him, for a three-week visit, receives an incomprehensible unsigned telegram. As he blithely acknowledges, "We Woosters are not very strong in the head, particularly at breakfast," so he asks Jeeves what it all means. Jeeves, although very strong in the head, compared to his employer, can't figure it out either. They proceed to the country house, where they encounter Bingo, an old friend of Bertie's who is currently tutoring Aunt Agatha's obnoxious son Thomas ("a fiend in human shape") in the hope of regaining money he has lost by gambling while his wife is away. Bingo has sent the mysterious telegram. Further developments include the presence of a disagreeable cabinet minister named Filmer, in whose vicinity one must neither drink nor smoke, and with whom Bertie must play a daily round of golf. Filmer gets stranded on an island, assailed by an angry swan, and rescued by Bertie in a torrential rainstorm. The obnoxious Thomas is responsible for the stranding, but Bertie gets blamed because Jeeves tells Aunt Agatha that his employer stole the boat by which Filmer had planned to return. This lie indirectly solves all problems. Jeeves has discovered that Aunt Agatha plans to entice Filmer into making Bertie (who is currently and perpetually unemployed, having enough money to live on rather nicely without working) his private secretary. He has also discovered a convenient water pipe by means of which Bertie can readily escape unnoticed. Thus Bingo keeps his job; Bertie doesn't have to have one; and Bertie and Jeeves get away from a disagreeable environment.

Fast-moving, unlikely, and comic, the sequence of events provides a framework for the linguistic performance that supplies so much delight for readers of the Jeeves stories. Both servant and master employ idiosyncratic speech patterns that, for me at least, never cease to give pleasure. Bertie, depicted as being indeed a bit weak in the head, relies heavily on the verbal habits of his peers— aristocratic slang, aristocratic decorum, and a lavish collection of clichés. Thus, when he comes down to breakfast feeling rather uneasy, he explains, "We Woosters are men of iron, but beneath my intrepid exterior at that moment there lurked a nameless dread." After this series of canned phrases, he summarizes to Jeeves, "I am not the old merry self this morning" (to which Jeeves, predictably, responds, "Indeed, sir?"). Multiplications of triteness convey the expressive difficulties of a man who has trouble knowing what he feels, at the same time that they remove any possible shadow of pathos from his situation.

The first dialogue between Bertie and his aunt demonstrates other effects that his language can create. Aunt Agatha issues orders. She announces that even Bertie must have heard of Mr. Filmer: "'Oh, rather,' I said, though as a matter of fact the bird was completely unknown to me. What with one thing and another, I'm not frightfully well up on the personnel of the political world." Aunt Agatha pronounces her commands. Bertie is not to smoke, not to drink, not to allude to the bar, the billiard room, or the stage door. He responds to the individual mandates with phrases like "Oh, I say!" and "Oh, dash it!" Aunt Agatha's final comments convince Bertie "that that was more or less that, and I beetled out with an aching heart."

That aching heart concludes the paragraph and the scene with comic completeness. Aristocratic speech, as deployed by Bertie, consists of clichés. Mostly the young man relies on exclamatory slang, altogether inadequate to communicate his feelings—which in fact, for one reason or another, he often seems reluctant to convey, even if he knows what they are. When he wants to tell the reader his emotion, all that occurs to him is a new cliché, the aching heart. Given the impoverishment of the speaker's language, that phrase emerges in conjunction with a ludicrously inappropriate bit of slang ("I beetled out"). The paragraph that records Bertie's responses to his aunt recklessly conjoins different linguistic registers. Thus "diplomatic personnel," a relatively precise phrase, consorts with "What with one thing and another," a characteristic Wooster evasion. The specific diplomat in question soon turns into a "bird," characteristic Wooster slang. Such comic conjunctions of slang and literary diction mark the entire story—indeed, all the stories.

Jeeves, like his master, employs language of surpassing predictability, never stepping out of his social role. Bertie wants to talk about Life; Jeeves insists on discussing the height of trousers. Bertie worries about whether Thomas might hit Mr. Filmer with a cutlass; Jeeves says that they can but wait and see, and that Bertie's tie needs a tighter knot. "What do ties matter, Jeeves, at a time like this?" Bertie replies. "Do you realize that Mr. Little's domestic happiness is hanging in the scale?" Jeeves's response: "There is no time, sir, at which ties do not matter." Bertie meditates on this: "I could see the man was pained, but I did not try to heal the wound. What's the word I want? Preoccupied. I was too preoccupied, don't you know. And distrait. Not to say careworn."

Bertie appears to have read some books. He has many words at his disposal, and he tends to dispose them, appropriately or not, when he feels put down by Jeeves, who, as in this scene of dressing for dinner, often succeeds in conveying disapproval by means of his performance of perfect propriety. Unlike Bertie's, Jeeves's language always suits the occasion. Jeeves by his perfect control and Bertie by his conspicuous lack of control both supply comedy.

Bertie, to be sure, has greater range. Fleeing an aggressive swan, he climbs up on a roof, ending up next to Mr. Filmer, who is roof-sitting for the same reason. The scene begins with the two men repeatedly saying "Hi" to each other from a distance. After the exchange of six hi's, Mr. Filmer says, "Oh!" and Bertie replies, "What ho!"—as he remarks, "sort of clinching the thing." He acknowledges that the conversation thus far has not attained a high level but thinks that "probably we should have got a good deal brainier very shortly," only the swan intervenes, causing him to climb rapidly and to comment, "The lad who bore 'mid snow and ice the banner with the strange device 'Excelsior!' was the model for Bertram."

Bertie alludes here to the Longfellow poem "Excelsior," which one might not expect to constitute part of his literary knowledge. But his head is full of bits and pieces; that's why his language seems so random. It goes in all directions, always entertaining, if filling sometimes obscure purposes.

Given the ways in which both Jeeves and Bertie epitomize their respective social classes, one might expect, or even surmise, that Wodehouse has satiric purposes in mind. If so, they express themselves with remarkable gentleness. One of the pleasures of reading this fiction is its lack of edge. Mr. Filmer, with no apparent redeeming qualities, has his rowboat stolen and is chased by a swan, exposed on a roof, and drenched with rain. Only the rowboat differentiates him from Bertie in these respects. Characters may experience public humiliation, but they recover quickly. The bad guys as well as the good ones often get what they want. A large tolerance envelops all. Bad guys usually don't want to be bad, apparently; they just turned out that way. Aunt Agatha can't help being Aunt Agatha, any more than Bertie can help being Bertie. Generalizing from such instances, one must conclude that the aristocracy as a class have just turned out that way. To laugh at them is quite appropriate, but not to chastise them.

The Wodehouse I used to enjoy hasn't changed a bit, but one aspect of reading him has changed conspicuously: I no longer understand why I was embarrassed. What this writer does, he does superbly. This particular pleasure now seems quite respectable.

John Collier also supplied guilty pleasures in my post-Ph.D. years. I read most of his short stories, justifying this activity to myself by the fact that they appeared from time to time in the *New Yorker*, acceptable reading matter, in my view, for a young intellectual. (I think, though I'm not quite sure, that Collier wrote one of my favorite stories of all time, about a man who murders his wife by hitting her over the head with a frozen leg of lamb. But maybe it was Roald Dahl, another of my indulgences.) I also read, with slightly less enthusiasm, Collier's novels. Novels and short stories alike were unserious reading, not works to be talked about. I seem to have jettisoned most of my once extensive Collier collection, but one novel survives: *Defy the Foul Fiend, or The Misadventures of a Heart,* first published in 1934. Rereading it proved a considerable surprise.

The fact is, I remember nothing at all from my first reading. My readings of multiple Collier works seem to have left me with a vague impression of acerbic wit, clever plotting, and a penchant for introducing the supernatural in unlikely contexts, nothing more. *Defy the Foul Fiend,* however, manifests only the first of these characteristics. Although a good deal happens in the course of the narrative, the plot is insistently, ostentatiously, commonplace. The supernatural does not intervene. And the target of the wit is often unexpected.

I open my book at random and find this paragraph:

> Lady Stumber . . . had the most inspiring, the most provocative, and the most inescapable bosom in all London. It was a sight to make an old man young, and as for young men—it is as well that their thoughts, on meeting creatures so superlatively shaped, should not be apparent in their entirety; otherwise these creatures would be continually surprised, flustered, outraged. . . . Drowning in her smile, [Willoughby] surveyed the pleasing eminence referred to, with something of that intensity with which a forlorn swimmer regards the unattainable dunes.

The series of adjectives for Lady Stumber's bosom shows Collier at his best, each of the modifiers pointed, precise, and surprising, and the sequence surprising as well. "Provocative" is predictable, but unexpected after "inspiring," a startling adjective for a bosom. "Inescapable" raises questions. Is that bosom inescapable because Lady Stumber goes everywhere? Because everyone is talking about it? Because the lady uses it deliberately as a sign of her presence? How are we expected to feel about this fact of inescapability? For that matter, how should we feel about the emotions hypothetically experienced by the superlatively shaped "creatures"? The paragraph makes me feel that something or someone is being mocked, but I'm not sure what or who is the target. Lady Stumber? But is it her fault she has a bosom? As for Willoughby, the novel's protagonist, he doesn't fare well either. Drowning in a lady's smile, regarding her breasts as the dunes that might save him from drowning, he seems—not for the last time—something of a dolt.

The hero as schlemiel makes a fairly frequent appearance in twentieth-century fiction, but the tone of works that contain him is usually genial. That adjective would not characterize the narrator of *Defy the Foul Fiend*, whose condescension toward his central character (and toward most of the other characters as well) may make the reader uneasy. The questions that occur to me when reading the paragraph about Lady Stumber lead me on for a while: I want to know how I am expected to judge the lady and her retinue. I don't need to read far, though, to realize that questions envelop every character. The narrator condescends to Willoughby for all sorts of reasons: "Our hero had for some time past indulged in humanitarian impulses of the highest spiritual level." Both the verb "indulged" and "the highest spiritual level" have stings in their tails. "'A name like a pearl on black velvet!' he cried. The fact is, he had become acquainted with the writers of the 'nineties." The reader is expected to share the narrator's scorn for writers of the nineties, and consequently for the youthful Willoughby, whose thoughts, emotions, and impulses provide targets for a steady undercurrent of mockery. For much of the novel, that mockery seems directed at him mainly because of his youth and inexperience, but it hardly diminishes when he turns into a grown man. At about the story's midpoint, the fatal question occurred to me: Why bother? I finished the book because I wanted to think about it—not because it absorbed me.

The familiar plot of the young man trying to make his place in the world gets a special twist here because of the circumstances of Willoughby's upbringing, if it can be called that. The illegitimate child of an aging and impoverished roué, albeit a titled roué, Willoughby grows up in the household of a disagreeable uncle, to whom his father has offhandedly entrusted him. His aunt, who is kinder, soon dies. Uncle Ralph abandons the house where they have lived, but, having promised his wife that Willoughby could stay, leaves Willoughby in it, making no arrangements for his care or education. The boy therefore grows up haphazardly, with no school, and with a spotty education, more focused on life than on orthodox objects of early study, and acquired from a stable hand.

As Willoughby reaches nominal adulthood, his uncle, reminded of his existence, approaches his father with the demand that the old man assume some responsibility for his son. As a result, Willoughby finds himself private secretary—knowing nothing of a secretary's duties—to stupid and incompetent Lord Stumber, spouse of the lady with the bosom. (Lord Stumber says that after a few trial weeks, they'll see what Willoughby can do. The narrator comments, "This statement, made by one who had seen as little as Lord Stumber to one who had done as little as Willoughby, filled the library and the future with the pleasant glow of optimism.")

From this point onward, through most of the rest of the novel, events are predictable. Willoughby's ambitions focus on making sexual connections. He yearns after Lady Stumber, gets fired, exists on the edge of various social groups, and has sex with a prostitute, a rich bitch, a nice middle-class girl, and assorted others. Eventually he marries the nice girl, Lucy, who by this time has acquired musical interests and training. The novel's ending, however, comes as something of a surprise. Having inherited his father's title, Willoughby also inherits the family estate, an impoverished rural establishment, with which he falls in love. After a year or so of marital bliss—the two young people are truly happy together at the outset—Lucy decides that she can no longer stand the lack of cultivated company and of cultural opportunity. She departs, and Willoughby settles happily into semi-impoverished country life, with his crop of apples stored on the library floor and much of his time spent shooting pigeons.

Up until this point, the plot has held little interest. It has provided opportunities for the narrator to convey his superiority to the characters, but the novel has appeared more concerned with tone than with content. At Lucy's departure I found myself startled into recalling the book's subtitle: "The Misadventures of a Heart." The heart in question presumably belongs to Willoughby, whose emotions I had not previously taken very seriously. I thought also of the epigraph from Shakespeare (*King Lear*) on the title page, no doubt intended to explain the book's title: "Keep thy foot out of brothels, thy hand out of plackets, thy pen from lenders' books, and defy the foul fiend." Willoughby has not followed this advice through most of his career, but as he shoots pigeons and orders his apples stored in the library he has settled into an existence that appears to be far from brothels, plackets, and lenders. Are we to take this as a happy ending? Has Willoughby finally discovered his heart?

The narrator's tone has modified, but it has not altogether lost its bite. "It must be confessed that [Willoughby] had passed a bold-eyed animal in the avenue that afternoon, a handsome stupid creature, an enterprising vendress of cakes." Plackets, it appears, are not so far away after all. Yet in the next paragraph, "He looked at his little valley. It was held for a moment in the last rays, a moment of golden pause, time enough to feel centuries in it. 'I will hold it,' he said. 'I will know it, and hold it. I will hold it in my mind.'" No trace of irony here.

On the whole, it feels like a happy ending, as well as, unexpectedly, a sentimental one—in which case the novel's moral might be that the heart never knows what it wants until it has it. Yet a happy ending doesn't suffice to rescue the book, at least not for me. Too much has depended on style rather than on substance. The vaguely sneering tone keeps the narrator at a distance from his subject. Willoughby's feelings get summarized rather than explored; he seems more a specimen than a person. The novel offers its readers nothing to care about—not even their own amusement, which Wodehouse, in contrast, always attends to.

Indeed, the contrast with Wodehouse is instructive. Like Collier, Wodehouse does not attempt realism. His characters are unmistakably literary inventions, bearing only incidental similarities to actual human beings. His plots as well as his tone, however, convey enveloping good humor that includes his ridiculous characters and, implicitly, his imagined readers. He does not invite us to take anything in his fiction seriously, but he invites us to enjoy the remarkable vagaries possible to imagine within the human condition. I feel better for reading a Jeeves story—and worse from reading this Collier novel, with its sour take on society and on individuals within and outside it.

These reflections leave me with a sense of wonderment about my earlier enjoyment of a novel toward which I now foster unambiguously negative feelings. Why did I like it once upon a time, when I so emphatically dislike it now? I appreciate its wit and, often, its economy and even brilliance of phrasing, but I did not enjoy it. Under other circumstances I would have stopped reading it about half-way through. Once, though, I saw a lot in it. Were wit and phrasing enough for me then? I don't think so, but I can't remember.

To try to reconstruct a younger self is by no means so satisfactory as remembering that self. Trying nonetheless to do exactly that, I surmise that the narrator's pose of seeing through just about everything—hungry, skeptical youths, delighted to be outsiders, as much as bourgeois, self-satisfied, successful grown-ups— seemed to me then a desirable state of sophistication. Unable to identify with any of the book's shallowly rendered characters, perhaps I identified instead with the knowing narrator and found my pleasure in that.

Defy the Foul Fiend is one guilty pleasure that no longer pleases. I appear to have outgrown it.

Arnold Bennett's works provided guilty pleasures utterly unlike those of Wodehouse or Collier. Virginia Woolf in effect declared it reprehensible to approve of Bennett's fictions, and I knew of her opinion during the period when I devoured them, devouring them nonetheless. It was a time not far removed from that when I enjoyed Wodehouse, although the two writers differ conspicuously in both tone and content. Bennett has nothing to do with the aristocracy or their upper servants. He draws heavily on his knowledge of mundane British actualities: what people ate, wore, accumulated to furnish their houses; how they conducted their courtships and reared their children; how they conformed to or deviated from their social roles. His tone wavers between straight reportage and mild historical condescension. Set in the waning years of the nineteenth century, the novel appeared in 1910. The narrator assumes, or purports to assume, the general superiority of 1910 customs and habits to those prevalent a quarter-century earlier.

In an essay from *The Common Reader: First Series*, Woolf groups Bennett with H. G. Wells and John Galsworthy as "materialists . . . concerned not with the spirit but with the body" ("Modern Fiction"). Bennett, she declares, is the best of the three, able to create characters that live. "But," Woolf adds, "it remains to ask how do they live, and what do they live for?" Their destiny, she concludes, is "an eternity of bliss spent in the very best hotel in Brighton." Implicit in her observations is her own kind of condescension, toward a set of bourgeois assumptions that in her opinion vitiate whatever capacity Bennett might possess to consider matters of the spirit.

Arnold Bennett was one of the novelists I discovered when studying for my Ph.D. oral exams. In general, I would read two or at most three books by writers whose works I didn't already know—my goal was range rather than depth. Bennett, though (along with Balzac), attracted more of my attention. I read many of his numerous (more than twenty-five) novels.

At this period, perhaps partly in reaction against my intellectually indiscriminate teens, discriminations of value concerned me greatly. The orals, of which I was terrified, would presumably test my qualifications for entering upon a career as a college teacher. One of those qualifications, I thought, was an ability to assess literary merit, to tell the good from the bad and especially to tell the good from the mediocre. My reading of Bennett, however, had nothing to do with this concern. I knew what Virginia Woolf had said of him. I knew that he was generally considered a second-rate novelist; I was quite prepared to agree. I only pretended to myself that I was reading his multitudinous works as preparation for an examination. Really, I read them because they soothed me. I assumed that my temporary addiction to Bennett was equivalent to the pleasure that others felt in reading detective fiction: mindless indulgence.

Two years later I married. We went to England and ravenously bought books. Every time I saw something by Bennett in a market bookstall, I snapped it up. The minute prices of such works suggested that no high value attached to the novelist even in his native country, but I continued to find him a pleasure to read. Strangely, I had altogether forgotten the contents of the books I had read before; I absorbed them again as though they were entirely new to me.

The same thing has now happened once more. Rereading *The Old Wives' Tale*, I had virtually no recollection of its plot, although that plot (contrary to Woolf's implication) turns out to be, at least in part, quite eventful. I still find the book soothing—partly because it doesn't seem necessary to pay much attention to the minutiae that fill its pages.

Paradoxically, though, those minutiae themselves account for much of the soothing effect: "The shop was narrow and lofty. It seemed like a menagerie for trapped silver-ware. In glass cases right up to the dark ceiling silver vessels and instruments of all kinds lay confined. The top of the counter was a glass prison containing dozens of gold watches, together with snuff-boxes, enamels, and other antiquities." The description goes on in this vein for ten lines more, constantly introducing new detail. The nature of this shop, site of one brief episode, matters hardly at all, nor does that of any particular thing in it. Not even the pervasive metaphors of entrapment carry much weight. Yet the accumulation of detail creates the impression that I, the reader, know everything I could possibly need to know about the scene, and know it without effort. If something matters, I will be told so. The novelist appears to make no demands on me.

Appears to make no demands. In fact, I think, Bennett requires rather a lot of his readers. Distant though he is from such modernists as Woolf, he too has his designs, and designs of a complicated sort.

It takes a while to notice. The novel occupies more than 600 closely printed pages in my edition, and for great stretches of it nothing much happens. Moreover, a lot of what does happen strikes one as altogether predictable. We first encounter the "old wives" of the title as sisters in their teens, daughters of shopkeepers in an industrialized Midlands town. Constance, the more compliant of the two, marries her parents' assistant in the shop: no surprise. Sophia, the beautiful, rebellious one, elopes with a charming commercial traveler (no surprise either) and disappears from view for a sizeable chunk of the narrative. Constance bears a son. Sophia's husband soon deserts her and is not heard of again until the novel's end, more than thirty years after his departure. Constance lives an uneventful life in Bursley; Sophia makes ends meet in Paris, equally uneventfully. Ultimately they reunite in their home town. They die, first Sophia, then Constance. End of story.

The "so what" question looms large. Although the novel fills its many pages with more event than I have summarized, few of its happenings have more inherent interest than the ones I have mentioned. The novelist disposes cavalierly of characters who become inconvenient or unnecessary. In an episode so arbitrary as to be unintentionally amusing, a Frenchman who is courting Sophia floats away in a balloon, never to be heard of again. The girls' parents die when they have filled their narrative function; nothing much is made of the fact.

Yet *The Old Wives' Tale* has its surprises. Although for the most part it remains resolutely on the surface of its occurrences, avoiding detailed accounts of its characters' thoughts and feelings, its designs on the reader ultimately concern the deep workings of consciousness. From the outset, the narrative presents itself as organized by contrasts between the sisters—contrasts of a sort familiar from fiction and film. Constance, conformist from the beginning, models herself on her mother and aspires to nothing more than her mother's life. Sophia yearns for more excitement, more possibility. She fancies herself as having vague intellectual aspirations, making her first effort at a life course beyond her parents' sphere by becoming a schoolteacher. Sophia lives in Paris; Constance stays in Bursley. Constance grows fat early (like her mother); Sophia remains slender. Sophia sends the occasional Christmas card to her family of origin, with no return address; Constance treasures every card. Sophia resolves never to return to the setting or the people of her girlhood; Constance cannot imagine living elsewhere.

Yet Sophia, too, ends up in Bursley. Convenient coincidence provides her with knowledge of her sister's widowhood and other family matters, and a further coincidence of timing provides that at just the right moment she sells the Parisian pension that she has run brilliantly for many years. She goes to England to visit her sister, and without ever quite deciding to do so, she stays, living in the house she inhabited as a girl. She concerns herself with such matters as the behavior of the family servant, who mistreats Sophia's poodle. Enjoying her new intimacy with Constance, she discusses household and local affairs with her. Often she finds herself feeling superior to her sister, despite the fact that she admires her "goodness." Often she fondly remembers Paris, although during her long sojourn there she remained convinced of the higher virtues of English ways and people.

The reader may feel bewildered by why Sophia stays. Early in what she still thinks of as a "visit," she reflects about Constance's defects and her considerable virtues, and about her own admiration for the English in general. She concludes, though, "But to be always with such people! To be always with Constance! To be always in the Bursley atmosphere, physical and mental!" The thought seems inconceivable. Yet she stays.

If the reader indeed feels conscious of bewilderment about the matter, the feeling is unlikely to seem urgent. Bennett's resolute avoidance of any sense of urgency marks all his literary effects. When Sophia's husband leaves her almost destitute in a foreign country, the text specifies the facts. It even adds harrowing details about the prolonged illness that ensues. But since Sophia herself hardly reflects on the situation; since she is promptly taken in by women who care for her through her sickness and subsequent weakness; since as soon as she feels better she devises immediate practical expedients for survival—since, in short, the marital desertion functions chiefly as a way of getting Sophia to the next stage in her career, its narration lacks emotional pressure.

Just so with Sophia's decision (apparently made unconsciously, and long unrecognized by its maker) to remain with her sister. It neither elicits nor responds to a sense of crisis. A definitive change in a protagonist's life occurs with little emphasis. At every crucial point in his narrative, the novelist avoids underlining emotional and psychological possibility or claiming the reader's impassioned attention.

That reader, however, needing to make sense of the story, may ponder the clues provided and realize that the contrasts established between the two sisters only obscure the more important truth that they resemble each other. Sophia has always seen herself as more glamorous and interesting than Constance, and smarter, better suited for life in the great world beyond Bursley. The morning after she arrives for her final "visit" with her sister, she looks out on the square that she has remembered as vast and impressive, finding it now small and ugly, and thinks, "It would kill me if I had to live here. It's deadening. It weighs on you. And the dirt, and the horrible ugliness! And the way they talk, and the way they think!" Certainly she talks in a more elegant way than that of the typical Bursleyite. About her thinking we must feel less sure, since in the more than 500 pages that precede her negative judgments of Bursley's square we have seen little beyond her mastery of practical affairs to reveal the quality of Sophia's thought.

A few pages after her morning meditations, Sophia encounters a Scottish doctor, more sophisticated than other Bursley residents and clearly disposed to feel strong interest in her. Hoping for conversation, he remarks that he has been reading a Zola novel. Sophia says that she has not read it. In fact, the narrator reveals, she has read almost nothing since 1870—more than twenty years earlier. The doctor tries again, making an effort to engage her in talk about the Siege of Paris, at the end of the Franco-Prussian War, which he knows she has lived through. She has little to say. The narrator observes that the doctor "might have been disappointed at the prose of her answers, had he not been determined not to be disappointed." As for Sophia, she can't understand why people make such a fuss about that siege. She feels no awareness that the war's events (which included the balloon departure of her would-be lover) have any interest or importance. She does not think about nations, or even about communities, except to the degree that they immediately affect her life.

In her lack of interest in books—indeed, in her lack of interest in happenings that do not directly concern her—Sophia bears a striking resemblance to her sister and to the other Bursley folk, objects of her condescension. Her sense of superiority, it emerges, rests on style rather than on substance. Not that she lacks substance—but then, neither does Constance, as Sophia would readily acknowledge. She never sees, however, that she shares with her sister traits that define them both.

Both, in fact, resemble their mother. Although Constance at times seems dithery and weak (notably in her vulnerability to the thoughtlessness of her spoiled son, a grown man by the time Sophia returns, and in her difficulties dealing with servants), she has unexpected force, acknowledged by the townsfolk who know and visit her. Like Sophia, they may patronize her, but they nonetheless defer to her. "[W]ith all her temperamental mildness," the narrator observes, "she had her formidable side." Young people think her old-fashioned: she remains serenely unaware of such judgments.

Unawareness provides a powerful defense for both sisters. Sophia feels nothing for or about her husband, once he leaves her. When he reappears, ill and destitute, however, she promptly and mysteriously dies. Constance consciously feels only delight about her sister's renewed presence in her life. When Sophia dies, though, she experiences a sense of relief: "the energetic and masterful Sophia had burst in upon her lethargic tranquility and very seriously disturbed the flow of old habits." Well before Sophia's death, Constance wins, and knows she has won, "the main point": she succeeds in remaining in the old house, after a brief experiment in hotel living. Sophia and the doctor plot to get her away from home, to give her a taste of and for luxury, to enable her to take pleasure in the money she has. But "lying there in the dark, the simple Constance never suspected that those two active and strenuous ones had been arranging her life for her, so that she should be jolly and live for twenty years yet." Both she and Sophia always manage not to know what they prefer not to know.

As for Sophia, although living with her sister allows her to preserve her sense of herself as relatively glamorous, accomplished, and smart, the novel's accumulating evidence demonstrates that her emotional range and intelligence are at least as limited as Constance's. After her early infatuation with the salesman, she has never come close to love. Constance, in contrast, has remained devoted to her husband and to the son she bears him. Blind to his deficiencies, she also blinds herself to her sister's. Sophia, however, needs to find inadequacies in others in order to maintain her own sense of superiority. Her life choices have appeared more ambitious than her mother's, but like her mother she nurtures a defensive conviction of her capacity always to know how others should act. Despite her courage in embarking on an innkeeper's career in France, she never ventures outside the confines of that role—to which she brings the maternal virtues of prudence, economy, and domestic skill.

Bennett's narrative, in short, deals not with a Madame Bovary—

like romantic and her stodgy, unimaginative sister but with a pair of women whose shared heredity and environment largely determine their possibilities. Sophia seems to escape Bursley and all it signifies, but she does not and cannot. The process by which the reader comes to realize this fact creates the novel's drama.

The plot of *The Old Wives' Tale* itself generates little drama. Indeed, as I have already hinted, Bennett apparently takes pains to make his story's large events as undramatic as possible. The several deaths related in the narrative—including those of the protagonists—occur with minimal emphasis. Characters act and suffer without elaboration. Internal excitement, after Sophia's youthful escapade, barely emerges. Yet a lot may happen in the reader's mind, as she gradually grasps that all is not quite what it seems in the Povey family.

Ideally, she grasps also why that family holds interest despite its mediocrity. Bennett's methods do not in the least resemble Woolf's. If Woolf considers his work trivial and uninteresting, he suggests by his practice that he would find her writing likewise trivial, although in a different sense. To dwell on the interior life, *The Old Wives' Tale* suggests, lends false importance to internal happenings that matter little in the great scheme of things. External circumstances and heredity matter more. An individual's sense of self may defend against this recognition, but only by achieving it can one have any hope of defining the self in new terms.

I hardly need say that none of this consciously occurred to me in my early readings of Bennett. I had neither the life experience nor the literary sophistication to grasp the nature of his accomplishment; nor, despite my incipient Ph.D., did I have the habits of analysis. It feels exciting now to find that *The Old Wives' Tale* actually deals with something important and to see how Bennett artfully leads his readers toward new realizations. Re-encountering the large cast of characters (some evoked with a few details; others richly developed through a long series of reported actions), I feel once more the relaxation and security that Bennett long ago induced—at the same time that I notice how much more goes on in this fiction than I previously saw. Reading *The Old Wives' Tale* again provides an exemplary experience of rereading's rewards. I need not be embarrassed about enjoying Arnold Bennett, either; I now know how to defend him.

I did not expect the results I got from rereading the three works discussed in this chapter. I anticipated, rather, that I would now scorn Wodehouse as a youthful indulgence that I had long outgrown and that I would find *The Old Wives' Tale* tedious. I expected that Collier would hold up as a source of entertainment. I appear, however, to have outgrown what I thought I would like and to like what I thought I would outgrow. It's a great pleasure to find Wodehouse still delightful and to be able to think about why. I disliked Collier so much this time around that I feel ashamed of ever having been a person who liked him. *The Old Wives' Tale* astonishes me by having turned into a first-rate novel instead of only a soothing one.

One way and another, then, I seem to have lost my guilty pleasures. I hope not all of them have disappeared—and with them the associated pleasures of hugging them to myself or of confiding them, under the right circumstances, to a treasured friend. Of course most books in the category of "guilty pleasure" are not books that one would think of rereading. Perhaps that's why so few come to my mind at the moment.

Conscious discriminations of value did not concern me when I read as a girl. Not the least of the many surprises that rereading always supplies is the discovery in unexpected places of kinds of value that I still feel comfortable upholding. Of course I read now in ways different from the ways of my youth—different even from my ways as a doctoral student. Professional training and both professional and nonprofessional experience have changed my habits. The enterprise of purposeful rereading in itself creates a kind of self-consciousness absent from my early engagement with books, and self-consciousness inheres in a teacher's reading, and a critic's. Self-consciousness, like any other state of mind, affects what I see in the book before me.

I'm a special case, in the close connection between my profession and my predilection for rereading. Anyone, though, who discovers by rereading apparent changes in a familiar text may be made aware of the clear association between how we read and what we read—what we understand ourselves as reading. The obvious contrast between concentrating on a book for the sake of understanding and skimming one in search of easy pleasure calls attention to two familiar ways of reading, but further possibilities include reading for aesthetic satisfaction, reading for the plot, reading in search of life lessons or information or comfort, and reading for escape. The list could easily continue. What we seek is often what we find; rereading can enlighten us about what we are looking for now and what we have sought in the past.

Reading Together

No one ever reads alone. When we encounter a book for the first time, perhaps devouring it in solitude, we participate in silent exchange with the book's author, whose efforts to shape our responses we encourage or resist or permit. Moreover, the obscure presences of those who have read the book before us—sometimes many generations of such readers—hover in the background. Perhaps we have heard of the book before we begin to read it. Perhaps we have been enticed by a current review, or by someone's casual or enthusiastic reference, or by an allusion in something else we've read. In any of these instances, we must realize, even if we barely notice, that we read in the company of others.

It may happen—for me, it has happened infrequently but memorably—that the company of others becomes literal and concrete. Such an experience has become familiar to many people in recent years, with the proliferation of book clubs, which predate Oprah (whose club started in 1996) but have certainly been encouraged by her influence. I know many women, and a few men, who belong to multiple clubs, often over a span of many years. Online reading groups, where the presence of others remains virtual, also foster the experience of reading in company. The "One Book, One City" program, which encourages every citizen of a given town, city, or state to read the same book at the same time and sometimes entails organized discussion, enlarges the cast of characters. Such phenomena testify to the attractiveness of sharing an intellectual and emotional experience with others—without the anxiety that may attend the idea of judgment associated with the classrooms of higher education.

I have participated in no such organized arrangement. Only occasionally have I read a book simultaneously with someone else, or even with many others: a rare and revelatory pleasure. In fact, I can only remember three specific episodes of reading with others, beyond the repeated privilege of reading with students in my classes. The first, reading with my mother, was the most powerful at the time and has had the strongest sustained effect. It happened during a summer before college. I would have been fourteen, perhaps. I brought home from the library *Islandia*, by Austin Tappan Wright, a book that I chose, almost certainly, because it was so thick. My father had ordained that I read no more than one book a day: he worried about my eyesight. This rule caused me to specialize in very big books. I was a fast reader; one book a day rarely satisfied my gluttony.

I can't imagine what made my mother pick up the novel—she customarily showed no interest in what I read—or, more surprising still, start reading it. Once she started, she was hooked. She and I read *Islandia* simultaneously—whoever got to it first on a given day hung onto it. We enjoyed it, and we talked about it.

This was an extraordinary event. "Get your nose out of that book," in my mother's disapproving voice, had echoed through my childhood. My mother didn't exactly deplore reading, but she thought that I did too much of it. I'm not quite sure what she wanted me to do instead: I was dutiful about making my bed and setting the table and washing dishes. Probably she thought I should play more, or get outdoors more, or just be more like "normal" children. She herself was vigorous, inventive, and always busy, indoors and out. She gardened, she mixed cement, she painted, she cooked brilliantly, she upholstered furniture and made curtains, as well as clothes for her daughters. In the evenings she often read: women's magazines, the *Reader's Digest*, travel books and biographies that I brought her from the library. But she didn't read the way I read, nor did she read the same books.

Until, in that one instance, she did.

Summer in Florida, in those days, made considerable demands. We had no air conditioning, and apparently we didn't know about ceiling fans. It rained just about every afternoon, and that helped a little, but one survived mainly by going swimming every day in the sixty-eight-degree water of central Florida springs. If stuck at home, my mother and I would appropriate the twin beds in my parents' bedroom, with heads toward the foot of the bed in order to get whatever breeze came through the windows, and with two big box fans strategically deployed. I don't recall where my sister was at these times, but she had a much livelier social life than I. Reading was my entertainment on hot days at home, a way of forgetting the heat. My mother would read too, or gaze out the window, or occasionally nap.

Into this sedentary—indeed, almost comatose—existence came *Islandia*. The copy I picked up recently in a second-hand store, a first edition, looks identical to the book I remember. It contains 1,013 pages of closely printed text, considerably cut by the author's daughter from the 2,300-page manuscript left after the author's death. Wright never planned to publish it. He had developed in leisurely fashion his account of an imagined island kingdom, its geology, its flora, its history and politics, its social institutions, and its residents, elaborating visions from his childhood. Killed in a

1924 accident, in his forties, Wright, a lawyer and professor of law, wrote no other fiction, but he left in manuscript form a "philosophic history" of Islandia and various other documents about the island's language and history. Amazon still sells two paperback editions of *Islandia*. The book has thirty-nine reader reviews, of which thirty-seven assign it the top, five-star rating.

I certainly would have given it five stars—and so would my mother. More surprising even than the fact that she read the book was the fact that she enjoyed it, apparently, as much as I did. We both felt most interested in the romance of the central character, John Lang, an American graduate of Harvard College (a member of the class of 1905, like his creator) and of law school, who comes to Islandia as American consul, after acquiring an Islandian friend in college and learning something of the language. He falls in love successively with two Islandian women, sleeps with one of them, but marries an American girl who joins him on his utopian island.

My mother and I had doubts about this marriage. Would it last, we wondered. Gladys doesn't quite seem to get the point about Islandia. Unlike her husband, she retains American standards. She tries repeatedly to get John to acknowledge the "immorality" of his previous sexual relations with an Islandian woman. Although she always subsides, given his insistence that there was nothing immoral about his affair, she never becomes convinced.

My mother, too, thought nonmarital sexual expression immoral and had made this clear to me well before we read *Islandia*, yet she never pressed the point in relation to the novel. Her interest focused on Gladys's psychology. Would it really be possible for a proper American woman to adjust to Islandian customs, to warm to Islandian people, to content herself with Islandian occupations? Would she come to resent her husband because of his harmonious adjustments? Would the placid life that John loved bore his wife? Mother raised such questions as though she were talking about an actual person and an actual place.

By the time I'd read all those pages and absorbed all that data, I, too, thought of Islandia as a real place and of the characters as living people. I responded to my mother in her terms and raised questions of my own based on similar assumptions. The nonmarital sex made me nervous; I did not wish to talk about it, partly because I found it hard to decide what I thought and didn't want maternal authority to govern my conclusions. But puzzles about the marriage preoccupied me, too.

We talked also, a lot, about Islandia as a place. If it were real, if it were possible to go there, to live there, would we want to do such a thing ourselves? My mother was skeptical; I felt more divided. I didn't like the idea of leaving my family, but the notion of a country where everyone spoke and lived honestly appealed to my idealism. My mother said that the Islandian system was impossible, that people were only honest when honesty was to their advantage. We argued a good deal about the issue. Her position confused me, since she had always responded severely to the slightest suspicion of a lie from one of her daughters.

The substance of our talk, however, hardly mattered. It mattered a lot that my mother and I were sharing an experience that I had inaugurated. True, I had chosen the book we read together on the basis of its bulk. Nonetheless, I had chosen it, and my mother had felt interested in my choice, and we were talking about it as equals. The thrill of this happening made the novel seem remarkable.

I don't think I ever spoke of *Islandia* to anyone, until I came upon it for sale and acquired a copy, battered and, by the looks of it, much read, for little money. It sat on my bookshelf for many months, unopened: I felt afraid to reread it. The magic would have vanished, I thought, and I'd be embarrassed by my earlier enthusiasm, and a happy memory of my mother would be contaminated. As I started thinking about the experience of reading with others, though, I knew that the time had come to open that book.

At first it seemed heavy going, written in rather flat prose and dwelling in detail that held little interest for me. John Lang goes to Harvard; John Lang meets Dorn, from Islandia; John falls in love but is "abruptly dismissed" by a young woman given little characterization. The love and the dismissal together occupy a single paragraph. He goes to work for his Uncle Joseph, who praises the life of a businessman. He unexpectedly wins the consulship and proceeds to Islandia; both he and the reader require much explanation in order to begin understanding the local way of life. He travels around the island, providing data about exactly what he sees. Despite the cavalier narrative disposal of John's first love, the novel's pace is generally leisurely, with no sense of urgency. The book reads as though it might go on forever. Although things keep happening, I did not feel conscious of much plot development. John narrates his own career, one thing after another, and it takes a long time for any intricacies to develop.

But it's a big book. There's plenty of room for taking a long time. Rereading *Islandia* caused me to ponder the special qualities of a long novel. For one thing, sheer bulk seems to generate conviction. I can understand now why—apart from our mutual lack of literary sophistication—my mother and I talked about Islandia as though it were a real place with real inhabitants. By the time I had made my way through about half the novel, I felt as though I was reading a genuine reminiscence of travel to a strange country. I had slogged through some slow sequences and had been soothed by meticulous reporting of mostly trivial events, of the look of things and the materials that compose them, of individual characters and their social and familial roles. John Lang himself, the narrator, doesn't until late in the book seem to have a very distinct personality. He reacts with asserted feeling to various happenings, but the claimed emotion rarely affects his serviceable prose. When it does, the effect tends to be awkward rather than moving. The subject of naked women, for instance, stimulates him, although he thinks that it should not: "The thought of a woman without clothes was associated with thoughts of desire. To [Islandians] this surely was not so. Could I put myself upon their level?" The stiffness of this comment gives way to a declaration that the idea of nakedness no longer matters, once he has seen Dorna, the Islandian woman whom he loves, without her clothes: "I could look into her eyes and smile and see the wet gleam of her bare shoulders and for a moment her breasts, frank, honest, and full." The idea of frank and honest breasts still perplexes me a bit, as it must have in my girlhood, but "honest" remains throughout the novel John Lang's favorite adjective for nakedness.

Austin Tappan Wright doesn't write well about emotion, and his prose never achieves stylistic distinction. It works nonetheless to give his narrative the solidity that encourages suspension of disbelief. The clumsiness about feelings only intensifies the sense of authenticity in the reporting about folkways and geography.

And politics. *Islandia* held many surprises for me in this second reading, and one of them concerned politics—an invisible topic to me in my earlier encounter with the text, this time appearing as one of the novel's dominant concerns. I remembered nothing about the international diplomatic struggle or the internal political conflict that in fact shapes much of the plot. As far as I was concerned, I think, this was a novel about a young man trying to marry and finally succeeding, with geographical and sociological detail attached to the story. The fact that John Lang's romantic encounters occur in an exotic setting added interest, as did the conception of the Islandian ethical system and the way of life associated with it, but the various love stories were the real point. I exaggerate, perhaps: it seems inconceivable now that I could have ignored so much. Did my mother's understanding shape mine? Did I cross out of my mind whatever failed to interest her? That hypothesis suggests that reading in concert with someone else may have its dark side, narrowing possibilities. To be sure, few imaginable co-readers have the kind of power a mother exercises over a daughter in her early teens. Rebellious though such a daughter may be (and I wasn't), her mother's voice carries great weight. Any people reading together, though, surely influence and perhaps constrict one another's responses. I saw this pattern in operation on my single visit to a book club, on an evening when the group was discussing *Pride and Prejudice*. The most authoritative sounding woman present announced that the plot was ridiculous, the characters implausible, and the language impenetrable. Everyone else promptly stopped talking about her enjoyment of the novel. I kept quiet: I knew I would sound like a teacher if I opened my mouth, and I was only a visitor.

I don't know that I should blame my mother, though, for my early blindness. It may be that I would have failed to notice the strong political emphasis in any case. Ours was not a political family: I can never recall my parents, staunch Republicans both, discussing political matters. I probably didn't know enough to be interested in a book's political notions.

I'm interested now, though, and I have come to realize that political and social concerns lie at the heart of Wright's enterprise. The novel's central issue is whether Islandia should engage with the rest of the world. Mineral deposits of great value allegedly lie beneath the island's surface. The Germans in particular are eager to get their hands on them and to build a railroad to transport ore to seaports. They hold forth a vision of "progress," of enabling Islandia to prosper in the modern world, of new machines, sewing machines to motor cars, and of new possibilities.

The Islandian legislature splits over the issue. Under the legislative leadership of a local proponent of progress, they have inaugurated a treaty that allows foreign countries to send diplomatic representatives. The treaty specifies, however, that no foreigner without diplomatic standing can stay in the country for more than a year. When John arrives, the time is rapidly approaching for a vote on whether to open the country further. The father of his friend Dorn leads the opposition to such a possibility.

John, as American consul, is expected to facilitate the commercial interests of his countrymen, whose proposals frequently challenge his ethical sense. Perceived as insufficiently supportive, he resigns under pressure, sadly realizing that he must leave within a year the country that he has grown to love. He increasingly believes that Islandia must preserve its separateness, that progress would come at the cost of individual and collective autonomy, and that the rest of the world has nothing to offer that Islandia needs. Considered an ally by Dorn and his friends, he helps to guard the frontier against invasion and heroically gives warning to prospective victims as invaders arrive. Wounded in his effort to protect the innocent, known as a hero to virtually all Islandians (it's a small country), he sees the legislature vote, as a result of the Dorn family's tactics, to protect Islandia's independence and to give John Lang, alone among foreigners, the right to stay, as a reward for valor.

I have elided a good deal in this account, but it at least sketches the central political drama. Wright engineers his narrative to support a conservative view: isolationism, preservation of the status quo, opposition to innovation. He makes this position plausible in relation to Islandia's unique conditions. Because of its lack of machinery, the country has developed an economy based on agricultural and craft activities. Although Islandia has a rudimentary class system, founded on landownership, in practice little distinction separates owners from tenants. Real distinction depends mainly on political leadership. No military class exists, since there has been little perceived danger from without. Individual lives typically do not contain much variety, and no one sees cause for complaint in this fact. One of its consequences appears to be widespread serenity. Deep love for one's land is so important that the Islandians have a special word for it (and one for sexual love, and one for the kind of love that leads to marriage). Equally pervasive is individual honesty and frankness, which work, in the John Lang plot, to assuage the protagonist's chagrin over the marriage to another (to the king, in fact) of his Islandian love.

I find myself dubious now about the utopian ideas that honesty and frankness never hurt anyone's feelings, that tenants never resent landowners, and that, partly because people invariably help one another, no serious poverty exists in an agricultural country. It seems unlikely that no other nation has previously attempted to invade Islandia and that few Islandians appear to worry about the possibility that some army might penetrate their borders. But utopian novels always require imaginative faith: one decides to credit an author's hypotheses and to enjoy the ways they play out. In *Islandia,* the playing out is benign, but the figure of Gladys supplies a skeptic, resistant to the ethos of openness, honesty, and agriculture.

In this way, Gladys fills a significant role—or perhaps it would be better to say that she *should* fill a significant role. My mother and I, in my earlier reading, failed to notice that the novel rushes toward its conclusion and brings up issues that it neglects to develop. The Lang marriage is indeed problematic, as we thought. That fact serves an important function in Wright's narrative scheme. It provides an opportunity to recapitulate explicitly some arguments for Islandia's isolationist, idealistic ethos and to reintroduce, rather cavalierly, important characters. Gladys, imbued with American notions, resists Islandian ideas. She specially resists John's notion of marriage, an advanced one for Wright's era. John, influenced by what he has learned in Islandia, wishes an equal partner, someone who belongs to herself, not to him, and who functions independently while remaining sensitive to his needs and desires. Gladys claims to want only to be his.

John has returned to America before deciding on his Islandian life, has accepted another position in his uncle's firm, and has worked hard in it. His uncle offers him a partnership after witnessing his effort and his apparent devotion. The offer promises great financial advantage—but it precipitates the young man's decision to go back to Islandia for good, a decision incomprehensible to his uncle and to the rest of his family and argued against strongly by the uncle.

The portion of *Islandia* concerned with John's time as a New York businessman consists almost entirely of overt or covert diatribe against the American way of life as it has developed in practice. Everyone, male and female, is strained and edgy. Neither work nor recreation satisfies human needs. The city is inhumane. John's brother Philip articulates the case for the American Way. It centers, in his view, on belief in progress, acceptance of reason as the only valid basis for decision, and ambition as the driving force of every worthy human being—indeed, ambition as a test of worth. When John expresses his longing to "feel more" rather than to govern all action by reason, Philip accuses him of being a hedonist, a charge he several times repeats. It is apparently the worst thing he can imagine calling anyone.

The account of business life and of city life in general has cartoonish intensity. The author's interest does not seem fully engaged in spelling out the charge against Western values, although his passionate conviction energizes the section on America. What matters most for the narrative is getting John Lang back to Islandia and getting him a wife—an operation also handled cavalierly.

John's love for Gladys, although frequently asserted, develops too rapidly to feel convincing. His love for Islandia, in contrast, carries great force.

Gladys recapitulates the argument for ambition in a discussion about her hypothetical children. She chides her husband for not feeling concerned that those children meet and associate with "the best people" and for apparently not caring whether they turn into anything other than farmers. She strongly believes in progress. She complains, or ostentatiously fails to complain, that their life on the farm John loves is boring. She quotes her mother as authority about matters ethical and social. Most of all, she expresses— repetitively, monotonously—her desire to be John's creature. She wants only to do what pleases him. She wants him to punish her, ideally to whip her, when she does wrong. She wants a master, a manly man.

John and Gladys resort to sex to solve their problems. The novel's last hundred pages or so report, in truncated, discreet, repetitive form, many couplings, all ending in some version of satisfaction for John. Such a "solution," to be sure, solves nothing at all, and John realizes this, although he can find no better expedient. *Islandia* finally offers, in a conclusion unsatisfactory to the reader, if at least temporarily pleasing to the characters, Gladys's pregnancy as a resolution to marital difficulty. A child will presumably supply her with responsibility and activity and will make her settle into her Islandian life.

This summary, I think, suggests that the last quarter of *Islandia* supplies more doctrine than drama. So it does, as though the author's imagination wore out in the stretch. The account of the marriage, partly because the courtship is so unconvincing, lacks the interest, as well as the detail, of earlier narratives within the novel, their characters and their situations. Earlier, the leisurely descriptions and explanations of Islandian people, land, and customs make the imagined realm both convincing and appealing. The rush through what's-wrong-with-America and how-to-get-a-wife, however, along with the effort to convey as quickly as possible the outlines of a marriage filled with sexual satisfaction and ideological discord, not only fails to convince. It also makes me suspect uneasily that hortatory rather than imaginative purpose drives the novel.

Perhaps my mother and I felt the same uneasiness when we worried about Gladys and about the health of the marriage. I still experience a sense of something wrong in the final two hundred pages or so, but I now interpret it differently. It seems now that Gladys is constructed as unsatisfactory in her resistance to Islandian ways and then abruptly turned satisfactory by her pregnancy, in a reversion to the patriarchal values that John Lang has apparently rejected. Or possibly the novel intentionally generates and preserves its readers' uneasiness as part of its intent to question the capitalist way of life and to argue for an alternative to ambition and wide engagement.

Clumsy in language, sometimes tedious in development, imperfect in plot, *Islandia* nonetheless continues to convey the energy of conviction and the imaginative power of a culture conjured up in full detail. To read it a second time did not prove as enchanting as my first reading; I can see the book's literary flaws as well as its virtues. Yet some of the original enchantment still hovers over *Islandia* for me. More than any other work I have re-read for this study, the novel evokes for me a special moment of my past. Enriched by my memory of shared experience, it has an aura that makes it impossible for me to dismiss it. Not even a clear-eyed literary assessment can alter that fact.

When, at the age of fifteen, I entered college, I lived in a small freshman dormitory, a frame house on the edge of a Florida lake, inhabited by twenty or thirty girls. (We didn't call ourselves women in those days, and we didn't act much like women.) I think there were eight of us, two to a room, on my corridor of the first floor.

The big literary event of the second semester—not for strictly literary reasons—was the publication of Edmund Wilson's *Memoirs of Hecate County*. The book consisted of six loosely linked short stories, and Wilson did not excel as a writer of fiction; I would not ordinarily have rushed to read his work in the genre. But one of the stories—marked, incidentally, by a penciled arrow in the table of contents of the second-hand copy I much later bought—was, by the standards of the time, scandalously erotic. The reviews and the gossip about the volume centered, always, on "The Princess with the Golden Hair," a novella narrated by a man who succeeds in having a love affair with a beautiful woman who wears a back brace.

Someone on our corridor bought a copy. She read the book first and reported in hushed tones that the novella was "very dirty." In due time she passed the volume along to another girl, and gradually it came about that each of us read it, titillated in advance by the idea of the "dirty story" and later by the fact. In the evenings we would assemble and talk about it. I don't recall much about the individual participants in these discussions, but they included at one extreme my roommate, a prim prospective music major and devout Christian, and at the other extreme a vivid Latina who had already taught the rest of us how to curse in Spanish. All of us, however, were, I think, fairly innocent of first-hand sexual knowledge.

Reading a dirty story with this group of my approximate contemporaries (I the youngest of the bunch but accepted as an equal) didn't feel much like reading *Islandia* with my mother, but like the earlier experience this seemed remarkable at the time and remains, for me, unique. I remember the talk far better than I remembered the story, which provided a pretext for discussion of issues that concerned us all. How should we feel about adultery—a question that occurs belatedly to the male protagonist who seduces (or is seduced by) a married woman? The woman, Imogen, at one point tells her would-be lover that they must stop seeing each other because she is married. His response: "You've been married for sixteen years, and Ralph has had you all that time. Don't you think I deserve something, too?" (Later, however, when he is suffering from gonorrhea, the lover turns to supporting the sanctity of marriage.) What would it be like to undress in front of a man? What would the story be like if told by the "princess" herself?

Eventually the narrative offers some fairly detailed sex scenes between Imogen and the unnamed narrator. While that narrator waits for Imogen to yield, he initiates a love affair with Anna, a working-class young woman whom he meets in a dance hall; at times he convinces himself that he's in love with her. That relationship too generates sexual encounters of some specificity, so it too produced material for our slightly hesitant but altogether enthralling evening conversations—questions about how, exactly, one "did it," about the nature of female orgasms, about physical details mysteriously alluded to in the text, about the erotic functions of various parts of our anatomy. In short, Wilson's story enabled us to talk about sex. This was the first time I had ever discussed sexual matters, except in uncomfortable exchanges with my mother in which she provided the information she thought I should know and often responded to questions by assuring me that I'd understand when I got older. No wonder I recall the talk more vividly than I recalled the story!

Indeed, I didn't really remember the story at all. I didn't remember that its action takes place in the 1920s, in an environment of speakeasies and dance halls as well as of suburban prosperity.

Its characters drink a great deal of bootleg liquor. Although the protagonist and Imogen spend the summer in New York suburbs ("Hecate County"), they also inhabit New York City. Imogen, the "princess," does not wear her back brace when making love, though I distinctly recall that she did. (The narrator, however, fantasizes about having sex with her as she remains confined in a brace; that vivid fantasy obviously lived in my mind.) Her back ailment is almost certainly delusional; I remembered it as real. The other woman important in the narrator's erotic life occupies a good deal of the text; I had forgotten her. Moreover, the narrator also sleeps with two women besides Imogen and Anna, both of whom had vanished from my consciousness. As far as I was concerned, Wilson's story concerned a sympathetic narrator (he now seems morally and psychologically unattractive) and a beautiful, flawed woman. The woman is there in the text all right, but her flaws turn out to be spiritual rather than physical. And, like *Islandia*, "The Princess with the Golden Hair" reflects social and political interests, an aspect that I either failed to notice in the first place or failed to recall.

All in all, my memories, assessed in the light of recent rereading, turn out to be mainly either false or distorted. The story Wilson wrote bears little relation to the one I read, which assumed its retrospective form, I now realize, mainly as a result of those dormitory conversations. Over the years I had elided most of what makes the story interesting to me now.

The stories in *Memoirs of Hecate County*, linked by their common narrator and common locale, are mostly ordinary or worse: trivial, pointless, repetitive, in one case crudely polemical. All in all, they seem forgettable—and indeed I remembered nothing about any of them except the central novella. It's possible that I didn't even read them when I was a freshman. There was strong demand to pass the book along, and it was quite clear that "The

Princess with the Golden Hair" exerted compelling force on everyone who had read it and not at all clear that the other stories were worth our attention. Reading them now, I'm struck by
their apparent lack of interest in the narrator, except as a story-
telling device. Only the last of them, "Mr. and Mrs. Blackburn at
Home," enlarges slightly the implications of "The Princess with
the Golden Hair," and it seems something of an afterthought.

· 259

To my surprise, however, "The Princess with the Golden Hair"
still proves compelling, for reasons that I didn't even glimpse six
decades ago. As social/psychological analysis, the novella develops subtle insights into a man who apparently lacks much insight
about himself. He castigates himself from time to time; he makes
short-lived resolutions of self-improvement; he explores various
life possibilities. None of these activities leads him to a more fruitful existence. Mostly, he engages in fantasy, much of it concerning
women.

This narrator lives in fairly comfortable circumstances. Edu-
cated at private school and a university where he eventually pursues a Ph.D. in economics, he inherits enough money to live on
and drops out of school before writing his dissertation. He decides
to combine his interests in art and economics to write about the
paintings of various historical periods as reflections of the life of
their times. The novella's action takes place in 1929. The Depression has begun; millions lack jobs and income, but the narrator
rents a small house in Hecate County and, in winter, an apartment
in New York City; a black maid attends to his needs and follows
him to the city when he temporarily moves there; he buys cocktail
shakers and bootleg liquor and sofas at will. He has dabbled from
time to time in Marxist theory and continues to allude glibly to it.

Although his direct self-revelations apparently try to establish
him as a serious person (near-Ph.D., interest in art and economics, efforts to write a book, Marxist intellectual paraphernalia), his

fantasies and his attempts to enact them suggest self-absorption and frivolity. Suddenly seeing the married Imogen as a "princess," he sets out to seduce her, imagining in varying detail what a liaison with her would be like. While the seduction pursues its lingering course, he encounters Anna, working class and of Lithuanian origins. She becomes his increasingly satisfactory mistress.

Imogen collaborates in constructing fantasies about life with the narrator. Around such diverse locales as a European castle, a Scottish retreat, or a small house on Cape Cod she weaves detailed stories about blissful joint existence. Her would-be seducer joins in the story making, until at last he becomes satiated and irritated, demanding a "real" consummation for their "love." Imogen agrees and duly comes to his apartment, wearing a new dress consciously intended to support one of her lover's early fantasies. She wears no brace; her body is unexpectedly perfect; she has beautiful breasts; she is physically eager for sexual union. Somehow, though, that union feels disappointing. The physical relationship does not last long.

The narrator's fantasies about Anna assume a different form, developing along with, not previous to, their sexual liaison. They focus most specifically on her as a member of the working class, the class most damaged by the Depression. At one point, her lover even talks to her about the role of the proletariat, although he soon realizes the inappropriateness of holding forth in this way. Anna is pragmatic and efficient. He is not. He admires her; he imagines living with her and her small daughter somewhere in Brooklyn. She, sensitive to the social disgrace of living with a man outside of marriage, has no interest in such a plan. The actual and pressing demands of her impoverished life leave no room for fantasy. The idleness of the narrator's mental life becomes increasingly apparent.

Indulging further in his proclivity for fantasy, this male protagonist finds a brutal way to end his affair with Anna. He convinces himself of her infidelity and accuses her. She leaves quietly and soon sends him a note informing him that she has agreed to wed another man, a Pole who has been wooing her and whom she does not wish to marry. She remains practical, however, and cuts her losses, not attempting to persuade an irrational, self-indulgent man of her loyalty to him.

· 261

The narrator does not report his reaction. This is not a story of education: he does not appear to have learned anything from his adventures. If there is a moral, it seems to be that women are always available if you want them. The immediate resolution to the narrator's difficulties is the return from California of his long-term girlfriend, Jo, who has to spend six months of every year in the West with her children. Jo, making no emphatic claims on him, remains good fun. When she's around, she seems always sexually accessible; and she leaves every year before her presence can cloy. In "Mr. and Mrs. Blackburn at Home," reporting events some years after those of "The Princess," the narrator is still vacillating about whether to marry her. He makes no decision. He travels west with her, and the final page reveals "that the tall intimidating presence of the forests of aspen and pine, with their alien life that excluded ours, only left us the more alone with the strain of our wrong relation."

One wrong relation after another: but the young man, even after he's not so young, never reflects seriously about why his relations infallibly go wrong. Edmund Wilson, though, manages to make his readers see more than his protagonist can. His representation reveals that the central character retreats into fantasy from the hard work of human relations, and that his fantasies about himself as a Communist serve purposes equivalent to those of his imaginings about women. When he engages in pursuit of a woman or enjoys a sexual connection, he indulges in dreams of committed happiness; when the pursuit's conclusion proves less blissful than the dream, or the fear of commitment outweighs the desire, his thoughts turn sour. To imagine himself as a Communist fosters his sense of superiority to the bourgeoisie who surround him. Thus, realizing that his affair with Anna "was saving me trouble and time," he concludes, at least briefly, that "since Imogen, on the other hand, was so difficult, . . . as a bourgeois 'escapist' she was not really worth having." His alleged Communism, however, results in no action. By the time of "Mr. and Mrs. Blackburn," he has written a book, but such an outcome seems unlikely in "The Princess with the Golden Hair," where writing occupies little of his time in comparison with that assigned to the pursuit or enjoyment of women or even to alcoholic indulgence.

The sexual detail, less shocking now than it was in my girlhood, still registers as explicit and insistent. The character's vivid awareness of physical facts and sensations contrasts with his apparent paucity of emotional reactions—except in his fantasy life. He does not take women seriously, except as instruments of pleasure. Revealingly, when he praises Anna's judgment and perception he formulates those qualities as "a clear little power of perception and a cool little faculty of judgment." The diminutives—which don't make sense—recur in later sequences of approving contemplation about Anna.

The narrator's superficiality, his alcoholic and sexual indulgence, his flirtation with Communism, his easy prosperity: all make him a figure that could serve as an almost allegorical representative of the 1920s. Wilson, writing with the perspective of the full Depression and of the war that followed, conveys superficial sympathy and more profound distaste, suggesting his indictment of a decade as well as of an imagined person.

My current response to the novella surprises me as much as the story itself astonished me. The discrepancy between then and now exceeds that of any other episode of reading and rereading in my experience, and it suggests once more that reading with others can obscure as well as reveal truths about the text considered and about the nature of a personal response. Group opinion may have distorting force. I suspected that when rereading *Islandia,* first read in a group of two; I suspect it more strongly after my new encounter with Edmund Wilson. To read together may affirm and enrich relationships, but it mediates responses to a text. I begin to think that one *should*—one *must*—reread works read initially in company in order really to know much about the works themselves.

Yet when I think back on that undergraduate experience, it occurs to me that there may be another explanation for the distortion, that it may reflect something about rereading in general as well as rereading in groups. The story I read in 1946 has little in common with the one I read recently—but surely I found in that novella long ago exactly what I needed. (Also, not incidentally, what my fellow freshmen needed.) We needed to ponder the subject of sexuality. The reassurance of the group made such pondering possible. Not just any story would do as a pretext for it, but "The Princess with the Golden Hair" worked perfectly for the purpose.

Differences between the diverse selves suggested by multiple readings of a single work must emerge partly as a consequence of different needs associated with different stages of development. Those needs are sometimes embarrassing, sometimes almost incomprehensible in retrospect, sometimes appealingly innocent, sometimes appallingly misguided—and often, whatever their nature, powerful. Especially in youth, before we develop habits of critical reading or sophisticated expectations of what texts may offer, individual needs can deform our understanding of what we read. I realize now, more forcibly than ever before, the urgency of rereading the great works I encountered before I was twenty-one.

Yet the experience of reading "The Princess with the Golden Hair"—not, by any reckoning, a "great work"—in conjunction with my classmates remains in my memory as an important moment in my college and my reading careers. Without the support of those other young women, I would probably have been unable to fulfill, or even to acknowledge, a crucial need of my own.

My third episode of reading with others, also retrospectively important, involved a large and complicated group. When I began teaching at Wellesley College, every member of the English Department taught at least one section of freshman composition. The course lasted for a full year, two semesters, and was required for all students: no exemptions. It involved a great deal of writing and quite a lot of reading, beginning with essays in the first semester and going on to fiction and poetry in the second. Every section had its own syllabus, devised by the individual instructor. The staff met regularly, every two or three weeks, to talk about goals and strategies. As a young instructor, I learned a great deal from these meetings. I learned, in fact (or so I believed), how to be a teacher. Although I had previously taught for two years at Indiana University and for a year at the University of Florida, I had never discussed the art and craft of teaching or even reflected much about it: the struggle of preparing each individual class absorbed me.

Four or five years after I arrived at Wellesley, one of the staff meetings took an unexpected direction. Although the long-established idea of the individual syllabus spoke to what seemed a universal desire for independence in the classroom, someone raised the question of whether it wouldn't be useful for the students to have at least one common experience. Much debate ensued, with eventual agreement that we would teach a single common text, in the context of other works of our own choosing, during the spring semester. A great deal more debate ended in specifying the text: Henry James's novella *The Spoils of Poynton*. In due time we all read it, the entire freshman class and the entire faculty of the English Department. The students, by and large, loved it. When it came time to decide on their class cheer—loudly and frequently employed throughout their college careers—they agreed to memorialize their common experience. "Fleda Vetch, Fleda Vetch, Fleda Vetch," they would yell. For four years we heard this from time to time, ringing reiterations of the name of James's protagonist.

I've frequently had the experience of reading something with my students, but never before or since have I read a book simultaneously with my academic colleagues. Still a young teacher, I felt awed and sometimes intimidated by many of those colleagues— not only by members of the tenured faculty, but by the experienced assistant professors, who seemed to me immensely smart and well-read. As for me, I had not previously read *The Spoils of Poynton*. I didn't dispute the decision, but I played little part in making it. Not for the first or the last time in my teaching career, I felt myself only a step ahead of my class—and well behind my fellow teachers.

But talking about the book with my colleagues was glorious. It is a sad and mysterious aspect of academic life in literature departments, at least in my experience of three state universities, one elite college, and one Ivy League university, that faculty members rarely talk with one another about books. Close individual friendships can allow such talk; I have been fortunate enough to have at least one such friendship at each of the three institutions where I taught longest. Conversation over the lunch table, however, more customarily concerns institutional (or, at best, pedagogical) and social rather than literary matters.

For several weeks, though, Wellesley encounters over lunch or coffee were likely to turn into enthusiastic discussions of Fleda

Vetch and her doings, or Henry James and his. Even if a conversation started out about teaching, it would soon become concerned with the substance of the text that we were all simultaneously confronting. Polite conversations could suddenly become arguments. Other people often joined in. Every day was exhilarating, challenging, rich in unexpected turns. I've never had another experience remotely like it.

266 ·

Both the "official" discussions of *The Spoils of Poynton* that we had in staff meetings and the informal ones that erupted everywhere compelled me to keep exploring different points of view about every aspect of the book. I remember thinking that I was engaging my students at a higher level as a result, and learning that they, too, responded well to challenge. And I remember that my confidence grew as a result of those weeks of lively exchange. I had never read *Spoils* before; I knew much less about James than many of my colleagues knew; yet it was clear to me that I too had something to contribute to the discussions, that I too was taken seriously by my colleagues, that I on occasion saw something that others failed to see.

All of this—the atmosphere of excitement, inside and outside the classroom; the sense of common purpose; the exhilaration of argument and of discovery—I remember vividly. I do not, however, remember a single thing about the content of all those conversations. I do not remember what I taught, or tried to teach, my students. I don't even remember how I understood the book or what I thought about it.

In all three of the instances of reading with others that I have recorded, it seems, conversation remains more vivid than text, and the substance of the conversation, in retrospect, matters less than its atmosphere. That atmosphere, recalled, retains sufficient power to drown out the book in memory. I try to recall what I thought of

The Spoils of Poynton at first reading; I recall instead the tone and
the thrill of arguments that no longer have any content.

So, I read the book again, for only the second time. In the years
that have intervened since that first reading, I appear to have convinced myself that I don't much care for Henry James. Even *Portrait of a Lady*, which I remember with conscious pleasure, I don't
pick up for casual rereading. It comes as a surprise to me now,
picking up *The Spoils of Poynton*, that James can be very funny,
even at his own expense. Thus: "Save on one other occasion, at
which we shall in time arrive, little as the reader may believe it,
she never came nearer." Who would expect that James could joke
about his own leisurely pace?

More surprise: I get almost immediately hooked by the story.
What a great book for freshmen to read, I think. It's all about instantaneous love and its consequences. It moves fast and contains
both much that entertains and much that puzzles. Its characters
have intricacy that challenges the reader. Even the male center of
the love triangle, declared by his own mother to be stupid, proves
to have unexpected depths. And the book seems even timelier now
than I can imagine it seeming back in my Wellesley days: it's all
about *things*—desire for things, hoarding of them, consequences
of possession.

The copy of *The Spoils of Poynton* that I recently reread is evidently the one from which I taught the book. It's full of marginal
notes in my hand, some in red ink, some in capital letters lavishly
underlined. Almost without exception, though, these notes have
faded into complete illegibility. In the rare instances when they
are readable, they make no sense to me. "Her ruling passion had
in a manner despoiled her of her humanity," James writes. I underlined that in red ink and wrote in the margin "General truth."
What on earth does that mean—I mean, what bearing does it have

on the book's enormous accomplishment? Alas, my effort to interpret my own cryptic comment now only leads me to suspect that I didn't teach freshmen about *The Spoils of Poynton* nearly as well as I thought I had done.

I wonder if they found it baffling, this sly piece of entertainment. Mrs. Gereth, the cultivated lady who in effect adopts Fleda because of the young woman's fine sensibility, reveals herself ever more clearly as a villain, obsessed with the fineness of objects, unconcerned with the feelings of humans. She bases her sense of superiority on her delicate taste, her connoisseurship. It justifies her, in her view, in stealing all the possessions that her husband has left to their son. Indeed, it justifies her in plotting against the son's intentions of marriage, trying to maneuver him into a match with Fleda rather than with the woman he has chosen and to whom he is engaged.

As for Fleda—well, in the first place, who but Henry James could name someone "Fleda Vetch," and then take her seriously, and make readers do likewise? Described early—metaphorically—as "a hungry girl," Fleda possesses a rich sensibility but virtually no resources for gratifying it. Mrs. Gereth provides her with the opportunity to enjoy without needing to possess the lavish products of a lifetime spent amassing the rare and beautiful. She flourishes in the new atmosphere of luxury and loveliness, only to discover its miasmal aspect.

If the novella's conflict only pitted Mrs. Gereth's desire to use Fleda for her own purposes against Fleda's determination not to be used, it might present little challenge. James, however, gives that conflict a double, perhaps a triple, twist. Fleda, it emerges, really loves Owen Gereth and wishes to marry him. He's handsome and good, she thinks, and perhaps not so stupid after all. If in fact he *is* stupid, that's all right too: she would feel happy to be the clever member of the family. Another surprise: Owen loves and yearns to marry her. What could be simpler?

But for James nothing is simple. Fleda sends Owen back to his fiancée, to do the right thing by confronting her openly. Passive if not stupid, the young man allows himself to be married to the wrong woman; and because Mrs. Gereth mistakenly believes her plot successful, Owen's vulgar wife gains full possession of all the beautiful things that she covets although she cannot appreciate them. Both Mrs. Gereth and Fleda lose forever the glories of Poynton, the Gereth estate. In a final unexpected plot development, Owen and his wife also lose them.

Mrs. Gereth has also lost her humanity, the narrator suggests, as a result of her obsession with things. She does not think of herself as a materialist: quite the contrary. She understands herself, rather, as a woman of feelings too subtle for the workaday world. From her point of view, it is women like Mona, her son's fiancée, who epitomize materialism. To be sure, Mona's desire simply to possess, with no interest in what she owns, constitutes a crasser form of the vice than does Mrs. Gereth's subtle appreciation: Mona is crudely covetous. Fleda avoids covetousness; she expresses no desire to own things, apparently content to enjoy her friend's possessions. Yet she embodies yet another form of materialism, feeling depleted when deprived of the opportunity to live among objects of beauty.

After Owen's disappearance from her life, Fleda continues to live with his mother, who is now in the process of beautifying, in a new, modest mode, the small house that her husband's will has allotted her. If Mrs. Gereth is angry at Fleda, she never says so, but their relationship no longer involves intimate communication. Fleda expects no happiness, nor does the older woman. They simply live, because living is what there is to do.

Into this resigned existence (one with undertones of rage, though) comes a letter from Owen, enjoining Fleda to go to Poynton in his absence (he and his wife are in India) and to take, as a gift from him, the most precious object she can find there. She cannot interpret this gesture. Perhaps she simply *will* not interpret it: she consciously, willfully, decides—presumably in order to avoid the suffering of speculation—to take it as meaning that Owen is so happy in his marriage that he has psychic space for such generosity. At any rate, she acknowledges her desire to do exactly what he commands. In her mind she contemplates the objects she remembers, thinking what she might choose. She takes her time. She does not tell Mrs. Gereth. Finally, she embarks on a solitary train trip to Poynton—only to discover that an unexpected catastrophe has destroyed the house and all its contents. She puts her face in her hands, she decides to return to London. Thus the novella ends.

It ends, in short, with puzzles. Has Fleda succumbed to Mrs. Gereth's malady, acquisitiveness merged with appreciation? Why, exactly, does she accept Owen's offer? Does the novella instruct us that *things* corrupt everyone, or only that they *can* corrupt anyone? Fleda's life has diminished since she sent Owen away; even her imagination has dimmed. Was she wrong to insist that her suitor behave impeccably? She might have married him forthwith, sorting out the matter of the jilted fiancée later; would the fuller life that such a course guaranteed justify the moral shortcut? Are moral shortcuts altogether beside the point in a society little concerned with morality? Or does Fleda's uprightness sustain her even when the outside world can offer her little?

James's ability to make such moral questions compelling, to make them the stuff of drama, animates his tale. He combines a rather flat narrative tone with abundant psychological detail and atmospheric suggestion to generate characters so vivid that they compel readers to ask themselves the kind of questions I have just raised, questions that shed a certain glare on life in twenty-first-century America. James so brilliantly establishes his own terms that they envelop the reader. The sense of having been drawn into another world lingers beyond the story's end.

Perhaps I thought these things when I read *The Spoils of Poynton* the last time: I wish I could remember. My happy memories of discussing the book with colleagues as well as students, though, suggest that the richness I found in my second encounter with the text owes something to the auxiliary delights of my initial reading.

Coda: What I Have Learned

To REREAD CELEBRATES the act of reading. Returning to a work read in the past, no matter what feeling or judgment attended the original meeting of book and mind, declares important the process of encountering and coming to terms with a text. We wrestle with difficult ideas, rejoice with elegant prose, empathize with or assess compelling characters, choosing once more to engage with meanings of words on a page, rejoicing once more in the choice.

My own rereading, as will have been obvious in many instances, involved (and involves) books printed on paper. The look of those books, especially if they are old, contributes to their meaning for me—not only to my sense of nostalgia, although certainly to that, but also to my sense of serious history. None of the actual books that I have recently reread belongs to a century before the twentieth, but even a book from the 1950s or 1960s speaks of the past, in its design, its typeface, and the degree and kind of wear it shows. Such reminders of a past cultural moment give me pleasure and inform my understanding.

I know, though, that many people rereading now do so from

electronic sources. In the era of Kindle and its successors, reading has changed. That change will make differences in the experience of rereading that I can't begin to imagine. The work you read will not bear physical signs of age; one part of the experience is gone. But new aspects, aspects unknown to me, will provide pleasure, presumably, that paper does not. If you have read a book the first time in paper form and reread it on the screen, will the experience resemble that of reading a favorite Russian novel in new translation? How will the impermanence of words on a screen (they disappear as you move on from them, even though they remain available) affect what rereading feels like? Will people feel more tempted to reread, or less? Or will the medium fail to modify the degree of temptation?

As I said, I can't begin to imagine. I can imagine, though—I *must* imagine—that readers will still read and that novels will still entice. Reading a novel supplies aesthetic pleasure, wisdom (moral, psychological, social), mental stimulation, excitement, entertainment, emotional stimulation and release, escape. Rereading that novel recalls and enlarges the satisfactions of the first reading (unless, in fact, it doesn't, in instances when a work has mysteriously lost its power over the reader). Encountered initially, *Middlemarch* excites, say, by its sheer inclusiveness, the scope of its concerns. A second reading perhaps focuses attention on the character of Dorothea and generates different excitement through gradual realization of the character's intricacies. The third time through, we might find ourselves absorbed in the problem of growth and change and immersed in the characters' different varieties of development or regression. In practice, we don't observe only one thing at a time. We notice, or partly notice, many aspects of a novel in every reading, but the specific things we see vary unpredictably, and so, therefore, does the total impression. Rereading implies accretion: each new reaction adds itself to the previous accumulation of insight, so that our knowledge of a book constantly reshapes itself.

I have suggested before the image of a palimpsest (an object with diverse layers beneath its surface; originally, writing paper used repeatedly after earlier material has been erased) as a model for rereading's richness. That image provides a precise metaphor for the results of repeated engagement with a single book. The layers of experience accruing from early readings, partly erased, remain partially discernible. Each new layer both adds to and subtracts from what has gone before. It subtracts in obscuring old reactions by new ones; it adds new responses to those still remembered. The final product—if one can ever speak of finality in connection with rereading—includes more than is readily visible. Although one never altogether recovers previous layers, they add texture and meaning to the ultimate version.

In the course of writing this book, I have learned, among other things, how much I have been shaped—personality, sensitivities, convictions—by reading. No family fills all its members' needs, but books, I now realize, can plug the gaps. Fiction has provided my models of behavior; fiction has supported and doubtless largely created my ideals; fiction has gratified emotional needs. Such effects depend on rereading. The repetitions and reinforcements of reiterated engagement with the same stories, the same language, the same characters enable the rereader to internalize what she needs, converting a novel into part of herself.

This vital function of rereading works in individual ways. Readers vary in what they gain from a book even on first reading. They make diverse discoveries and have unpredictable emotional experiences. Readers diverge from one another in the books they choose and in the ways they read those books, in how they process the reading and the rereading, in the time that elapses between one reading and the next, in the judgments they make and the pleasures they receive. There are no rules. All readers, though, change as a result of their experiences with books, and the changes generated by rereading can run deep. Rereading, as I observed earlier, is a way of paying attention. It takes books seriously and allows them to do their work: work that includes the changing of one's self and consequently of one's life, although in the nature of things we never quite glimpse the changes as they occur.

Both the stability and the change that ground rereading's appeal can seem alternately illusions and facts: so the experience of writing this book leads me to conclude. The stability, or relative stability (textual changes, usually minor but sometimes major, can take place as a result of new editorial discoveries or techniques), of a text is a fact of knowledge but often not of experience. Particularly if a long time has elapsed between readings, the sense of change can feel so persuasive as to override rationality. Emotional rather than factual knowledge grounds the conviction that change has taken place—and, indeed, *something* has certainly changed in order to generate such a conviction. That "something" is the reader's consciousness. The scope and degree of shift—radical alterations in assessment, radical mutations of perception—can be startling: reminders, if seriously contemplated, that we remain always works in progress. Writing in the *American Scholar* about the plasticity of the brain, the neuroscientist Richard Restak uses rereading as an example. People wonder, he points out, why it is that a once valued book no longer appeals, and why it once meant so much. "We didn't enjoy the book that second time around," he explains, "because, as a result of the lifetime plasticity of our brain, we're literally a different person from the person who read the book the first time."

To think about my own rereading has encouraged a sense of humility, especially when it comes to questions of value. I set out with the conviction that I could dependably discriminate value, and with the associated conviction that it is important to do so. Although I still hold that the question of value deserves pondering in relation to everything read, I'm no longer sure that such reflection produces solid results in any individual instance. My uncertainty comes from my reversals over the years. Although *Pride and Prejudice* and *Middlemarch* and *Alice in Wonderland* seem as marvelous as ever, revealing new reasons to admire them, *The Golden Notebook*, of whose merits I was once deeply convinced, has dwindled, like *The Catcher in the Rye*, like *Gone with the Wind*. Earlier in my life I held forth about the weaknesses of *Herzog;* now I think it an important novel. And so on.

The really unsettling part is that my standards remain the same. I value complex characterization, effective and elegant prose, meaningful and engaging plot, large import. I find exactly these qualities, however, where I did not find them before; and they have disappeared where once I readily discerned them. If *Herzog* has meanings that I was earlier unable to detect; if *The Golden Notebook*, with large pretensions, now seems relatively trivial in import; if the facts of a book's nature can shift in such ways, value judgments, too, must be less stable than they appear. I can say, facilely, that taste differs from judgment and that value involves concerns quite different from those entailed in merely liking a book, but that observation only opens new questions. Pleasure and instruction constitute literature's essential contributions: so classical critics held, and I agree. Then if the pleasure a reader takes in a book bears no relation to the standards she holds, something must be wrong with the standards.

Such puzzles inhere in first readings as well as in rereadings. Rereading, however, makes them more emphatic and inescapable. It heightens consciousness: of the act of reading and its implications, and of what goes on in the work reread. It encourages thought,

even as it may overwhelm the reader with feeling. Always, it involves discovery—at worst, discovery that a book once loved no
longer enthralls; at best, a host of new meanings and new pleasures in a familiar text, or even in one only half-remembered. For
me, *The Sacred and Profane Love Machine* was an especially delightful surprise. I read it first at a time when I was reading all
of Murdoch's novels as they appeared, in rapid succession. One
blurred into another in my consciousness. I liked them all, with
varying degrees of enthusiasm, but none remained sharp in my
memory. Rereading the book years later, in a new context, brought
it to life as a remarkable and piercing exploration of human relations in all their comedy and profundity. My discovery of *The
Wizard of Oz* as a book to be taken seriously, not for buried meaning but for superb execution, also delighted me. But every discovery, large and small, brings its own delights, reminding me over
and over why I need not feel guilty over rereading instead of exploring new ground. Rereading *is* exploring new ground—new
ground in familiar territory. By the criterion of pleasure, it ranks
high; and its evocation of fresh meanings gives it weight also as a
source of instruction.

    The activity necessarily entails awareness of time's passage and
of what it means (and has meant). Time brings enlightenment, rereading often makes one feel. What formerly was fuzzy emerges
into clarity. The once overlooked is newly seen; the incomprehensible personality becomes transparent. Yet time also brings nostalgia, a force of anti-clarity that can envelop works read long ago in
an unearned glow. If my rereading were in the service of rigorous
literary criticism, I would regret such a glow and try to penetrate
it. In actuality, I often, on the contrary, treasure it as a benign
form of memory. Predictably, it occurs most often in relation to
children's books, but it can come unexpectedly in other contexts

as well, frequently recalling forms of happiness no longer readily available. Rereading insists on awareness of the past, and such awareness can in itself provide pleasure.

Indeed, the pleasures offered by rereading prove almost as various as its forms of insight. The unpleasures mainly assume two forms: disappointment in a book and disappointment with the self. The previous pages have recorded my own disappointments in books; disappointments with the self have provided a less conspicuous subject. Self-judgment, however, almost inevitably accompanies changes of opinion. Although I have also experienced, in the course of my rereading, unexpected bursts of affection for the past self that devoured every book in sight, I have often felt inclined to repudiate that earlier self for its gullibility, its blindness, its undependable or unaccountable judgments. Yet surely we should be charitable to our past selves, if only because we realize that, granted another decade of perspective, we may judge our current selves equally inadequate. Perspective on and insight into the self is yet another of rereading's gifts.

I really have trouble here, though. As a teacher, I have considered myself primarily obligated to teach students how to read. If they look for the right things, if they exert the proper kind of attention, if they allow themselves to feel, I believe that they will have a valuable experience. They will, I like to believe, perceive their reading as valuable even if they don't approve of a specific book, and they will come to appropriate conclusions, learning to judge as well as to enjoy. What, in the light of these assumptions, am I to make of my own recent experience, with its recognition of conflicting feelings and judgments? I must be a "bad reader" in the present or have been one in the past—a disturbing hypothesis for a professional teacher and critic. I prefer, obviously, to think that the "badness" belongs to the past, that my current understanding constitutes an advance over previous versions. The change, then, suggests that no matter how my students read in the present, they may well read better in the future—and that my interventions may make no difference.

Rereading has turned out to be rich in paradox. A conservative activity that holds on to the past, it is also potentially revolutionary, overturning judgments and repudiating assumptions. What once you failed to notice jumps up to alarm or delight you. Rereading gives the self permission and space to think, to play, and to meditate. It can feel like self-enlargement. In some ways it proves more personal even than initial acts of reading, given its engagement with earlier versions of the self.

I have realized most forcefully, in this regard, the power of individual desire to shape interpretation. This realization helps me forgive myself for "bad reading" and enables me, retrospectively, to forgive many undergraduates for what might have seemed their perverse understandings of works we read together. What one wants helps to determine what one gets. Wanting to please my mother, I read *Islandia* as she did; wanting to understand my own sexuality, I read "The Princess with the Golden Hair" as only about sex. (I'm struck, retrospectively, in the light of this realization, by the fact that many reviewers of Wilson's book read it exactly the same way.) Rereading, however, I understand them in new ways. The discoveries of each new reading of a given text—"bad readings" included—add up to a richer interpretation than a single reading could offer. If, or as, desires change, readings change likewise, and past perversities come into view.

Just as we develop stories about our lives (indeed, as part of those stories), I now think, we evolve private narratives about the books in our lives. The books we have read take form in our memories partly in accord with our individual fantasies and the needs associated with them. The distortions of nostalgia create a subset of these shapings. Books help to form us, and we in turn help to form them. If I have undermined my own confidence in the possibility of critical authority, I have also heightened my understanding of the vital part that reading and rereading have played in my life and encouraged my speculation about the purposes they serve for others. Rereading, given my protracted thought about it, turns out to be a much more complicated process than I initially assumed.

Acknowledgments

The insight of others has enriched this book and encouraged me in the writing of it. Deborah Kaplan, Nancy Sommers, and Myra Jehlen read and remarked on parts of my work in progress in ways that urged me toward deeper thought and increased precision. Their comments, as always, have stimulated and enlightened me. Conversations with Jude Spacks and with Liliane Greene frequently clarified my thinking. John Kulka, my editor at Harvard University Press, once more provided warm and invaluable support as well as keen critical judgment. Christine Thorsteinsson, manuscript editor of *On Rereading*, rescued me from infelicities large and small. I am grateful to all of them.